THE

FITNESS OF HOLY SCRIPTURE

FOR

UNFOLDING THE SPIRITUAL LIFE OF MEN.

II.

CHRIST THE DESIRE OF ALL NATIONS,

OR, THE

UNCONSCIOUS PROPHECIES OF HEATHENDOM:

BEING

THE HULSEAN LECTURES

FOR M.DCCC.XLV. AND M.DCCC.XLVI.

BY

RICHARD CHENEVIX TRENCH, M.A.,

VICAR OF ITCHEN-STOKE, HANTS; PROFESSOR OF DIVINITY, KING'S
COLLEGE, LONDON, EXAMINING CHAPLAIN TO THE LORD
BISHOP OF LONDON; AND LATE HULSEAN LECTURER.

From the Second London Edition, Revised by the Author.

WIPF & STOCK · Eugene, Oregon

Wipf and Stock Publishers
199 W 8th Ave, Suite 3
Eugene, OR 97401

The Fitness of Holy Scripture
for Unfolding the Spiritual Life of Men,
Christ the Desire of All Nations, or,
the Unconscious Prophecies of Heathendom
By Trench, Richard Chenevix
Softcover ISBN-13: 978-1-7252-9900-9
Hardcover ISBN-13: 978-1-7252-9901-6
eBook ISBN-13: 978-1-7252-9902-3
Publication date 1/29/2021
Previously published by H. Hooker, 1850

This edition is a scanned facsimile of
the original edition published in 1850.

ADVERTISEMENT.

I HAVE not felt myself at liberty to make more than a few verbal alterations, or here and there to recast a sentence, or add a clause, in these Lectures, on the occasion of their second appearance. I have inserted indeed a few brief passages, which, originally belonging to the Discourses, had been omitted in the delivery, and have to the Second Series appended a considerable number of Notes, in confirmation or illustration of statements made in the text. These having been asked for in more quarters than one, I trust may not be found unacceptable to some readers.

ITCHEN-STOKE, Nov. 19, 1847.

CONTENTS, FOR THE YEAR 1845.

LECTURE I.

INTRODUCTORY LECTURE

PSALM CXIX. 18.

Open thou mine eyes, that I may behold wondrous things out of thy law, ... 13

LECTURE II.

THE UNITY OF SCRIPTURE

EPHESIANS I. 9, 10.

Having made known unto us the mystery of his will, according to his good pleasure, which he hath purposed in himself; that in the dispensation of the fulness of times he might gather together in one all things in Christ, both which are in heaven and which are on earth; even in him, ... 32

LECTURE III.

THE MANIFOLDNESS OF SCRIPTURE.

MATTHEW XIV. 20.

They did all eat, and were filled, ... 51

LECTURE IV.

THE ADVANCE OF SCRIPTURE

HEBREWS I. 1, 2.

God, who at sundry times and in divers manners, spake in time past unto the fathers, by the prophets, hath in these last days spoken unto us by his Son, . . 73

LECTURE V.

THE PAST DEVELOPMENT OF SCRIPTURE.

JOHN XII. 16.

These things understood not his disciples at the first; but when Jesus was glorified, then remembered they that these things were written of him, . . . 91

LECTURE VI.

THE INEXHAUSTIBILITY OF SCRIPTURE

ISAIAH XII. 3.

With joy shall ye draw water out of the wells of salvation, ... 108

LECTURE VII.

THE FRUITFULNESS OF SCRIPTURE

EZEKIEL XLVII. 9.

And it shall come to pass, that every thing that liveth, which moveth, whithersoever the rivers shall come, shall live, ... 126

LECTURE VIII.

THE FUTURE DEVELOPMENT OF SCRIPTURE.

REVELATION VI. 2.

Conquering and to conquer, ... 143

CONTENTS, FOR THE YEAR 1846.

LECTURE I.
INTRODUCTORY LECTURE.
Haggai II. 7.

The Desire of all nations shall come, ... 163

LECTURE II.
THE VANQUISHER OF HADES
Mark XVI. 3.

Who shall roll us away the stone from the door of the sepulchre? 184

LECTURE III.
THE SON OF GOD
Acts XIV. 11.

And when the people saw what Paul had done, they lifted up their voices, saying, in the speech of Lycaonia, The gods are come down to us in the likeness of men, ... 202

LECTURE IV.
THE PERFECT SACRIFICE
Micah VI. 6, 7.

Wherewith shall I come before the Lord, and bow myself before the high God? shall I come before him with burnt offerings; with calves of a year old? Will the Lord be pleased with thousands of rams, or with ten thousands of rivers of oil? shall I give my first-born for my transgression, the fruit of my body for the sin of my soul? . . . 220

LECTURE V.

THE RESTORER OF PARADISE.

Genesis V. 29

And he called his name Noah, saying, This same shall comfort us concerning our work and toil of our hands, because of the ground which the Lord hath cursed, 239

LECTURE VI.

THE REDEEMER FROM SIN

Romans VII. 21, 23.

I find then a law, that, when I would do good, evil is present with me. For I delight in the law of God after the inward man: but I see another law in my members, warring against the law of my mind, and bringing me into captivity to the law of sin which is in my members, ... 256

LECTURE VII

THE FOUNDER OF A KINGDOM

Hebrews XI. 10.

A city which hath foundations, whose builder and maker is God, ... 277

LECTURE VIII.

CONCLUDING LECTURE.

1 Thess. V. 21.

Prove all things; hold fast that which is good, . . 297

THE FITNESS OF HOLY SCRIPTURE

FOR

UNFOLDING THE SPIRITUAL LIFE OF MEN.

PSALM CXIX. 18.

Open thou mine eyes, that I may behold wondrous things out of thy law.

It was with a true insight into the sad yet needful conditions of the Truth militant in a world of error, that he who has of such just title given his name to these Lectures, which I am now permitted to deliver in this place, devoted so largely of his temporal means to the securing among us a succession of discourses, having more or less nearly to do with the establishing and vindicating of that Truth against all gainsayers and opposers. For such apologies of our holy Faith as he desired by this and other kindred foundations of which he was the author, to promote and set forward, are deeply grounded in the very nature of tha Faith itself—and this, whether they be defensive or aggressive, whether they be of the Truth clearing itself from unjust aspersions, or carrying the war, as it must often do, into the quarters of error, and proving itself not merely to be true, but to be Truth absolute, to the exclusion of all rival claims. We know, as a matter of history, that Christian literature did begin, as far back as we can trace it, with works of this character; they are among the earliest which have reached us; probably among the earliest which existed. Nor do they belong merely to the first ages of the Church's being, however in them they may naturally have had a special importance. The Truth, like Him who gave it, will *always* be a sign which shall be spoken against. The forms of the enmity may change; the coarser and more brutal accusations of one age may give place to subtler charges of another; but so long as an ungodly world exists, the enmity itself will remain, and will find utterance. The Truth, therefore, must ever be succinct, and prompt to give an answer for itself; and this it does the more readily, as knowing that not man's glory, but God's glory is at hazard, when *it* is assailed; as being infinitely removed from that pride which might tempt to the keeping silence, because it knows that the accusations made against it are unjust; being rather full of that humility and love, which make it willingly condescend to the most wayward, if haply it may win them to the service of its King.

And this is not all: the Truth cannot pause when it has thus refuted and thrown back the things that it knew not, which yet were laid to its charge. In its very nature it is aggressive also. How should it not be so? how should it not make war on the strongholds of falsehood and error, when its very task in the world is to deliver them that were prisoners there? how should it not seek to gather men under its banner,—being moved, as it ever is, with an inward bleeding compassion for all them that are aliens from the faith of Christ, as knowing that every man, till he has found himself in Him, is estranged from the true home of his spirit, the right centre of his being? How should it not press its treasures upon each, commend its medicines to all, when they are medicines for every man's hurt, treasures which would make every man rich? when it knows that it has the reality, of which every lie is the counterfeit; that when men are the fiercest set against it, then are they the most madly at strife with their own blessedness?

But this, it might be said, would sufficiently explain the uses of Christian apology before a world which resists, or puts by, the Faith; it would explain why the Truth should count itself happy to stand, as it did once in the person of Paul, before Festus and Agrippa, and in presence of Gentile and Jew, to make answer for itself. But allowing this, what means it when before a congregation of faithful men, when at one of the great centres of Christian light and knowledge in our own land, a preacher undertakes, and that at large and from year to year, the handling some point of the evidences of our Religion? Might not this seem at first as superfluous a form, as when, upon a day of coronation, a champion rides forth, and with none but loyal hearts beating in unison with the multitudinous voices which have hailed his king and theirs, flings down his glove, and challenges any that will gainsay the monarch's right to the crown which has just been set upon his brows? Our task might indeed be superfluous as this, were its only purpose to convince opposers. There is, blessed be God, a foregone conclusion in the minds of the faithful, drawn from all which they have known themselves of the life and power of the Truth, which suffers them not for an instant to regard it as something yet in debate, and still to be proved; since it has already approved itself in power and blessing unto them.

And yet even for them a work of Christian apology may be so constructed as to have its worth and meaning. If it widen the basis on which their Faith reposes, if it help them to take count of and use treasures, which before they had, but which they knew not before save in part; if it cause them to pass from belief to insight; if it bring out for them the perfect proportions of the Truth, its singular adaptations to the pre-established harmonies of the world, as they had not perceived these before; if it furnish them with a clue for guiding some perplexed and wandering brother from his dreary labyrinth of doubt and error— if in any of these ways it effectually serve, surely it has not been in vain. Such uses we acknowledge in Evidences of our Faith, when we constitute them a part of our discipline in this University; which assuredly we do, not as presuming that we have to deal with any who are yet aliens from that Faith, who have yet need to be brought to the acknowledging of the truth as it is in Jesus; but rather as desiring to put them who already have drawn in their faith, and that from better sources, from the lips of their mothers, from the catechisms of their childhood, from among the sanctities of their home, in possession of the scientific grounds of that belief, which already, by a better and more immediate tenure, is theirs.

Nor may we leave wholly out of sight that in a time like our own, of great spiritual agitations, at a place like this, of signal intellectual activity, where oftentimes the low mutterings of distant controversies, scarcely heard elsewhere, are distinctly audible—there can hardly fail to be some perplexed with difficulties, harassed, it may be, with doubts which they do not welcome, but would give worlds to be rid of for ever —doubts which, perhaps, the very preciousness of the Truth in their sight alone magnifies into importance; for they feel that they are going to hang upon that Truth all that is dear to them for life and for eternity, that it must be to them as their spirits' bride; and therefore they cannot endure upon it the faintest breath of suspicion. I say, brethren, that we may not leave wholly out of mind that one and another in such perplexity of spirit may be among us here. Happy above measure he who has "a mouth and wisdom" given him to meet the necessities of such an one among his brethren; who shall help to bring him into the secure haven of belief, into the confession that in Christ Jesus are indeed laid up "all," and those infinite "treasures of wisdom and knowledge."

But if discourses of the kind which I am commencing to-day, are indeed to be of profit to any, there appear to be one or two preliminary conditions in the choice of a subject, most needful to be observed; which failing to observe, we shall, of sure consequence, fall wholly short of those ends of usefulness which we desire.

And first, a work of Christian defence will be marred, if the subject which we select be one upon which none of the great and decisive issues of the mighty conflict between Truth and error depend; as when in jousts and tournaments a knight touches the shield of some feeble adversary, passing by and leaving the stronger and more accomplished unchallenged. For thus it is with us, when we go off upon some minor point, which, even were it plainly won, would leave *us* in no essential degree the better, nor an adversary the worse; which he might yield without being dislodged from his strongholds of unbelief, without even feeling them less tenable than before.

Or again, it will be to little profit that we deal with hinderances to men's belief, which once indeed were real and urgent, but of which the urgency and reality have long since departed; if we take our stand in some part of the battle-field from which the great turmoil of the conflict has now ebbed and shifted away; or conjure up phantom forms of opposition, which once indeed were living and strong, but now survive only in the tradition of books, and at this day practically weaken no man's faith, disturb no man's inner peace. This, too, were a fatal error, to have failed to take note of that great stream of tendency, which has borne *us* amid other shoals, and near other rocks, from those among which our forefathers steered with manful hearts the bark of their faith, and of God's great mercy made not shipwreck of that faith amidst them all.

Or, once more, Christian apology fails in its loftiest aim, when it addresses, not the whole man, but the man only upon one side, and that not the highest, of his being; when it addresses, not the conscience, the affections, the will, but the understanding faculties alone. How often do we meet in books of Christian evidence the attempt made to substitute a logical or mathematical proof of our most holy Faith for a moral one; to ascend to that proof by steps which can no more be denied than the successive steps of a problem in geometry, and so to drive an adversary into a corner from whence there shall be no escape. But there *is* always an escape for those that in heart and will are alienated from the truth. At some stage or other of the process they will successfully break away, or even if they are brought to the end, they remain not with us long. And we may thank God that it is so; for it is part of the glory of the Truth that it leads in procession no chained, no unwilling captives —none that do not rejoice in their captivity, and share in the triumph which they adorn. It is not therefore that arguments which address themselves to lower parts of man's being than the highest, are to be rejected—but only their insufficiency acknowledged; that they of themselves will never introduce any to the inner sanctuary of the Faith; but can only lead him up to the doors. Most needful are they in their place; most needful that Christianity should approve itself to have a true historic foundation; that as a fact in history it should stand as rigid a criticism as any other fact; that the books which profess to tell its story should vindicate for themselves an authentic character; that the men who wrote those books should be shown capable and credible witnesses of the things which they deliver; that the outworks of our Faith should be seen to be no less defensible than its citadel. But, after all, the heart of the matter is not there; when all is done, men will feel in the deepest centre of their being that it is the moral which must prove the historic, and not the historic which can ever prove the moral; that evidences drawn from without may be accepted as the welcome *buttresses*, but that we can know no other *foundations*, of our Faith than those which itself supplies. Revelation, like the sun, must be seen by its own light; being itself the highest, the ultimate appeal with regard to it cannot lie with any lower than itself. There was indeed a sense in which Christ received the witness of John, but there was another in which He received not witness of any man, only his own witness and his Father's. Even so is it with his Word and his doctrine. There is a witness which they can receive of men; there is also a witness which no other can yield them than themselves.

I trust, then, that taking for my argument *The fitness of Holy Scripture for unfolding the spiritual life of men*, and finding in its adaptations for this a proof of its divine origin, I shall not fail in these primary conditions, however immeasurably I shall of necessity fall below the greatness and grandeur of my theme.

For first, this question, Whether Scripture be not a book capable of doing, and appointed to do, an higher work than every other book, cannot be regarded as one which is not vital. It is felt to be vital by all those whose aim and purpose is to prove that it is but a book as other books, and therefore underlying the same weakness and incompletenesses as every other work of men's hands. And these are many; since for one direct assault on Christianity as a delivered fact, there are twenty on the records of Christianity, or the manner of its delivery. Many a one who would not venture boldly to enter on the central question, whether the Christ whom the Church believes, whom not any one passage alone, but the collective sum of the Scriptures has delivered to us, be not the highest conceivable revelation of the Invisible God, and his Incarnation the necessary outcoming of the perfections of the Godhead, will yet hover on the outskirts of the conflict, and set himself to the detecting, as he hopes, a flaw in this narration, or to the proving the historic evidence for that book insufficient. They who pass by the consideration as one which never rose up before their minds, whether there has not been a great education of our race, reaching through all ages, going forward from the day that God called Abraham from among his fathers' idols; and whether this great idea be not as a golden thread, running through the whole woof and tissue of Scripture—they who shun altogether considerations such as these, will yet set themselves diligently to look for petty discrepancies between one historic book and another, or for proofs which shall not be put by, of some later hand than that of Moses in some notice in the book of Genesis. And however paltry and petty this warfare may be, it is no doubt a true instinct of hate which makes them hope to discover vulnerable points in Scripture, as knowing that could they really find such, through them they might effectually wound Him, of whom the Scripture is the outcoming and the Word.

Nor, again, can it be said that this is a matter, which though once brought into earnest debate, is now so no more; or that the earnestness of the struggle has been now transferred to other parts of the great controversy between the kingdoms of light and of darkness. It is not so: the Porphyrys, the Celsuses, and the Julians of an earlier age, have never wanted their apt scholars, their worthy successors. The mantle of the false prophet is as surely dropped and bequeathed, as the mantle of the true. Who that knows aught of what is going forward among a people, who not in blood only, but in much besides, are most akin to us of all the nations of Europe, will deny that even now God's Word is tried to the uttermost; that it still has need to make good its claims; or knowing this, will presume to say how soon we may not find ourselves in the midst of controversies, which assuredly have not yet run themselves out, nor by the complete victory of the Truth brought themselves to a quiet end?

Nor shall we with this theme be lingering about the outer precincts of our Faith. Not the external authority with which these books come to us, but the inner seal with which they are sealed, the way in which, like Him of whom they testify, they receive not witness of men, but by all which they are, by all which they have wrought, bear witness of themselves that they are of God, even the witness of power, this is our high argument.

And to it perhaps there will be no fitter introduction than a few general remarks on the connexion in which a book may stand to the intellectual and spiritual life of men. And would we appreciate the importance of a book received as absolute law, for the mental and moral culture of those who in such wise receive it, the influences which it will exert in moulding them, if only that book contain any elements of truth; let us consider for an instant what the Koran has been and is to the whole Mohammedan world; how it is practically the great bond and band of the nations professing that spurious faith, holding fast in a community, which is a counterpart, however feeble, of a Christendom, nations whom every thing else would have tended to separate; how it has stamped on them the features of a common life, and set them, however immeasurably below the Christian nations, yet well nigh as greatly above all other nations of the world;—let us consider this, and then what the book is that has wrought the mighty effects —the many elements of fraud and folly which are mixed up with, and which weaken, the truth which it possesses; and then let us ask ourselves what by comparison must be a Bible, or Scripture of absolute truth, to the Christian world!

Or to estimate the shaping moulding power which may lie in books, even when they come not as revelations, real or pretended, of the will of God, let us attempt to measure the influence which a few Greek and Latin books, (for the real effective books are but few,) exert and have exerted on the minds of men, since the time that they have been familiarly known and studied; the manner in which they have modified the habits of thought, coloured the language, and affected the whole institutions of the world in which we live; how they have given to those who have sedulously occupied themselves in their study and drunk in their spirit, a culture and tone of mind recognisably different from that of any other men; and this, although they come with the seal of no absolute authority; although, on the contrary, we feel that on many points (and some of these the very chiefest) we stand greatly above them. Let us take this into account, and we shall allow that it is scarcely possible to overrate the influence of a book which *does* come with highest sanction, to which men bow as containing the express image of the Truth, and which is, as those are, only for a longer period and in a higher region of the spiritual life, the appointed instrument for calling out the true humanity in every man.

At first, indeed, it seems hard to understand how any *written* word should possess such influence as that which we attribute to this; difficult to set a dispensation of the Truth in that form at all upon a level in force and influence with the same Truth, when it is the living utterance of living men, or to ascribe to it powers at all equal to theirs. But when we consider more closely, the wonder disappears; we soon perceive how, by the Providence of God, a written word, be it of man's truth or of God's Truth, should have been charged with such important functions to fulfil. For first, it is plain that the existence of a written word is the necessary condition of any historic life or progress whatsoever in the world. If succeeding generations are to inherit aught from those that went before, and not each to begin anew from first rudiments,—if all is not to be always childhood,—if there is to be any manhood of our race,—it is plain that only thus, only through such an instrument could this be brought about.

And most of all it is evident that through a Scripture alone, that is, through a written record, could any great epoch, and least of all an epoch in which great spiritual truths were revealed or reasserted, transmit itself unimpaired to the after world. For every new has for a long while an old to contend with, every higher a lower, which is continually seeking to draw it down to itself. The most earnest oral tradition will in a little while lose its distinctness, undergo essential though insensible modifications. Apart from all desire to vitiate the committed word, yet, little by little, the subjective condition of those to whom it is intrusted, through whom it passes, will infallibly make itself felt; and in such treacherous keeping is all which remains merely in the memories of men, that after a very little while, rival schools of disciples will begin to contend not merely how their master's words were to be accepted, but what those very words were themselves.

Moreover it is only by recurrence to such witnesses as are thus secured for the form in which the Truth was at the first delivered, that any great restoration or reformation can proceed; only so can that which is grown old renew its youth, and cast off the slough of age. Without this, all that is once let go would be irrecoverably gone—all once lost would be lost for ever. Without this, all that did not interest at the moment, all which was laid deep for the uses of a remote posterity, of which they were first to discover the price and value, would long before it reached them have inevitably perished. And when the Church of the Apostolic age, with that directly following, is pointed to as an exception to this general rule,—as a Church existing without a Scripture,— even as no doubt for some while the Church did exist with a canon not full formed, but forming, and for a little while without *any* Scriptures peculiarly its own, it is left out of sight that the question is not, whether a Church could so *exist*, but whether it could *subsist* —not whether it could be, but whether it could *continue* to be. That for a while, under rare combinations of favourable circumstances, with living witnesses and fresh memories of the Lord's life and death in the midst of it, a Christian Church without any actual writings of its new Covenant could have existed, is one thing; and another, whether it could so have survived through long ages; whether without them it could have kept ever before its eyes any clear and distinct image of Him that was its founder, or stamped any lively impress of Him on the hearts of its children. No; it is assuredly no happy accident of the Church that it possesses a Scripture; but if the wonders of the Church's first becoming were not to repeat themselves continually, if it was at all to know a natural evolution in the world; then, as far as we can see, this was a necessary condition of its very subsistence.

This then, brethren, will be the aim of these Lectures which I am about to deliver in your hearing. I shall desire reverently, and with God's grace assisting, to discover what I may, of the inner structure of this Book which is so essential a factor in the spiritual life of men—humbly to trace where I can, the wisdom with which it is laid out to be the nourisher and teacher of all men, and of all men in all ages and in all parts of their complex being; also to show, where I am able, how it has effectually approved itself as such.

And yet, brethren, such considerations may not be entered on without one or two needful cautions, which I should wish to keep ever before myself, which I should wish to commend also to you. And first, let us beware lest contemplating this goodly fabric, we be contemplators only; as though we were to stand without Scripture and admire it, and not to stand within it and obey it. That were a mournful self-deceit—to see and marvel at its fitness for every man, and never to have made proof of that fitness for the needs of *one* heart, for the healing the deep wound of one spirit, even of our own. And, indeed, only in this way of love and of obedience shall we enter truly into any of the hidden riches which it contains; for that only which we love, we know. No book, much less the highest, yields its secrets, reveals its wonders, to any but the reverent, the loving, and the humble. To other than these, the door of higher understanding is ever closed. We must pass into and unite ourselves with that which we would know, ere we can know it more than in name.

And then, brethren, again, when we propose to consider the structure of Scripture, it is not as though this were needed before men could enter into its fullest and freest enjoyment. It is far from being thus; for as a man may live in an house without being an architect, so may we habitually live and move in Holy Scripture, without consciously, by any reflex act, being aware of any one of the wonders of its construction, the secret sources of its strength and power. To know simply that it is the Word of God has sufficed thousands and tens of thousands of our brethren; even as, no doubt, in this one affirmation is gathered up and anticipated all that the most earnest and devout search may unfold. We may say this, that it is God's Word, in other language, we may say this more at large, yet more than this we cannot say; after the widest range we shall only return to this at the last.

But while this is true, it remains true also that "the works of the Lord are great, sought out of all them that have pleasure therein," if only leisure and opportunities are theirs—that if love is the way of knowledge, knowledge also is the food of love, the appointed fuel of the sacred fire; that, if the affections are to be kept lastingly true to an object, the reasonable faculties, supposing them to have been actively called out, must find also in that object their satisfying employment. Many among us here have, or will have, not merely to live on God's Word ourselves, but, as our peculiar task, to unfold its secrets and bring forth its treasures for others. We therefore cannot draw from it that *unconscious* nutriment which do many. Whatever may be the danger of losing the simplicity of our love for it, and coming to set that love upon other grounds than those on which the love of the humblest and simplest of our brethren reposes, and so of separating ourselves in spirit from him; this, like any other danger of our spiritual life, must not be shrunk from, by shrinking from the duty to which, like its dark shadow, it cleaves; but in other and more manful ways must be met and overcome. We all of us have need, if not all from our peculiar functions, yet all from our position as the highest educated of our age and nation, as therefore the appointed leaders of its thoughts and feelings, not merely to prize and honour this Book, but to justify the price and honour, in which we hold it ourselves, in which we bid others to hold it.

May some of us be led by what shall be here spoken

to a fuller recognition of those treasures of wisdom and knowledge which are or may be, day by day, in our hands. May we be reminded of the high privilege which it is to have *a* book which is also, as its name declares, *the* Book; which stands up in the midst of its brethren, the kingly sheaf, to which all the others do obeisance (Gen. xxxvii. 7;)—not casting a slight upon them, but lending to them some of its own dignity and honour. May we in a troubled time be helped to feel something of the grandeur of the Scripture, and so of the manifold wisdom of that Eternal Spirit by whom it came—and then petty objections and isolated difficulties, though they were multiplied as the sands of the sea, will not harass us. For what are they all to the fact, (I am here using and concluding with words far better than my own,) that "for more than a thousand years the Bible collectively taken has gone hand in hand with civilization, science, law, —in short, with the moral and intellectual cultivation of the species, always supporting, and often leading the way? Its very presence as a believed book, has rendered the nations emphatically a chosen race, and this too in exact proportion as it is more or less generally studied. Of those nations which in the highest degree enjoy its influences, it is not too much to affirm that the differences, public and private, physical, moral and intellectual, are only less than what might be expected from a diversity in species. Good and holy men, and the best and wisest of mankind, the kingly spirits of history enthroned in the hearts of mighty nations, have borne witness to its influences, have declared it to be beyond compare the most perfect instrument, the only adequate organ, of humanity; the organ and instrument of all the gifts, powers, and tendencies, by which the individual is privileged to rise above himself, to leave behind and lose his dividual phantom self, in order to find his true self in that distinctness where no division can be,—in the Eternal I AM, the ever-living WORD, of whom all the elect, from the archangel before the throne to the poor wrestler with the Spirit until the breaking of day, are but the fainter and still fainter echoes."

LECTURE II.

THE UNITY OF SCRIPTURE.

Ephesians I. 9, 10.

Having made known unto us the mystery of his will, according to his good pleasure, which he hath purposed in himself; that in the dispensation of the fulness of times he might gather together in one all things in Christ, both which are in heaven and which are on earth, even in him.

It is the necessary condition of a book which shall exert any great and effectual influence, which shall stamp itself with a deep impression upon the minds and hearts of men, that it must have a unity of purpose: one great idea must run through it all. There must be some single point in which all its different rays converge and meet. The common eye may fail to detect the unity, even while it unconsciously owns its power: yet this is necessary still; this growing out of a single root, this subordination of all the parts to a single aim, this returning of the end upon the beginning. We feel this in a lower sphere; nothing pleases much or long, nothing takes greatly hold, no work of human genius or art, which is not at one with itself, which has not *form*, in the highest sense of that word; which does not exclude and include. And it is hardly necessary to add, that if the effects are to be deep and strong, this idea must be a great one: it must not be one which shall play lightly upon the surface of their minds that apprehend it, but rather one which shall reach far down to the dark foundations out of sight upon which reposes this awful being of ours.

Now what I should desire to make the subject of my lecture to-day is exactly this, that there is one idea in Holy Scripture, and this idea the very highest; that all in it is referable to this; that it has the unity of which I spake; that a guiding hand and spirit is traceable throughout, including in it all which bears upon one mighty purpose, excluding all which has no connexion with that,—however, from faulty or insufficient views, *we* might have expected it there; however certainly it would have intruded itself there, had this been a work of no higher than human skill. I would desire to show that it fulfils this condition, the necessary condition of a book which shall be mighty in operation; that it is this organic whole, informed by this one idea;—how this one explains what it has and what it has not; much in its form, and yet more in its substance; why it should be brief here, and large there; why it omits wholly this, and only touches slightly upon that; why vast gaps, as at first sight might seem to us, occur in some portions of it; infinite minuteness of detail in others; how things which at first we looked to find in it, we do not find, and others, which we were not prepared for, are there.

And this unity if it can be shown to exist, none can reply that it was involved and implied in the external accidents of the Book, and that we have mistaken the outward aggregation of things similar for the inward coherence of an organic body: since these accidents, if the word may be permitted, are all such as would have created a sense of diversity: and it is only by penetrating through them, and not suffering them to mislead us, that we do attain to the deeper and pervading unity of Scripture. Its unity is not, for instance, that apparent one which might be produced by a language common to all its parts. For it is scarcely possible, I suppose, for a deeper gulf to divide two languages than divides the two in which severally the Old and the New Testament are written. Nor can it be likeness of form which has deceived us into believing that unity of spirit exists; for the forms are various and diverse as can be conceived; it is now song, now history; now dialogue, now narration; now familiar letter, now prophetic vision. There is scarcely a form of composition in which men have clothed their thoughts and embodied their emotions which does not find its archetype here. Nor yet is the unity of this volume brought about through all the parts of it being the upgrowth of a single age, and so all breathing alike the spirit of that age; for no single age beheld the birth of this Book, which was well nigh two thousand years ere it was fully formed and had reached its final completion. Nor can its unity, if it exists, be accounted for from its having had but one class of men for its human authors: since men not of one class alone, but of many, and those the widest apart, kings and herdsmen, warriors and fishermen, wise men and simple, have alike brought their one stone or more, and been permitted to build them in to this august dome and temple which God through so many ages was rearing to its glorious height. Deeper than all its outward circumstances, since these all would have tended to an opposite result, this unity must lie—in the all-enfolding seed out of which the whole book is evolved.

But this unity of Scripture, where is it? from what point shall we behold and recognise it? Surely from that in which those verses which I have taken from the Epistle to the Ephesians will place us; when we regard it as the story of the knitting anew the broken relations between the Lord God and the race of man; of the bringing the First-begotten into the world, for the gathering together all the scattered and the sundered in Him; when we regard it as the true *paradise Regained*—the true *De Civitate Dei*,—even by a better title than those noble books which bear these names—the record of that mystery of God's will which was working from the first, to the end "that in the dispensation of the fulness of times He might gather together in one all things in Christ."

And all nearer examination will show how true it is to this idea, which we affirm to lie at its ground. It is the story of the divine relations of men, of the divine life which, in consequence of those still subsisting relations, was struggling to the birth with more or less successful issues in every faithful man; which came perfectly to the birth in the One, even in Him in whom those relations were constituted at the first, and perfectly sealed at the last. It is the story of this, and of nothing else; the record of the men who were conscious of a bond between earth and heaven, and not only dimly conscious, for *that* all people who have not sunk into savage hordes have been, but who recognised these relations, this fellowship, as the great undoubted fact with which God had underlaid their life—the support not merely of their personal being, but as that which must sustain the whole society of earth—whether the narrower society of the Family, or the wider of the State, or the all-embracing one of the Church.

How many temptations there were to wander out of and beyond this region, which yet every one of us must recognise at once to be the true region in which only an Holy Scripture should move; how many other regions in which, had it been other than what it is, it might have lost itself! For instance, other so called sacred books almost invariably miss the distinction between ethics and physics, lose themselves in theories of creation, endless cosmogonies, subtle speculations about the origin of the material universe. Such a deep ground has this error, so willing are men to substitute the speculative for the practical, and to lose the last in the first, that we find even after the Christian Faith had been given, a vast attempt to turn even that into a philosophy of nature. What, for example, was Manicheism, but the attempt to array a philosophy of nature in a Christian language, to empty

Christian truths of all their ethical worth, and then to use them as a gorgeous symbolic garb for clothing a system different to its very core? But Scripture is no story of the material universe.* A single chapter is sufficient to tell us that "God made the heavens and the earth." Man is the central figure there, or, to speak more truly, the only figure; all which is there besides serves but as a background for him; he is not one part of the furniture of this planet, not the highest merely in the scale of its creatures, but the lord of all—sun and moon and stars, and all the visible creation, borrowing all their worth and their significance from the relations wherein they stand to him. Such he appears there in the ideal worth of his unfallen condition; and even now, when only a broken fragment of the sceptre with which once he ruled the world, remains in his hand, such he is commanded to regard himself still.

It is one of Spinoza's charges against Scripture, that it does erect and recognise this lordship of man, that it does lift him out of his subordinate place, and ever speak in a language which takes for granted that

* Compare the remarkable words of Felix the Manichæan, and the fault which he finds with it on this very ground (Augustine *Acta c. Felice Manichæo*, l. 1, c. 9) Et quia venit Manichæus et per suam prædicationem docuit nos initium medium et finem, docuit nos de fabricâ mundi, quare facta est et unde facta et qui fecerunt, docuit nos quare dies et quare nox, docuit nos de cursu solis et lunæ, quia hoc in Paulo non audivimus, nec in cæterorum apostolorum scripturis, hoc credimus, quia ipse est Paraclitus.

nature is to serve him, and not he to acquiesce in nature, that the Bible every where speaks rather of a God of men than a Creator of the universe. We accept willingly the reproach; we acknowledge and we glory in its entire truth,—that the eighth Psalm is but a single distinct utterance of that which all Scripture proclaims; for *that* every where sets forth man as the crown of things, the last and the highest, the king to rule over the world, the priest to offer up its praises—and deals with nature not as co-ordinated with him, much less as superior; but in entire subordination; "Thou makest him to have dominion of the works of thy hands, and thou hast put all things in subjection under his feet." And herein Holy Scripture is one, that it is throughout the history of man as distinct *from* nature, as immeasurably above nature —that it is throughout ethical, and does never, as so many of the mythic accounts of heathen religions, resolve itself on nearer inspection into the mere setting forth of physical appearances.

It is then the history of man; yet not of all men, only of a chosen portion of our race; and such, if we have rightly seized the purpose and meaning of a Scripture and what it is intended to tell, it must needs be. It is true that this too is often brought against it as a short-coming. It is a frequent sneer on the part of the master-mocker of France, that the Bible dedicates its largest spaces, by far the greatest number of its pages, to the annals of a little tribe, which occupied, to use his very words, a narrow strip of mountainous territory, scarcely broader than Wales, leaving almost unnoticed the mighty empire of Egypt and Assyria; and he goes on to observe, that from a book which professes to go back, as this does, to the very beginning, and to be in possession of all authentic history from the first, to have in its keeping the archives of our race, we should gladly have received, even as we might have reasonably expected, a few notices of these vast empires; which had been cheaply purchased by the omission or abridgment of lives and incidents now written with such a special minuteness.

Now it is no doubt remarkable, and a fact to awaken our earnest attention, that in a Book, wherein, if in any, all waste of room would have been spared, the lives of an Abraham, a Joseph, a David, fill singly spaces so large; while huge empires rise and fall, and all their multitudes pass to their graves almost without a word. These vast empires are left in their utter darkness, or if a glimpse of light fall upon them for a moment, it is only because of the relations in which they are brought to this little tribe; since no sooner do these relations cease, than they fall back into the obscurity out of which they emerged for a moment.

But strange as this may at first sight appear, it belongs to the very essence of Scripture that it should be thus and no otherwise. For that is not a world-history, but a history of the kingdom of God; and He who ever chooses "the weak things of the earth to confound the things which are mighty," had willed that in the line of this family, this tribe, this little people, the restoration of the true humanity should be

LECTURE II.

effected: and each man who at all realized the coming Restorer, each in whom that image of God, which was one day to be perfectly revealed in his Son, appeared with a more than usual distinctness, however indistinctly still,—every such man was singly a greater link in the world's history than all those blind millions of whom these records have refused to take knowledge. Those mountains of Israel, that little corner of the world, so often despised, so often wholly past over, was yet the citadel of the world's hope, the hearth on which the sparks that were yet to kindle the earth were kept alive. There the great reaction which was one day to find place against the world's sin was preparing; and just as, were we tracing the course of a stream, not the huge morasses, not the vast stagnant pools on either side, would delay us; we should not, because of their extent, count *them* the river; but *that* we should recognise as the stream, though it were the slenderest thread, in which an onward movement and current might be discerned; so it is here. Egypt and Assyria and Babylon were but the vast stagnant morasses on either side; the man in whose seed the whole earth should be blest, he and his family were the little stream in which the life and onward motion of the world were to be traced.

For indeed, properly speaking, where there are no workings, conscious or unconscious, to the great end of the manifestation of the Son of God in the flesh,—conscious, as in Israel, unconscious, as in Greece,—where neither those nor these are found, there history does not and cannot exist. For history, if it be not the merest toy, the idlest pastime of our vacant hours, is the record of the onward march of humanity towards an end. Where there is no belief in such an end, and therefore no advance toward it, no stirrings of a divine Word in a people's bosom, where not as yet the beast's heart has been taken away, and a man's heart given, there history cannot be said to be. They belong not therefore to history, least of all to sacred history, those Babels, those cities of confusion, those huge pens into which by force and fraud the early hunters of men, the Nimrods and Sesostrises, drave and compelled their fellows: and Scripture is only most true to its idea, while it passes them almost or wholly in silence by, while it lingers rather on the plains of Mamre with the man that "believed God, and it was counted to him for righteousness," than by "populous No," or great Babylon, where no faith existed but in the blind powers of nature, and the brute forces of the natural man.

And yet, that there were stirrings of a divine life, longings after and hopes of a Deliverer, at work in Israel, had not been, of itself, sufficient to exalt and consecrate its history into a Scripture. These such a history must contain, but also something more and deeper than these; else all in Greece and elsewhere that was struggling after moral freedom, that was craving after light, all that bore witness to man's higher origin and nobler destinies, might have claimed by an equal right to be there. But Holy Scripture, according to the idea from which we started, is the history of men in a constitution—of men, not seeking relations with God, but having them, and whose task is now to believe in them, and to maintain them. Its mournful reminiscences of a broken communion with heaven are evermore swallowed up in the firm and glorious assurances of a restored. The noblest efforts of heathenism were seekings after these relations with God, if haply man might connect himself anew with a higher world, from which he had cut himself loose. But here man does not appear as seeking God, and therefore at best only dimly and uncertainly apprehending him; but rather God appears as seeking man, and therefore not seeking in vain, but ever finding—and man only as seeking God, on the ground that God has already sought and found *him*, and has said to him, "Seek my face," and in that saying has pledged Himself that the seeking shall not be in vain. With this, Scripture excludes all mere feelings after God, not as counting them worthless,—for precious and significant in the eyes of a Paul was the altar "To the unknown God" reared at Athens,—but excludes them, in that they belong to a lower stage of religious life than that to which it ministers, and in which it moves. It has no mythology; no ideal which is not also real; no dreams and anticipations of higher things than it is itself destined to record as actually brought to pass. These may be deep out-speakings of the spiritual needs of man, precious recollections of a state which once was his, but which now he has forfeited; yet being only utterances of his want, cries of his need, confessions of his loss, sharing, too, as they must ever, in the imperfections of which they testify, therefore they can find no place in a Bible. For *that* is in no way a record of man's various attempts to cure himself of the deep wound of his soul; it is no history of the experiments which he makes, as he looks round him to see if he may find on earth medicinal herbs that will meet his need; but it presents him already in an hospital of souls, and under a divine treatment. Heathen philosophy might indeed be a preparation for Christianity —heathen mythology, upon its better side, an unconscious prophecy of Christ; yet were they only the negative preparation and witness; Jewish religion was the positive; and it is with the positive alone that a Scripture can have to do.

Thus we have seen what, under some aspects, such a book must be: we have seen why it is not that, which men superficially looking at it, or in whom the speculative tendencies are stronger than the moral needs, might have desired to be. In the first place, that it is not the history of nature, but of man; nor yet of all men, but only of those who are more or less conscious of their divine original, and have not, amid all their sins, forgotten that great word, "We are God's offspring;"—nor yet even of all these, but of those alone who had been brought by the word of the promise into immediate covenant relations with the Father of their spirits. We have seen it the history of an election,—of men under the direct and immediate education of God—not indeed for their own sakes only, as too many among them thought, turning their election into a selfish thing, but that through them he might educate and bless the world. That it does not tell the story of other men—that it does not give a philosophy of nature, is not a deficiency, but is rather its strength and glory; witnessing for the Spirit which has presided over its growth and formation, and never suffered aught which was alien to its great plan and purpose to find admission into it—any foreign elements to weaken its strength or trouble its clearness.

Nor less does Holy Scripture give testimony for a pervading unity, an inner law according to which it unfolds itself as a perfect and organic whole, in the epoch at which growth in it ceases, and it appears henceforth as a finished book. So long as humanity was growing, it grew. But when the manhood of our race was reached, when man had attained his highest point, even union with God in his Son, then it comes to a close. It carries him up to this, to his glorious goal, to the perfect knitting again of those broken relations, through the life and death and resurrection of Him in whom God and man were perfectly atoned. So long as there was any thing more to tell, any new revelation of the Name of God, any new relations of grace and nearness into which he was bringing his creatures,—so long the Bible was a growing, expanding book. But when all is given, when God, who at divers times spake to the world by his servants, had now spoken his last and fullest Word by his Son, then to this Book, the record of that Word of his, there is added no more, even while there is nothing more to add;—though it cannot end till it has shown in prophetic vision how this latest and highest which now has been given to man, shall unfold itself into the glory and blessedness of a perfected kingdom of heaven.

For thus, too, it will mark itself as one, by returning visibly in its end upon its beginning. Vast as the course which it has traced, it has been a circle still, and in that most perfect form comes back to the point from whence it started. The heaven, which had disappeared from the earth since the third chapter of Genesis, reappears again in visible manifestation, in the latest chapters of the Revelation. The tree of life, whereof there were but faint reminiscences in all the intermediate time, again stands by the river of the water of life, and again there is no more curse. Even the very differences of the forms under which the heavenly kingdom reappears are deeply characteristic, marking as they do, not merely that all is won back, but won back in a more glorious shape than that in which it was lost, because won back in the Son. It is no longer Paradise, but the New Jerusalem—no longer the *garden*, but now the *city*, of God, which is on earth. The change is full of meaning; no longer the garden, free, spontaneous, and unlaboured, even as man's blessedness in the state of a first innocence would have been; but the city, costlier indeed, more stately, more glorious, but, at the same time, the result of toil, of labour, of pains—reared into a nobler and more abiding habitation, yet with stones which, after the pattern of the "elect corner-stone," were each in its time laboriously hewn and painfully squared for the places which they fill.

And surely we may be permitted to observe by the

way, that this idea, which we plainly trace and recognise, of Scripture as a whole, this its architectonic character, cannot be without its weight in helping to determine the Canonical place and worth of the Apocalypse, which, as is familiar to many among us, has been sometimes called in question. Apart from all outward evidences in its favour, do we not feel that this wondrous book is needed where it is?—that it is the key-stone of the arch, the capital of the pillar—that Holy Scripture had seemed maimed and imperfect without it,—that a winding up with the Epistles would have been no true winding up; for in them the Church appears as still warring and struggling, still compassed about with the weaknesses and infirmities of its mortal existence—not triumphing yet, nor yet having entered into its glory. Such a termination had been as abrupt, as little satisfying as if, in the lower sphere of the Pentateuch, we had accompanied the children of Israel to the moment when they were just entering on the wars of Canaan; and no book of Joshua had followed to record their battles and their victories, and how these did not cease till they rode on the high places of the earth, and rested each man quietly in the lot of his conquered inheritance.

And again, this oneness of Holy Scripture, when we feel it, is a sufficient, even as it is a complete, answer to a very favourite topic of Romish controversialists. They are fond of bringing out how much there is of accident in the structure, nay, even in the existence of Scripture,—that we have one Gospel (the third) written at a private man's request,—another, (the fourth) because heresies had risen up which needed to be checked—epistles owing their origin to causes equally fortuitous—one, because temporary disorders had manifested themselves at Corinth,—another, because an Apostle, having promised to visit a city, from some unexpected cause was hindered—a third, to secure the favourable reception of a fugitive slave by his master—that of the New Testament at least, the chiefest part is thus made up of occasional documents called forth by emergent needs. And the purpose of this slight on Scripture is evident, the conclusion near at hand—which is this, How little likely it is that a book so formed, so growing, should contain an absolute and sufficient guide of life and rule of doctrine—how needful some supplementary teaching.

But when once this inner unity of God's Word has been revealed to us, when our eye has learned to recognise not merely the marks and signs of a higher wisdom, guiding and inspiring each several part, but also the relations of each part to the whole; when it has risen up before us, not as aggregated from without, but as unfolded from within, and in obedience to an inner law, then we shall feel that, however accidental may appear the circumstances of its growth, yet this accident which seemed to accompany its production, and to preside in the calling out of the especial books which we possess, and no other, was no more than the accident which God is ever weaving into the woof of his providence, and not merely weaving into it, but which is the staple out of which its whole web is woven.

LECTURE II.

Thus, brethren, we have been led to contemplate these oracles of God in their deep inner unity; we have seen not merely how they possess, but how we can reverently trace them in the possession of, that oneness of plan and purpose, which should make them effectual for the unfolding the spiritual life of men. We have seen how men's expectations of finding something there which they did not find, with their disappointments at its absence, have ever grown out of a mistaken apprehension of what a Scripture ought to be; how the presence of that which they miss would indeed have marred it, would have contradicted its fundamental idea, would have been a discord amid its deep harmonies, even as the discords which men find in it come oftentimes as its highest harmonies to the purged ear.

Nor is it without its warning to ourselves, that these murmurings and complaints do most often evidently grow out of a moral fault in them that make them. Men have lost the key of knowledge—the master-key which would have opened to them every door; and then they wander with perplexed hearts up and down this stately palace which the Eternal Wisdom has builded, but of which every goodlier room is closed against them, till, in the end, they complain that it is no such peerless palace after all, but only as other works which man's art has reared. Nor is this conclusion strange; for unless they bring to it a moral need, unless that moral need be to them the interpreter of every part, and gather all that is apparently abnormal in it under a higher and reconciling law the Book, in its deepest meaning and worth, will remain a riddle to them still.

But this moral need, what is it? It is the sense that we are sundered and scattered each from God, each from his fellow-man, each from himself—with a belief deep as the foundations of our life, that it is the will of God to gather all these scattered and these sundered together anew—this, with the conviction which will rise out of this, that all which bears on the circumstances of this recovering and regathering is precious; that nothing is of highest worth which does not bear upon this. Then we shall see in this Word that it is the very history which we require—that altogether, nothing but that—the history of the restoring the defaced image of God, the re-constitution of a ruined but godlike race, in the image of God's own Son—the deliverance of all in that race, who were willing to be delivered, from the idols of sense, from the false gods who would hold them in bondage, and would fain make them their drudges and their slaves.

And, brethren, what is it that shall give unity to our lives, but the recognition of the same great idea which gives unity to this Book? Those lives, they seem often broken into parts, with no visible connexion between one part and another; our boyhood, we know not how to connect it with our youth, our youth with our manhood: the different tasks of our life, we want to bind them up in a single sheaf, to feel that, however manifold and apparently disconnected they are, there is yet a bond that binds them into one. Our hearts, we want a central point for them, as it were a heart within the heart, and we oftentimes seek this in vain. Oh, what a cry has gone up from thousands and ten thousands of souls! and this the burden of the cry, I desire to be one in the deep centre of my being, to be one and not many—to be able to reduce my life to one law—to be able to explain it to myself in the master-light of one idea, to be no longer rent, torn, and distracted, as I am now.

And whence shall this oneness come? where shall we find, amid all the chances and changes of the world, this law of our life, this centre of our being, this keynote to which setting our lives, their seeming discords shall reveal themselves as their deepest harmonies? Only in God, only in the Son of God—only in the faith that what Scripture makes the end and purpose of God's dealing with our race, is also the end and purpose of his dealing with each one of us, namely, that his Son may be manifested in us—that we, with all things which are in heaven and all things which are in earth, may be gathered together in Christ, even in Him.

LECTURE III.

THE MANIFOLDNESS OF SCRIPTURE.

MATTHEW XIV. 20.

They did all eat, and were filled.

It was the aim of my preceding Lecture to trace the unity which reigns in Scripture, that it has a law to which each part of it may be referred, a root out of which it all grows. It will be my purpose in the present, to bring out before you how this Book, which is one, is also manifold; a fact which we may not be so ready to recognise the instant that it is presented to us, as the other. For the truth which occupied us last Sunday, of the Bible as one Book, not merely one because bound together in the covers of a single volume, but as being truly one, while it testifies in every part of one and the same Lord, while it is every where the utterance of one Spirit; this, whether consciously or unconsciously, has strong possession of men's minds in this our land. We feel, and rightly, that every attempt to consider any of its parts in absolute isolation from the other, rent away from the connexion in which it stands is false, and can lead to no profitable result; and it is hardly possible to estimate too highly the blessing of this, that the band which binds for us the parts of this volume together is unbroken even in thought; that we still feel ourselves to have, not a number of sacred books, but one sacred Book, which, not merely for convenience sake, but out of a far deeper feeling, we comprehend under one name.

Yet, on the other hand, there are other truths which, if we mean to enter into full possession of our treasures, we need also to make thoroughly our own. This idea of the *oneness* of Holy Scripture is incomplete and imperfect, till it pass into the higher idea of its *unity;* till we acknowledge that it is not sameness which reigns there; that, besides being one, it is also many; that as in the human body we, having many members, are one body, and the perfection of the body is not the repetition of the same member over and over again, but the harmonious tempering of different members, all being instinct with one life—not otherwise is it with Scripture. For in that, whether we look at the Old or New Testament, the same richness and variety of form reveal themselves, so that it may truly be said, that out of the ground of this Paradise, the Lord God has made "to grow every tree that is pleasant to the sight and good for food;" all that the earth has fairest appearing here in fairer and more perfect form—the fable, only here transformed into the parable—the ode transfigured into the psalm—oracles into prophecies—histories of the world into histories of the kingdom of heaven. Nor is tragedy wanting, though for Œdipus, we have the man of Uz; nor epos, though for "the tale of Troy divine," ours is the story of the New Jerusalem, "coming down out of heaven as a bride adorned for her husband." And it will be my desire to show how this also was needful, if it was to be the Book which should indeed leaven the world, which should offer nutriment, not merely for some men, but for all men; which should not tyrannically lop men till they were all of one length, but should encourage in every man the free development of all which God had given him. Thus it must needs have been, if the Spirit by this Word was to sanctify all in every man which was capable of being sanctified; which, coming originally from God, could be redeemed from the defilements of this world, and in purer shape be again restored unto Him.

It will be my task then to consider to-day the relations of likeness and difference in which various parts of Scripture stand to one another; to show how the differences are not accidental, but do plainly correspond to certain fixed differences in the mental and moral constitutions of men; how there is evidently a gracious purpose of attracting all men by the attractions which shall be most potent upon them; of spreading a table at which all may sit down and find that wherein their soul delights, till those words of our text, "They did all eat and were filled," shall not be less true in regard of all the faithful now,—true rather in a higher sense,—than they were in regard of those comparatively few, whom the Lord nourished with that bread of wonder in the wilderness. And truly this Book, in the plainness and simplicity of many, and those most important, parts of it, might be likened well to the five barley-loaves of the Lord's miracle. Seeing them about to be set before the great spiritual hunger of the world, seeing the multitudes waiting to be fed, even disciples might have been tempted to exclaim, "What are they among so many?" But the great Giver of the feast confidently replies, "Make the men sit down;" and they *have* sat down—wise men and simple, philosophers and peasants, "besides women and children,"—and there has been enough and to spare; all have been nourished, all have been quickened; none have been sent empty away.

And first, let us take those books which must ever be regarded as the central books, relating as they do to the central fact, to the life of our blessed Lord, and which will afford the fullest illustration of my meaning. It is a fact which would at once excite every man's most thoughtful attention, were it not that familiarity had blunted us to its significance, that we should have, not one history only, but four parallel histories, of the life of Christ—a fact which indeed finds a slight anticipation in the parallel records which the Old Testament has preserved of some portions of Jewish history. None will call this an accident, or count that the Providence which watches over the fall of a sparrow, or any slightest incident of the world, was not itself the bringer about of a circumstance which should have so mighty an influence on all the future unfolding of the Church. It is part, no doubt, of this spreading of a table for the spiritual needs of all, that we have thus not one Gospel, but four; which yet in their higher unity, may be styled, according to

that word of Origen's, rather a four-sided Gospel*
than four Gospels, even as out of the same instinctive
sense of its unity, the whole Instrument, which contained the four, was entitled *Evangelium* in the early
Church.

And if we follow this more closely up, we can trace,
I think, a peculiar vocation in each of the Evangelists
for catching some distinct rays of the glory of Christ,
which the others would not catch, and for reflecting
them to the world—so that the terms, Gospel *according* to St. Matthew, *according* to St. Mark, and so
on, are singularly happy, and imply much more than
we, for whom the words are little more than a tech-
nical designation of the different gospels, are wont to
find in them. The first *is* the Gospel *according to*
St. Matthew—the Gospel as it appeared to him. This
which he has portrayed is *his* Christ: under this aspect the Deliverer of men appeared to him, and in
this he has presented Him to the world; and so also
with the others. For Christ, ever one and the same,
does yet appear with different sides of his glory re-
flected by the different Evangelists. They were themselves men of various temperaments; they had each
the special needs of some different classes of men in
their eye when they wrote their Gospels; and as these
classes, though under altered names, still subsist, they
have in this respect also, as ministering to these various
needs, an everlasting value.

* Ευαγγελιον τετραγωνον. Thus too Augustine (*In Ev. Joh.*,
Tract. 26·) Quatuor Evangelia, vel potius quatuor libri unius
Evangelii.

Thus the first Gospel, that of St. Matthew, was evidently a Gospel designed for the pious Israelite, for him who was waiting the theocratic King, the Son of Abraham, the Son of David; who desired to find in the New Testament the fulfilment of the prophecies of the Old, and in Christianity the perfect flower, of which Judaism was the root and stem. And as among the Epistles that of St. James, so among the Gospels, this of St. Matthew was to serve as the gentle and almost imperceptible transition for so many as clung to the forms of Old Testament piety; and desired to hold fast the historic connexion of all God's dealings from the first.

But the second Gospel, written, as all Church tradition testifies, under the influence of St. Peter, and at Rome, bears marks of an evident fitness for the practical Roman world—for the men who, while others talked, had done; and who would not at first crave to hear what Christ had spoken, but what He had wrought. It is eminently the Gospel of action. It is brief; it records comparatively few of our Lord's sayings, almost none of his longer discourses; it occupies itself mainly with his works, with the mighty power of his ministry, into which ministry it rushes almost without a preparatory note. Some deeper things it has not, but presents a soul-stirring picture of the conquering might and energy of Christ and of his Word.

But the third Gospel, that of St. Luke, composed by the trusted companion of St. Paul, and itself the correlative of his Epistles, while it sets forth one and the same Christ as the two which went before, yet in some respects sets Him forth in another light. Not so much, with St. Matthew, "Jesus Christ, a minister of the circumcision for the truth of God, to confirm the promise made unto the fathers"—not so much, with St. Mark, Jesus Christ, "the Lion of the tribe of Judah," rushing as with lion-springs from victory to victory; but Jesus Christ, the Saviour of all men, is the object of his portraiture. This is what he loves to dwell on,—the manner in which not Israel alone, but the whole heathen world, was destined to glorify God for his mercy in Christ Jesus; he describes Him as the loving physician, the gracious healer of all, the Good Samaritan that bound up the wounds of every stricken heart; in whom all the small and despised and crushed and down-trodden of the earth should find a gracious and ready helper. Therefore, and in accordance with this, his plan, has he gathered up for us much which no other has done; he sets the seventy disciples for the world over against St. Matthew's twelve Apostles for Israel; he breaks through narrow national distinctions—tells of that Samaritan, that alone showed kindness—of that other, who, of ten, alone remembered to be thankful; and his, too, and his only, the parable of the Prodigal Son, itself a gospel within the Gospel.

But to hasten on from these characteristics of the earlier three, which might well detain us much longer, something was yet wanting;—a Gospel in which the higher speculative tendencies, which were given to men not to be crushed or crippled, should find their

adequate satisfaction—a Gospel which should link itself on with whatever had occupied the philosophic mind of heathen or of Jew—the correction of all which in this was false—the complement of all which was deficient. And such he gave us, for whom the Church has ever found the soaring eagle as the fittest emblem*
—he who begins with declaring that the Word of God, whereof men had already learned to speak so much, was also the Son of God, and had been made flesh, and had dwelt among us, full of grace and truth, —who, too, has brought out the inner, and, so to speak, the mystical relations of the faithful with their Lord, as none other before him had done.†

It is true that this fulness under which the life of our Lord has been set forth to us, being, as it is, one of the gracious designs of God for our good, has been laid hold of by adversaries of the Faith, who would fain wrest it to their ends. Taking the difference, where it is the most striking, they have bidden us to

---

* Thus the Christian poet:

Cœlum transit, veri rotam	Volat avis sine metâ
Solis ibi vidit, totam	Quo nec vates, nec propheta
Mentis figens aciem	Evolavit altius.
Speculator spiritalis	Tam implenda quàm impleta
Quasi Seraphim sub alis	Nunquam vidit tot secreta
Dei videt faciem.	Purus homo purius.

† See Origen's interesting discussion (*Comm. in Joan., Tom.* I.) on the relation of the Gospels to the other Scriptures, and their relation, within themselves, one to another. On this latter subject he expresses himself thus: Τολμητέον τοίνυν ειπειν ἀπαρχὴν μεν πασῶν γραφῶν ειναι τὰ εναγγέλια, τῶν δὲ εὐαγγέλιων ἀπαρχὴν τὸ κατὰ Ἰωάννην.

note how unlike the Christ of the first three Gospels and of the fourth; and what a different colouring is spread over this Gospel and over those; and they would draw their conclusion, that either here or there historic accuracy must be wanting, that both portraits cannot be faithful. We allow the charge, so far as the *difference*, and only reject it when it assumes a *diversity*, of setting forth. There *are* features of our Lord which we should have missed but for his portraiture who lay upon the Lord's bosom; deep words which he has caught up, for which no other words that any other has recorded would have been adequate substitutes. But what then? This is not a weak point with us, but a strong. We rejoice and glory in this, rather than seek to gloss it over or conceal it. So far from being first detected by a hostile criticism, an early Father of the Church had expressed this very distinction in words which in sound perhaps are almost over-bold, styling the first three Gospels, ευαγγελια σωματικα, and the fourth an ευαγγελιον πνευματικον. Yet it is needless to observe, that herein he meant not to cast the faintest slight on those by comparison with this, but would only imply that those set forth more the outer, and this the inner, life of Christ.

And for the fact itself, do we not find analogies to it, however weak ones they may be, in lower regions of the spiritual life? To take an example which must be familiar to every scholar,—how different the Socrates of Xenophon, and the Socrates of Plato. Yet shall we therefore leap to the conclusion, that if the one has painted the master truly, then the other has portrayed him falsely? Such a conclusion may lie upon the surface; it might appear to us an easy solution of the difficulty; yet were it a very different solution from that to which all the profoundest inquirers into the matter have arrived. Were it not wiser to suppose, with them, that each of the great scholars of the Sage appropriated and carried away, as from a rich and varied treasure-house, that which he prized the most, that which was most akin to himself and his own genius, that which by the natural process of assimilation he had made most truly and entirely his own;—the practical soldier, the man of strong common sense, appropriating and carrying away his world-wisdom, his popular philosophy; the more meditative disciple taking as his portion the deeper speculations of their common Master concerning the Good and the True? And if thus it prove with eminent servants of the Truth—if they are so rich and manifold that they present themselves under divers aspects to divers men, it being appointed them in their lower sphere to feed many,—if, like some rich composite Corinthian metal, they yield iron for this man's spade, and gold for the other's crown, how much more was this to be looked for from Him, who was the King of Truth, who was to feed and enrich, not some, but all; and *this*, not in some small and scanty measure, but who was to *satisfy* all in all ages with goodness and truth? How inevitable was it that He, the Sun of the spiritual heaven, should find no single mirror large enough to take in all his beams—should only be adequately presented to the world, when many from many sides did, under the direct teachings of God's Spirit, undertake to set him forth.

Doubtless the pregnant symbol of the early Church, according to which the four Gospels found their type and prophecy in the four rivers of Paradise, that together watered the whole earth, going each a different way, and yet issuing all from a single head;—a symbol, which we find evermore repeated in the works of early Christian art, wherein, from a single cross-surmounted hill, four streams are seen welling out; this symbol was so great and general a favourite, because it did embody under a beautiful image, this fact, namely, how the Gospels were indeed four, and yet in their higher unity but one.* And so not less, when the Evangelists were found, as they often were, in the four living creatures of Ezekiel's vision, of whom each with a different countenance looked a different way, and yet all of them together upheld the throne and chariot of God, and ever moved as being informed by

---

* Allusions to it are frequent in the early hymnologists. Thus, one of them in a hymn, *De SS. Evangelistis:*

Paradisus his rigatur,	Horum rivo ebretatis
Viret, floret, fæcundatur,	Sitis crescat caritatis,
His abundat, his lætatur,	Ut de fonte Deitatis
Quatuor fluminibus.	Satiemur plenius.
Fons est Christus, hi sunt rivi,	Horum trahat nos doctrina
Fons est altus, hi proclivi,	Vitiorum de sentinâ,
Ut saporem fontis vivi	Sicque ducat ad divina
Ministrent fidelibus.	Ab imo superius

Another, too, in a hymn, *De S. Joanne Evangelistâ:*

Inter illos primitivos	Toti mundo propinare
Veros veri fontis rivos	Nectar illud salutare
Joannes exilut,	Quod de throno prodiit.

one and the self-same Spirit; this too was something more and better than a mere fanciful playing with Scripture; there was a deep truth lying at the root of this application, and abundantly justifying its use.*

* The first that we know of who connected these with the four Evangelists was Irenæus. He says (*Con. Hær.*, l. 3, c. 2, § 8,) Τετράμορφα γὰρ τὰ ζῶα, τετράμορφον καὶ τὸ εὐαγγέλιον, and draws out at length the fitness of each to represent each, on which see Suicer's *Thes.*, s. v. εὐαγγελιστής. It was taken up by many after him, thus by Jerome, *Comm. in Ezek.* c. 1 ; *Prol. in Comm. super Matth.*; and *Ep.* 50: Matthæus, Marcus, Lucas, et Johannes, quadriga Domini, et verum Cherubim, per totum corpus oculati sunt, scintillæ emicant, discurrunt fulgura, pedes habent rectos et in sublime tendentes, terga pennata et ubique volitantia Tenent se mutuò, sibique perplexi sunt, et quasi rotâ in rotâ volvuntur, et purgunt quoquumque eos flatus Sancti Spiritûs perduxerit. Cf. Augustine, *De Cons. Evang.* l. 1, c. 6, and the Christian poet sings thus:

Circa thronum majestatis
Cum spiritibus beatis
Quatuor diversitatis
Astant animalia.

Formam primum aquilinam,
Et secundum leoninam;
Sed humanam et bovinam
Duo gerunt alia.

And another:

Curam agens sui gregis
Pastor bonus, auctor legis
Quatuor instituit:
Quadri orbis ad medelam,
Formam juris et cautelam
Per quos scribi voluit.

Circa thema generale
Habet quisque speciale
Sibi privilegium,

Formæ formant figurarum
Formas Evangelistarum,
Quorum imber doctrinarum
Stillat in Ecclesiâ.

Hi sunt Marcus, et Matthæus,
Lucas, et quem Zebedæus
Pater misit tibi, Deus,
Dum laxaret retia

Quos designat in propheta
Formâ pictus sub discretâ
Vultus animalium.

His quadrigis deportatur
Mundo Deus, sublimatur
Istis arca vectibus.
Paradisi hæc fluenta
Nova fluunt sacramenta,
Quæ irrorant gentibus.

And as we have a Gospel which stands thus foursquare, with a side facing each side of the spiritual world, so have we a two-fold development of the more dogmatic element of the New Testament. For, like as the seed, one in itself, yet falls into two halves in the process of its fructifying, or as the one force of the magnet manifests itself at two opposing poles, exactly according to the same law, reappearing in the spiritual world, we have two developments of the same Christian theology, which make themselves felt from the very first, whereof St. Paul may be taken as chief representative of the one, and St. John of the other. We cannot do more than trace the distinction in some of its broadest features. We see then St. Paul making man the starting point of his theology. The divine image in man, that image lost, the impossibility of its restoration by any powers of his own; the ever deeper errors of the sin-darkened intellect; the ever vainer struggles of the sin-enslaved will;—it is from this human side of the truth that he starts; these are the grounds which he first lays,—as eminently in his great dogmatic Epistle to the Romans. And only when he has brought out this confession of a fall, of an infinite short-coming from the true ideal of humanity, and from the glory of God, only when the cry, "Oh, wretched man that I am, who shall deliver me?" has been wrung out from the bond-slaves of evil, does he bring in the mighty Redeemer, and the hymn of praise, the "I thank God through Jesus Christ" of the redeemed. But St. John, upon the other hand, starts from the opposite point, from the theology in the more restricted sense of the word; in this justifying the title ὁ Θεολογός, which he bears. His centre and starting point is the Divine Love, and out of that he unfolds all; not delineating, as his brother Apostle, any mighty birth-pangs, in which the new creature is born; since rather in that passing from death unto life, and in that abiding in the Father and in the Son which follows therefrom, the discovery of sin does not run long before, but rather goes hand in hand with, the discovery of the grace of God for forgiving, and the power of God for overcoming, that sin which by the Spirit of Christ is gradually revealed. Thus we have man delivered in St. Paul, God delivering in St. John; man rising in the one, God stooping in the other; and thus each travels over a hemisphere in the great orb of Christian Truth, and they, not each singly, but between them, embrace and encircle it all.

For this is part of the glory of Christ as compared with his servants, as compared with the chiefest of his servants, that He alone stands at the absolute centre of humanity, the one completely harmonious man, unfolding all which was in that humanity *equally* upon all sides, *fully* upon all sides—the only one in whom the real and ideal met, and were absolutely at one. Every other man has idiosyncrasies, characteristics— some features, that is, of his character, marked more strongly than others, fitnesses for one task rather than for another, more genial powers in one direction than in others. Nor even are the greatest, a St. Paul or a St. John, exempted from this law; but, according to this law, are made to serve for the kingdom of God; and the regeneration, even that mighty transformation itself, does not dissolve these characteristics, but rather hallows and glorifies them, using them for the work of God. And thus, in the power of these special gifts, that which lay as a fruitful germ in the doctrine, or, more truly, in the facts of our Lord's life, was by his two Apostles developed upon this side and upon that.

And as it was meant that the Gospel of Christ should embrace all lands, should fix, at its first entrance into the world, a firm foot upon either of its two great cultivated portions, so in these two, in St. Paul and in St. John, we recognise wondrous preparations in the providence of God for the winning to the obedience of the cross both the western and the eastern world. Who can fail to see in the great Apostle of Tarsus, in his discursive intellect, in his keen dialectics, in his philosophic training, the man armed to dispute with Stoic and Epicurean at Athens; who should teach the Church how she should take the West for her inheritance?—nor less was he the man who, by the past struggles of his inner life and the consequent fulness and power with which he brought out the scheme of our justification should become the spiritual forefather of the Augustines and Luthers, of all them who have brought out for us, with the sense of personal guilt, the sense also of personal deliverance, the consciousness of a personal standing of each one of us before God. And in St. John, the full significance of whose writings for the Church is probably yet to be revealed, and, it may be, will not appear till the coming in of the nations of the east into the fold, we have the progenitor of every mystic, in the nobler sense of that word—of every contemplative spirit that has delighted to sink and to lose itself, and the sense of its own littleness, in the brightness and in the glory of God. Shall we not thank God, shall we not recognise as part of his loving wisdom, that thus none are left out; that while there are evidently among men two leading types of mind, he has made provision for them both—for the discursive and the intuitive,—for the schoolman and the mystic,—for them who trust through knowing to see, and for them also who believe that only through seeing they can know;—that, whatever in their intellectual condition men may be, the net is laid out to catch them? For then, when once they are taken, all that might have been in them of overbalance in one direction, all of faulty excess, is gradually done away and redressed, till they and those that have been brought in by an opposite method, are more and more led to a mutual recognition and honouring of the gifts each of the other, and to the unity of a perfect man in Christ Jesus.

Nor is it only that there is different nourishment for different souls, but the same nourishment is also so curiously mixed and tempered, that it is felt to be for all. As, perhaps, the most signal example of this, let us only seek to realize to ourselves what the Book of Psalms, itself, according to that beautiful expression of Luther's, 'a Bible in little,' has been, and for whom—how men of all conditions, all habits of thought, have here met, vying with one another in expressions of affection and gratitude to this book, in telling what they owed to it, and what it had proved to them. Men seemingly the most unlikely to express enthusiasm about any such matter—lawyers and statists immersed deeply in the world's business, classical scholars familiar with other models of beauty, other standards of art—these have been forward as the forwardest to set their seal to this book, have left their confession that it was the voice of their inmost heart, that the spirit of it past into their spirits as did the spirit of no other book, that it found them more often and at greater depths of their being, lifted them to higher heights than did any other—or, as one greatly suffering man, telling of the solace which he found from this book of Psalms in the hours of a long imprisonment, has expressed it,—that it bore him up, as a lark perched between an eagle's wings is borne up into the everlasting sunlight, till he saw the world and all its trouble for ever underneath him. I can imagine no fairer volume than one of such thankful acknowledgments as I have described, and it is a volume which might easily be gathered, for such on all sides abound; not a few of them as large, as free, as rapturous as that of our own Hooker, which must be present to the minds of many of us here. Nor is it wonderful that there should be such; for, to quote but one noble utterance[*] in relation to this book, "the conflict of naked

[*] Maurice's *Moral and Metaphysical Philosophy* in the *Encyclop. Metropolitana.*

power with righteousness, of the visible with the invisible, of confusion with order, of the devilish with the divine, of death with life, this is its subject. And because this is the subject of all human anxieties, this book has been that in which living and suffering men in all ages have found a language, which they have felt to be a mysterious anticipation of, and provision for, their own especial wants, and in which they have gradually understood that the Divine voice is never so truly and distinctly heard, as when it speaks through human experience and sympathies."*

* The reader may be well pleased to see a few more of these brought at a single glance under his eye. St. Basil may fitly lead. In a passage *Hom. I in Psalmos*, quoted at much greater length in Suicer's *Thes.* s. v. Ψαλμός, Ψαλμὸς δαιμόνων φυγαδευτήριον· τῆς τῶν ἀγγέλων βοηθείας ἐπαγωγή· ὅπλον ἐν φόβοις νυκτερινοῖς, ἀνάπαυσις κόπων ἡμερινῶν· νηπίοις ἀσφάλεια ἀκμάζουσιν ἐγκαλλώπισμα πρεσβυτέροις παρηγορία γυναιξὶ κόσμος ἁρμοδιώτατος τὰς ἐρημίας οἰκίζει· τὰς ἀγορὰς σωφρονίζει· εἰσαγομένοις στοιχείωσις, προκοπτόντων αὔξησις, τελειουμένων στήριγμα, ἐκκλησίας φωνή. οὗτος τὰς ἑορτὰς φαιδρύνει οὗτος τὴν κατὰ Θεὸν λύπην δημιουργεῖ. Ψαλμὸς γὰρ καὶ ἐκ λιθίνης καρδίας δάκρυον ἐκκαλεῖται Ψαλμὸς τὸ τῶν ἀγγέλων ἔργον, τὸ οὐράνιον πολίτευμα, τὸ πνευματικὸν θυμίαμα, κ τ λ. St. Ambrose, as it was often his manner to reproduce what he found in the Greek Fathers to his purpose, would seem to have had this passage of his great eastern contemporary in his mind when he composed his not less beautiful laud of the Psalms. *Enarr. in Ps.* i. Here too it is but a fragment which can be quoted. Historia instruit, Lex docet, prophetia annunciat, correptio castigat, moralitas suadet: in libro Psalmorum profectus est omnium, et medicina quædam salutis humanæ. Quicunque legerit, habet quo propriæ vulnera passionis speciali possit curare remedio...Quantum laboratur in Ecclesiâ ut fiat

THE MANIFOLDNESS OF SCRIPTURE. 69

Indeed, in the fact of such a book as the Psalter forming part of our sacred Instrument, we trace a most gracious purpose of God. For in the very idea of a Revelation is implied rather a speaking of God

silentium, cum lectiones leguntur! Si unus loquatur, obstrepunt universi: cùm psalmus legitur, ipse sibi est effector silentii. Omnes loquuntur, et nullus obstrepit. Psalmum reges sine potestatis supercilio resultant. In hoc se ministerio David gaudebat videri. Psalmus cantatur ab imperatoribus, jubilatur à populis. Certant clamare singuli quod omnibus proficit. Domi psalmus canitur, foris recensetur. Sine labore percipitur, cum voluptate servatur: psalmus dissidentes copulat, discordes sociat, offensos reconciliat ..Certat in Psalmo doctrina cum gratià simul. Cantatur ad delectationem, discitur ad eruditionem. Nam violentiora præcepta non permanent: quod autem cum suavitate perceperis, id infusum semel præcordiis, non consuevit elabi. And Augustine (*Confess*, l. 9, c. 4,) speaks of the manner in which he exulted in the Psalms at the time of his first conversion: Quas tibi, Deus meus, voces dedi cum legerem psalmos David...et quomodo in te inflammabar ex eis, et accendebar eos recitare si possem toto orbe terrarum adversùm typhum humani generis...Quàm vehementi et acri dolore indignabar Manichæis, et miserebar eos rursus, quod illa sacramenta, illa medicamenta nescirent, et insani essent adversùs antidotum quo sani esse potuissent.

Jeremy Taylor, in his Preface to the *Psalter of David*, speaking of the manner in which, by the trouble of the civil wars, he was deprived of his books and his retirements, and how in his deprivation he found comfort here, thus goes on: "Indeed, when I came to look upon the Psalter with a nearer observation, and an eye diligent to espy any advantages and remedies there deposited...I found so many admirable promises, so rare variety of the expressions of the mercies of God, so many consolatory hymns, the commemoration of so many deliverances from dangers and deaths and enemies, so many miracles of

to men than of men to God; and such a speaking from
heaven predominantly finds place in all other books
of Holy Scripture. Yet how greatly had we been
losers, had there been no corresponding record of the
answering voices that go up from earth unto heaven.
How earnestly should we have craved a standard by
which to try the feelings, the utterances of our spirits,
—a rule whereby to know whether they were healthy
and true, the same voices, the same cries, as those of
each other regenerate man. Such a rule, such a
standard we have here; man *is* speaking unto God;

mercy and salvation, that I began to be so confident as to believe there could come no affliction great enough to spend so
great a stock of comfort as was laid up in the treasure of the
Psalter, the saying of St. Paul was here verified, 'If sin' and
misery 'did abound, then did grace superabound;' and as we
believe of the passion of Christ, it was so great as to be able
to satisfy for a thousand worlds, so is it of the comforts of
David's Psalms, they are more than sufficient to repair all the
breaches of mankind." And Donne, (*Sermon* 66,) taking his
text from Ps. lxiii. 7, proceeds: "The Psalms are the manna
of the Church. As manna tasted to every man like that that
he liked best, so do the Psalms minister instruction and
satisfaction to every man in every emergency and occasion.
David was not only a clear prophet of Christ himself, but a
prophet of every particular Christian, he foretells what I, what
any, shall do and suffer and say. And as the whole book of
Psalms is *oleum effusum,* an ointment poured out upon all sorts
of sores, a searcloth that supples all bruises, a balm that
searches all wounds, so are there some certain psalms that are
imperial psalms, that command over all affections, and spread
themselves over all occasions, catholic universal psalms that
apply themselves to all necessities."

that which came from heaven is returning to heaven once more. Here we have insight into the mystery of prayer; streams of life are rising up as high as the heights from which first they came down; the mountain-tops of man's spirit are smoking, but smoking because God has descended upon and touched them.

These are but a few examples, brethren,—time will allow us to adduce no more,—of that which all Scripture will abundantly supply,—the evidences, namely, of its own adaptation for the needs of all, for all the needs of each. And these things being so, let us for ourselves gladly enter into this many-chambered palace of the Truth, whereof the doors stand open to us evermore. Let us thankfully sit down at this feast of many spiritual dainties, which is spread for us and for all. And if not every one of them at once delight us; if of some we have rather to take the word of others that they are good than as yet proved it so ourselves, let us believe that the cause of this lies rather in the sickness of our palate, than in the faulty preparation of that which the great Master of the feast has set before us;—and let us ask, not that these be removed, but that our true taste be restored; and this the more, seeing that unnumbered guests, who in time past have sat down, or are now sitting down, at this heavenly banquet, have borne witness that these meats which may be dull and tasteless to us, were life and strength to them, "yea, sweeter than honey and the honeycomb." We are sick, and these are medicines no less than food; and for us that word must stand fast, *Non corrigat æger medicamenta sua.* Let us thus bear ourselves towards Holy Scripture, and then presently, in that which seemed a stranger face we shall recognise the countenance of a gracious, a familiar friend. We shall more and more see how this Scripture was laid out by One who knew what was in man, One who desired also to unfold us on all sides of our moral and spiritual being; who, too, in the largeness of his love, would send none empty away; but who does herein open his hand, that He may fill all things living with plenteousness.

LECTURE IV.

THE ADVANCE OF SCRIPTURE.

HEBREWS I. 1, 2.

God, who at sundry times and in divers manners spake in time past unto the fathers by the prophets, hath in these last days spoken unto us by his Son.

We have seen how in Holy scripture one idea is dominant, the idea of a lost, defaced, and yet not wholly effaced, image of God in man, with God's scheme for its restoration and renewal: we have seen how that, which is one in having this for its subject, and in knowing no other subject, has yet a manifold development, marvellously corresponding to the manifold necessities of his nature to whom it is addressed, and who by its help should be renewed. But the progressive unfolding of God's plan in Scripture, may well afford matter for another discourse, and will supply our theme for this day.

Nor shall I herein be wandering from my argument, since this progressiveness of Scripture is an important element in its fitness for the education of man. For this we claim of a teacher to whom we yield ourselves with an entire confidence, that there be advance and progress in his teaching; not indeed that this should be at every moment distinctly perceptible, but that it should be so when long periods and courses of his teaching are contemplated together. The advance may sometimes be rather in a spiral than in a straight line, yet still on the whole there must be advance; he must not eddy round in ceaseless circles, leaving off where he began, but evidently have a scheme before him, according to which he is seeking to lead on unto perfection those that have committed themselves to his teaching. It is of the essence of a true teacher, be that teacher book or person, thus to carry forward. If it be a book claiming to educate, it must be itself the history of an education, the record of an intensive, as well as extensive development. We look for this, and we rest our expectation on a yet deeper feeling. We feel that as each individual man was meant to go on from lower to higher, and in the end to have Christ fully formed in him, so the Church as a living body could not have been intended to be a stationary thing, always conning over the same lessons, but rather advancing in a like manner to perfection;—not in this advance leaving aught behind which God has taught it; but ever carrying with it into its higher state, as part of its realized possession, all which it has gotten in a lower. And if so, that Book which was to be the record and interpreter of these dealings of God, ever running parallel with them, growing with their growth, explaining them as they unfolded themselves, that must bear the stamp and impress of the same progress.

Does a nearer examination of Holy Scripture bear out this our expectation? Does it speak of itself as a progressive revelation of the Name of God? And if so, can we discern it to be such, to be the gradual unfolding of the ideas of the kingdom, and of men's relations to it, to be a continual calling out in them the sense of new relations and new faculties and powers? I think, both. And, first, Revelation speaks of itself in such language. "I have many things to say unto you; but ye cannot bear them now;" surely this was what God had been saying to his elect from the first, till that crowning day of Pentecost, when they were made capable of all mysteries and had the unction of the Holy One, and knew all things;—and with much before us, it needs not to tarry with the proofs of this.

And as regards ourselves, we can trace, I think, the Scripture to be this which it affirms itself to be. Who, for instance, can help feeling that in the three memorable epochs by which it marks the greatest unfoldings of the kingdom of God,—I mean, in the calling of Abraham, the giving of the Law by Moses, the Incarnation of the Son of God,—we have the childhood, the youth, the manhood of our race, of that elect portion of it, at least, which God had gathered into a Church and constituted for the while the representative of all; and that we have this with marvellous correspondencies of these epochs to similar periods in the lives which we ourselves are living?

In Abraham and the Church of the patriarchal age, we have that which exactly answers to childhood. Their relations to God were as a child's to a father, —the same undoubting, unquestioning affiance; with as yet no fixed code of law; the deeper evils of the heart not as yet stirring, the awful consciousness of those evils as yet unawakened. So Abraham and the patriarchs walked before God, in the beauty and the simplicity of a childlike faith—love seeming as yet the only law, and no other law being needed, since not yet the whole might of the rebellious will had been aroused, since a sheltering Providence had hitherto kept aloof many temptations which should afterwards arrive.

But a very different stage of man's history begins with Moses. The father is thrown for awhile into the background by the lawgiver; God appears the giver of a "fiery law:" and the race having outgrown its childlike estate, with all the blessed privileges of that time, appears now as the youth, aware of this terrible law, and struggling against it; and in this struggle brought to a consciousness of that which before was hidden from it, namely, the deep alienation of its will from the perfect will of God. This seems, at first sight, as though it were a retrograde step in man's progress, and regarded apart from the final issues it were; as the Apostle himself confesses, when he says, "I was alive without the law once, but when the commandment came, sin revived, and I died." Yet nor 'he, nor any, could have done without this coming in of the law. The opposition of his will to God's will being in man, most needful was it that it should not remain latent, but be brought out, yea brought out in all its strength, as a holy law could alone bring it out; for thus only was it in the way of being subdued. God having made himself known as a God of love, most needful was it that men should know Him also the God of an absolute righteousness; since without this that love itself had shown in men's eyes as a poor 'thing, as a weak toleration of their evil, instead of being, as it is, that which more than all else makes Him a consuming fire for all impurity and evil.

But with the entering of the Son of God into our nature, the manhood of the race begins—that which it was meant in its final perfection to be—that, for the sake of which it passed through those lower stages. The consciousness of the filial relation has again revived in all its full strength, and the suspended privileges are restored. "Abba, Father!" is once more on the lips of the Church, only with deeper accents and a fuller sense than at that earlier day of all which in these words is included. The sense of God's love which belonged to its childhood, of God's righteousness which predominated in its youth, are reconciled; they have met and kissed each other. His love is seen to be righteous, and his righteousness to be loving. His law is no longer struggled against, for it is written in the heart, and it reveals itself as that which to keep is the truest blessedness.

And how mysteriously, brethren, does this teaching of our race, which was thus written large, and acted out upon a great scale in the history of God's chosen people, repeat itself evermore in the smaller world, in the microcosm of elect souls, which are under the same divine education. Is there not many a one who can trace in himself the same process and progress as we have been following here? First was our childhood, corresponding to Abraham's state—the undeveloped, yet true affiance on a heavenly Father,—when we needed no more than this; when as yet we had not looked down into the abysmal deeps of evil in our hearts, when we too were alive without the law, and dreamt not of the rebel, who was ready, when occasion came, to take arms against his Lord, though that rebel was no other than ourselves.

But the years went on, with all which they brought, with their good and with their evil: and childhood was left behind; and to us, too, the time arrived for the giving of the law; and then us, too, God led apart into the wilderness, separated us from every other living soul, made us feel the mystery of our awful personality, and spoke to us as He had never spoken before, even face to face,—revealing Himself to us no longer merely as the God of our fathers, but with a higher revelation, as the I AM, the Holy One. For us, too, was that terrible giving of the law in the deep of our souls, which he who has known will say boldly, that Sinai with its thunders and lightnings, its blackness and its darkness, its unendurable voice which he who heard craved that he might hear no more, was not *more* terrible;—and sin is no longer a word but a reality, is no longer felt as the transient grieving of a parent's heart, but as the violation of an eternal order, a violation which cannot remain unavenged or unredressed. But dreadful as this law is, terrible and threatening shape as it rises over the soul, does not each man make the same experience as did Israel of old, and find out its helplessness for the true ends of his life? It can kill the sinner, but it cannot kill the sin: *that* only shrinks deeper into its hiding-places in the soul, and needs another charmer to lure it out. This is *our* state of condemnation, which is yet most needful for a right entering into the state of life and freedom: this is the law preparing for, and handing over unto, Christ.

And as there was the manhood of the race, as the Church which God had been training and disciplining so long, was introduced into the fulness of its inheritance, when Christ, who had upheld it always, came visibly into the midst of it; so is it in like manner when God brings his First-begotten into the inner world of any single heart. Then that heart understands all the way by which it had been led, and sees how all things have worked for the bringing it into that grace in which now it stands. Then the child's faith returns; only is it now a mightier faith, a more heroic act of affiance, for it is a faith in God *despite of* and in full knowledge of our evil, instead of a faith in God *in ignorance of* our evil.

Marvellously does He thus run oftentimes the lives of his children parallel with the life of the Church at large, as that life is unfolded in Sacred Writ, bringing each in particular under the same teaching as the whole. Yet this is not all: we have not merely in Scripture God carrying Israel his Son through successive stages, which may serve to explain to us the stages of our own innermost spiritual life; but we may trace

there another sequence, another progress—that by
which He is training his people into a sense of ever-
widening relationships, and this also making answer
to the sequence in which He trains each one in particular of his children into the same, and serving as a
pattern thereto. For what are the great fellowships
of men, which rest not upon man's choice, but upon
God's will, which are not self-willed associations into
which men gather of themselves, but societies wherein
they are set by the act of God? Each will at once
reply, The Family, The State, The Church. And
this too is their order; the Family must go before the
State, being itself the corner-stone on which the State
is built; and the State, which is the fellowship of certain men to the exclusion of others, waits to be taken
up into the Church, which is the fellowship of all men
who believe in the risen head of their race.

And this sequence is that maintained in the Bible;
for what is the early history of the Bible, but predominantly the history of the Family? of the blessing
which awaits reverence for the family order, of the
sure curse which avenges its violation. On the one
side, we have the men who were true to this divine
institute; who, amid many weaknesses, recognised and
honoured it—the Seths and Enochs before the flood,
the Abrahams and Isaacs, the Jacobs and Josephs
after. On the other side we have the Lamechs and
Tubal Cains, and at a later day, the builders of Babel,
the men who thought to associate *themselves*, to say,
A confederacy, where God had not said it, to knit
themselves into a body by bands of their own, instead

of owning that God had knit them already—skilled masters, as we learn, in the arts of life, starting up, as we are told, into a premature civilization; yet having in themselves, through violations, which we can plainly trace, of that family order, of the primal institutes of humanity, the seeds of a sure and swift decay: so that presently they are lost to our sight altogether; while the Patriarchs, the honourers and sanctifiers of these relations, walk before us heads of a nation, of that kingly and priestly nation in which all other nations should be blest.

But Holy Scripture does not linger here. It passes on, and its middle history is the history of this nation, of national life; showing us, by liveliest example, all that can exalt, all that can degrade, a people: how Israel, so long as it believed in its invisible Lord and King, its righteous Lawgiver, was great and prosperous—how, when it lost that faith and bowed to idols of sense, it became of a surety inwardly distracted, externally enslaved—forfeiting those very outward gifts for the sake of which it had turned its back upon the Giver—righteousness and truth and justice perishing between man and man, while He in whom alone these have any substantial existence was no longer held fast to and believed.

And then in the New Testament, not the conditions under which the Family can exist, not the conditions under which the State, but the idea of the Church, of that fellowship, which, including all, may itself be included by none, is unfolded to us. There we behold the laws of the universal kingdom, and Christ, not the

King of a single nation, but the Head of humanity, the Saviour of all.

And this order of Sacred Scripture, is also the order of our lives. I mean not that we first become members of a family and then of a State, and lastly of a Church; but this is the order in which we become conscious of relations. For what is it that a child first discovers? that it is the member of a family— that it has kindred. What are its earliest duties? a faithful entering into these relations; its earliest sins? a refusal to enter into them. And what next? that there is a wider fellowship than this of home-love and home-affections, to which it belongs; that there are other men to whom it owes other duties; that it is the member of a State no less than a family, that it must be just as well as loving. And last of all is perceived that there is yet another fellowship at the root of both these fellowships, which gives them their meaning, which alone upholds and sustains them against all the sin and selfishness which are continually threatening their dissolution—a fellowship with the Lord of men, and in Him with every man of that race which He has redeemed, of that nature which He has taken. And so the cycle of God's teaching is complete, and that cycle in which the Scripture shows us that He taught the world, is found here also again to be the cycle in which he teaches the individual soul.

But to pass to quite another province of our subject:—we must not leave unobserved the manner in which prophecy bears witness to this progressive unfolding of God's purpose with our race. Often we dishonour prophecy, when the chief value which it has in our eyes is the use to which it may be turned as evidence; when we regard it as serving no nobler ends, as having no deeper root in the economy of God than in this are presumed; when it is for us merely a *miraculum scientiæ*, which, with the miracles properly so called, the *miracula potentiæ*, may do duty in proving against cavillers the divine origin of our Faith; when all that we can find is that the doers of the works and the utterers of the words did and said what was beyond the reach and scope of common men. But the fact that prophecy should constitute so large an element in Scripture finds its explanation rather in that law which we have been tracing throughout *all* Scripture—the law, I mean, of an orderly development, according to which there is nothing sudden, nothing abrupt or unprepared in his counsels, all whose works were known to him from the beginning. It is part of this law that there should ever be prefigurations of the coming, that truths so vast and so mighty as those of the New Covenant, so difficult for man's heart to conceive, should have their way prepared, should, ere they arrive in their highest shape, give pledge and promise of themselves in lower forms and in weaker rudiments.

Thus was it good that before the appearing of the Son of God in the flesh, there should be, in the language of Bishop Bull, "preludings of the Incarnation," transient apparitions of Him in a human form, though not in the verity of our human nature.—Thus was it ordered that each one of the mighty acts of our Lord's life should not stand wholly apart, and without analogy in any thing which had gone before, but ever find in something earlier its lineaments and its outlines. Weak and faint these lineaments may have been, weak and faint they must have been, when compared with the glory that excelleth; yet sketches and outlines and foreshadowings still of the glory to be revealed. Thus, more than one was wonderfully born, with many circumstances of a strange solemnity, with heavenly announcements, with much that went beyond human expectation, ere HE was born, by the annunciation of an Angel, through the overshadowing of the Holy Ghost, whose name should be called Wonderful, The Mighty God. So we may say that in the shining of Moses' face, as he came down from the mount of God, we have already a weaker Transfiguration, a feeble fore-announcement of that brightness which, not from without, but breaking forth from within, should clothe with a light which no words could adequately utter, not the face only, but the whole person, of the Son of God. So again, in the translation of Elijah, the lineaments of *his* Ascension appear, who, not rapt in a chariot of fire, not needing the cleansing of that fiery baptism, nor requiring that commissioned chariot to bear him up, did in the far sublimer calmness of his own indwelling power arise from the earth, and with his human body pass into the heavenly places.* And once more, in the dividing of the Spirit

* Gregory the Great (*Hom. in Evang.*) Elias in curru le-

THE ADVANCE OF SCRIPTURE.

which Moses had, upon the seventy elders of Israel, so that they all did prophesy, we recognise an earlier though a weaker Pentecost; in which, however, the later was surely implied: for if from the servant could be imparted of his spirit, how much more and in what larger measure from the Son? All these should be contemplated as preparatory workings in a lower sphere of the same Spirit, which afterwards wrought more gloriously in the later and crowning acts; as knit to those later by an inner law, as sharers of the same organic life with them.

The rending away of isolated passages, and then saying, This Psalm, or That chapter of Isaiah, is prophetic, and has to do with Christ and his kingdom,— and this without explaining how it comes that these have to do, and those nearest them have not, can never truly satisfy; men's minds resist this fragmentary capricious exposition. The portions of Scripture thus adduced very likely are those in which prophecy concentrates itself more than in any other: they may be the strongest expressions of that Spirit which quickens the whole mass; but it has not forsaken the other portions to gather itself up exclusively in these.

Rather the subtle threads of prophecy are woven

gitur ascendisse, ut videlicet apertè demonstraretur, quia homo purus adjutorio indigebat alieno. Per angelos quippe facta et ostensa sunt adjumenta, quia nec in cœlum quidem aerium per se ascendere poterat quem naturæ suæ infirmitas gravabat Redemtor autem noster non curru, non angelis sublevatus legitur quia is qui fecerat omnia, nimirum super omnia suâ virtute ferebatur.

through every part of the woof and texture, not separable from thence without rending and destroying the whole. All the Old Testament, as the record of a divine constitution pointing to something higher than itself, administered by men who were ever looking beyond themselves to a Greater that should come, who were uttering, as the Spirit stirred them, the deepest longings of their souls after *his* appearing, is prophetic; and this, not by an arbitrary appointment, which meant thus to supply evidences ready to hand for the truth of Revelation, in the curious tallying of the Old with the New, the remarkable fulfilments of the foretold, but prophetic according to the inmost necessities of the case, which would not suffer it to be otherwise.

For how could God, bringing to pass what was good and true, do other than make it resemble what was best and truest, which he should one day bring to pass? Raising up holy men, how could he avoid giving them features of likeness to the Holiest of all? appointing them functions and offices in which to bless their brethren, how could these otherwise than anticipate his functions and his office, who should come in the fulness of blessing to his people? Inspiring them to speak, stirring by the breath of his Spirit the deepest chords of their hearts, how could He bring forth from them any other notes but those which made the deepest music of their lives; their longings, namely, after the promised Redeemer, their yearnings after the kingdom of his righteousness,—mere longings and yearnings no longer now, since the Spirit that inspired such utterances, being the very Spirit of Truth, gave pledge, in sanctioning and working the desire, that the fulfilment of that desire in due time should not be wanting? If the poet had right when he spake of

"the prophetic soul
Of the great world, dreaming of things to come,"

by how much higher reason must a prophetic soul have dwelt in Israel, by which it not vaguely dreamed, but in some sort felt itself already in possession, of the great things to come, whereof it knew that the seeds and germs were laid so deeply in its own bosom? We may say of Judaism, that it bore in its womb the Messiah, as the man-child whom it should one day give birth to, and only in the forming and bearing of whom it found its true meaning. This was its function, and according to the counsel of God it should have been saved through this child-bearing; though by its own sin it did itself expire in giving birth to Him who was intended to have been not its death but its life.

This, then, is another remarkable aspect under which the progressiveness of God's dealings, and of that Book which is their record, presents itself to us—this long and patient training of his people through many a preceding word and institution and person into the capacity of recognising his glory, of whom all that went before was but the shadow and the symbol. In all this was a prelude to prepare the spiritual ear for the full burst of a later, and but for that, an overwhelming harmony;—a purpling of the east, which might tell in what quarter the Sun of Righteousness would appear, and whither the straining eyes must turn, that would catch the first brightness of his rising.

Nor is it unworthy of observation, that prophecy did never run before that actual development, which alone would enable it to speak a language which men should understand. It did not paint upon air; but ever claimed forms of the present in which to array its promises of the future. Thus we have no mention of Christ the Prophet till a great Prophet had actually arisen, till Moses could say, "The Lord thy God will raise up unto thee a Prophet like unto me." We hear nothing of Christ the King, till there were kings in Israel—theocratic kings—who should give the prophecy a substance and a meaning; who should make men know, though with many imperfections, what a sceptre of righteousness was, and a king ruling in judgment. And thus (did time allow) we might trace in much more detail how not only in the idea of type and prophecy there is obedience to that law of advance and progress, which we have every where been finding, but in the very order and sequence of the prophecies themselves. Yet this matter we must leave. Sufficient for us to have seen how in prophecy are the outlines and lineaments which shall indicate, and fit men to know the very body of the Truth, when that at length shall come;—to have considered under another aspect to-day, how Scripture is its own witness, gives proof that it is what it affirms itself to be, a Book for the education of men,—in that it plainly contains the gradual unfolding of a great idea, such a thought as only could have entered into the mind of God to conceive, such a thought as He only who is the King of ages could have carried out.

And without question, for ourselves, brethren, the lessons which the Scripture contemplated as this Book of an ever-advancing education may suggest, are not very far to seek. And this first. God has taken our whole race by the hand that He may lead it on together; even so will he lead every single soul that will trust itself to Him. He will speak to us first as "little children," then as "young men," and then as "fathers." His Word in our hearts shall be as the blade, and the ear, and the full corn in the ear. He will give us, as we are faithful, an ever larger horizon, a widening horizon of duty, with an increasing consciousness of powers and faculties for fulfilling that duty.

And our second lesson lies also at the door,—that seeing, as we do in Scripture, what the school has been in which all God's saints have been trained, we be well content to learn in the same, nor count that we can learn better in any other. The study of this Scripture shows us how, through the everlasting ordinances of the Family, the State, the Church, God trains into nobleness and freedom the souls and spirits of men; how he calls out in their strength, first the affections, then the conscience, and last of all, the reason and the will of men. It teaches us that, not in self-willed separation from common duties, but in a lowly and earnest fulfilling of them, men have grown up to their full stature as men. Often in that evil pride which makes us rather to follow after that which will divide us from our brethren, than that which will unite us to them, we have counted, it may be, that we could discipline ourselves better, that we could train ourselves higher, than by those common ways in which all our fellows are being trained,—better than through the ordinances of the family, better than through the duties which devolve on us as citizens, better than by the teaching and Sacraments of Christ's Church. It has seemed to us a poor thing to walk in those trite and common paths wherein all are walking. Yet these common paths are the paths in which blessing travels, are the ways in which God is met. Welcoming and fulfilling the lowliest duties which meet us there, we shall often be surprised to find that we have unawares been welcoming and entertaining Angels; and nurturing ourselves upon these, it shall be with us in our souls and spirits as it was with Daniel and his young companions, when they showed fairer and better liking, and had more evidently thriven upon their common food, their ordinary pulse, than had all their compeers upon their royal dainties, their profane meats, brought from the table of the Babylonian king.

LECTURE V.

THE PAST DEVELOPMENT OF SCRIPTURE.

JOHN XII. 16.

These things understood not his disciples at the first; but when Jesus was glorified, then remembered they, that these things were written of him.

THE subject of the Lectures which I am now permitted to resume, is the fitness of Holy Scripture for unfolding the spiritual life of men, and the arguments which we may from this fitness derive for its being the gift of God to his reasonable creatures, whom He has called to a spiritual fellowship with Himself. So many who are now present cannot have heard the earlier discourses, so little have I a right to expect that those who did, should vividly retain them in their memories, that I shall just mention at this resumption of the course the point at which I have arrived, not attempting to retrace even with hastiest steps, but indicating merely by lightest hints, the way by which we hitherto have gone. Passing by, then, the external arguments, not as comparatively unimportant, but as not belonging to the domain of my peculiar subject, I have sought, after some preliminary observations which filled the chief part of my first Lecture, in the second to trace the oneness of Scripture; how there runs through it one idea, that of the kingdom of God, and how by that one are knit into unity its most diverse parts and elements; in the third, how this Scripture, which is one, is also manifold, so laid out that it shall nourish all souls, and make wonderful answer to the moral and intellectual needs of all men; and then in the fourth, the latest of that series, I endeavoured to show how Scripture is fitted to be the Book of our education, the furtherer of our spiritual growth, through itself being the history of the progressive education of our race into the fulness of the knowledge of God.

An ample task remains for us still: this day's portion of that task will consist in an attempt, it must be indeed a most imperfect one, to show how this treasure of divine Truth, once given, has only gradually revealed itself; how the history of the Church, the difficulties, the trials, the struggles, the temptations in which it has been involved, have interpreted to it its own records, brought out their latent significance, and caused it to discover all which in them it had; how there was much written for it there as in sympathetic ink, invisible for a season, yet ready to flash out in lines and characters of light, whenever the appointed day and hour had arrived. So that in this way the Scripture has been to the Church as their garments to the children of Israel, which during all the years of their pilgrimage in the desert waxed not old, yea, according to rabbinical tradition, kept pace and measure with their bodies, growing with their growth, fitting the man as they had fitted the child,

THE PAST DEVELOPMENT OF SCRIPTURE. 93

and this, until the forty years of their sojourn in the wilderness had expired. Or, to use another comparison which may help to illustrate our meaning, Holy Scripture thus progressively unfolding what it contains, might be likened fitly to some magnificent landscape on which the sun is gradually rising, and ever as it rises, is bringing out one headland into light and prominence, and then another; anon kindling the glory-smitten summit of some far mountain, and presently lighting up the recesses of some near valley which had hitherto abided in gloom, and so travelling on till nothing remains in shadow, no nook nor corner hid from the light and heat of it, but the whole prospect stands out in the clearness and splendour of the brightest noon.

And we can discern, I think, in some measure, causes which in the wisdom and providence of God worked together to constitute Scripture as this glorious landscape which should ever reveal new features of wonder and beauty, this boundless treasure with riches laid up for all future times and all future needs. The apostolic Church—that of which the sacred writings of the New Covenant are a living transcript—was not merely one age and one aspect of the Church, but we have in it the picture and prophecy of the Church's history in every future age. All which in those after ages should only slowly declare itself, is there presented in one great image,—the most amazing contrasts, the best and the worst, the highest and the lowest, the noblest assertions, and the deadliest perversions, of the Truth. It is, if we may so speak, a rapid rehearsal of the great drama of God's providence with His Church, which should afterwards be played out at leisure on the world's stage. Nothing, which was after to be, was not there; although, by the necessities of the case, all compressed and brought into narrowest compass, and, so to speak, all foreshortened, and, as a picture of the future, wanting in perspective and in distance. But this glimpse once vouchsafed to us of all, the wondrous picture dislimns and dissolves again; that era in which were all other eras wrapped up, closes, and the period of gradual development begins; but yet not this, before every error and the antidote of every error had been set down, every heresy which should afterwards display itself full-blown, had budded, and the witness against it had been clearly borne; not till it had been seen how Jewish legality and heathen false liberty would equally seek to corrupt the Truth, and with what weapons both were to be encountered; not till missions to the Jew and missions to the heathen had alike been founded, and the manner of conducting them been shown; not till many Antichrists had rehearsed and prefigured the final one, and tried the faith of God's elect. And thus it was ordained that the canonical Scriptures, which seem to belong only to one age, should indeed belong to all ages; inasmuch as that age, that fruitful time, that middle point of the world's history, in which an old world died and a new world sprang to life, had the germs and rudiments of all other times within its bosom.

It is this fact,—that the Holy Scripture contains

THE PAST DEVELOPMENT OF SCRIPTURE. 95

within itself all treasures of wisdom and knowledge, but only renders up those treasures little by little, and as they are needed or asked for,—which justifies us in speaking of a development of doctrine in the Church, and explains much in her inner history that might else startle or perplex. But about this matter so much has lately been spoken, and another theory of the manner in which the Church unfolds her doctrine, looking at first sight the same as this, but at heart entirely different, has so diligently been put forth,—and *that* with purposes hostile to that sound form of faith and doctrine, which it is given us to maintain and defend,—that it might be worth our while to linger here for a little, and consider wherein the essential difference between the false theory and the true is to be found, and in what sense, and in what only, the Church may be said to develop her doctrine. It is familiar to many who have watched with interest the course of the controversies of our day, that those who have given up as hopeless the endeavour to find in Scripture, or in the practices or creeds of the early Church, evidence for the accretions with which they have overlaid the Truth, have shifted their ground, and taken up a position entirely new. True, they have said, these additions are not there, but they are the unfolding of the Truth which *is* there; they are but the producing of the line of Truth, the later numbers of a series, whereof the earlier in Scripture are given; they are necessary *developments of doctrine,* such as the Church has ever allowed to herself, and which will alone explain many of the appearances which she presents.

Now doubtless there is a true idea of Scriptural developments, which has always been recognised, to which the great Fathers of the Church have set their seal;* and it is this, that the Church, informed and quickened by the Spirit of God, more and more discovers what in Holy Scripture is given her; but it is not this, that she unfolds by an independent power any thing farther therefrom. She has always possessed what she now possesses of doctrine and truth, only not always with the same distinctness of consciousness. She has not added to her wealth, but she has become more and more aware of that wealth; her dowry has remained always the same, but that dowry was so rich and so rare, that only little by little she has counted over and taken stock and inventory of her jewels. She has consolidated her doctrine, compelled thereto by the provocation of enemies, or induced to it by the growing sense of her own needs. She has brought together utterances in Holy Writ, and those which apart were comparatively barren, when thus married, when each had thus found its com-

---

* Thus Augustine (*Enarr. in Ps.* LIV. 22) Multa enim latebant in Scripturis, et quum præcisi essent hæretici, quæstionibus agitaverunt Ecclesiam Dei; aperta sunt quæ latebant, et intellecta, est voluntas Dei....Numquid enim perfectè de Trinitate tractatum est antequam oblatrarent Ariani? numquid perfectè de pœnitentibus tractatum est antequam obsisterent Novatiani? Sic non perfectè de baptismate tractatum est antequam contradicerent foris positi rebaptizatores. Cf. *Enarr. in Ps.* lxvii. 31, and *Confess.*, 1. 7, c. 19. Improbatio hæreticorum facit eminere quid Ecclesia sentiat, et quid habeat sana doctrina.

plement in the other, have been fruitful to her. Those which apart meant little to her, have been seen to mean much, when thus brought together and read each by the light of the other. In these senses she has enlarged her dominion, her dominion having become larger to her.

And yet all this which she has laboriously won, she possessed before, implicitly though not explicitly, —even as the shut hand is as perfect a hand as the open; or as our dominion in that huge island of the Pacific is as truly ours, and that region as vast in extent now, as it will be when every mountain and valley, every rivulet and bay, have been explored and laid down in our maps, and the flag of England has waved over them all. All, for example, which the later Church slowly and through centuries defined upon this side and that, of the person of the Son of God— of the relation of his natures and the communication of their properties—of his divine will and his human, —all this the earliest had, yea and enjoyed, not having arrived at it by analytic process, not able, perhaps, as not needing, to lay it out with dialectic accuracy, but in total impression, in synthetic unity. She possessed it all, she lived in the might and in the glory of it; as is notably witnessed by the prophetic tact, if one may venture so to call that divine instinct, by which she rejected all which was alien to and would have disturbed the true evolution of her doctrine, even before she had fully elaborated that doctrine; by which she refused to shut the door against herself; and even in matters which had not yet come before her for decision and definition, preserved the ground clear and open from all that would have embarrassed and obstructed in the future.

We do not object to, rather we fully acknowledge, the theory of the development of religious Truth so stated. We no more object, than we do to a Nicene Creed following up and enlarging an Apostolic, which rather we gladly and thankfully receive as a rich addition to our heritage. But that Nicene creed in the same manner contains no new truths which the Church has added to her stock since the earlier was composed, though it may be some which she has brought out with more distinctness to herself and to her children,—as it contains broader and more accurately guarded statements of the old. But the essential in this progress of Truth is, that the later is always as truly found in Scripture as the earlier—not as easy to discover, but when discovered, as much carrying with it its own evidence;—and there, not in some obscure hint and germ, putting one in mind of an inverted pyramid, so small the foundation, so vast and overshadowing the superstructure—as for instance, the whole Papal system, which rests, as far as Scripture is adduced in proof, on a single text—nor yet there in some passage which is equally capable of a thousand other turns as that given; as, for example, when the worship of the Blessed Virgin is found prophesied and authorized in the Lord's answer to her at the marriage in Cana of Galilee.

But with these limitations the scheme is altogther different from that which some of late have put for-

THE PAST DEVELOPMENT OF SCRIPTURE.

ward,—different not in degree only, but in kind; and it is that mere confusion of unlike things under like terms, which is so fruitful a source of errors in the world, to call by this same name that theory which, refusing the Scriptures as, first and last, authoritative in and limitary of the Truth, assumes that in the course of ages there was intended to be, not only the discovery of the Truth which is there, but also, by independent accretion and addition, the further growth of doctrine, *besides* what is there; which recognises such accretions, when they fall in with its own notions, for legitimate outgrowths, and not, as indeed they are, for noxious misgrowths, of doctrine; and which thus makes the Church from time to time the creator of new Truth, and not merely the guardian and definer and drawer out of the old. This is all that she assumes to be; whatever she proclaims, she has ever the consciousness that she is proclaiming it as the ancient Truth, as that which she has always borne in her bosom, however she may not have distinctly outspoken it till now; as part of the Truth once delivered *to* her, though, it may be, not all at once apprehended *by* her.

Thus was it felt in the ages long past of the Church; thus also was it at the Reformation; for that too was an entering of the Church on a portion of the fulness of her heritage, on which she had not adequately entered before. It is hardly too much to say, that the Reformation called out from their hiding-places the Epistle to the Romans, the Epistle to the Galatians, and generally the Epistles of St. Paul, which then became to the faithful all which they were intended to be. It is not, of course, implied that these were not read and studied and commented on before, or that much and varied profit was not drawn from them in every age, or that they had not been full of blessing for unnumbered souls. But with all this, men's eyes were holden, and had been for long, so that the innermost heart of them, the deepest significance, was not seen. For they were the needs of souls, the mighty anguish of men's spirits, which were the true interpreters of these portions of God's Word. When that vast and gorgeous fabric, the Papal Christendom of the middle ages, dissolved and went to pieces,—that which, as one contemplates it on its bright side or its dark, one is inclined to regard as a glorious realization, or an impious caricature, of the promised kingdom of Christ upon the earth;— when the time arrived that men could no longer live by faith that they were members of that great spiritual fellowship, (for it was felt now to be only the mockery of such;) when each man said, "I too am a man, myself and no other, one by myself, with my own burden, my own sin, the inalienable mystery of my own being, which I cannot put off on another, and, as such, I must stand or fall; it helps me nothing to tell me that I belong to a glorious community, in which saints have lived and doctors taught, wherein I am bound in closest fellowship with all the ages that are past; this helps me nothing, unless I too, by myself, am a healed man, with the deep wound of my own spirit healed, unless you show me how my own personal relations to God,

THE PAST DEVELOPMENT OF SCRIPTURE. 101

which sin has utterly disturbed, may be made firm and strong again;—then, when men thus felt, where should they so naturally turn as to those portions of Scripture especially designed to furnish a response to this deep cry of the human heart, and which are occupied with setting forth a personal Deliverer from this personal sense of guilt and condemnation? And not any thing else but this mighty agony of souls would have supplied the key of knowledge to the Epistles of St. Paul, which had remained otherwise to the faithful as written in a strange language, to be admired at a distance, but dealing with matters in which they had no very close concern. But with this preparation, and thus initiated by suffering, men came to them with ineffable joy, as to springs in the desert, and found in them all after which their inmost spirits had yearned and thirsted the most.

Thus at the Reformation the relations of every man to God, consequent on the Incarnation and death and resurrection of the Son of God, were those for which the Church mainly contended;—that those relations were perfect,—that by one oblation Christ had perfected for ever them that were sanctified, that nothing might come between God and the cleansed conscience of his children, to bring them nearer than they were brought already,—no pope, no work, no penance,—that all which pretended to intrude and come between was a lie. And by consequence those records of Scripture which were occupied with declaring the perfectness of these relations, were those most sedulously and most earnestly handled; bright beams of light flashed out from them, at once enlightening and gladdening and kindling, as they had never done until now.

But in our own day, as we see in that country where alone a speculative philosophy, with which theology has to put itself in relation, exists, the controversy has drawn, as was to be looked for, even nearer yet to the very heart of the matter. For now it is not, What is the meaning for us of this constitution in the Son? but whether there is such a constitution at all? it is not what follows on the relations which the Incarnate Word established between God and men, but whether there have been any such relations at all established—any meeting of heaven and earth in the person of Jesus of Nazareth,—whether all which has been spoken of such has not been merely dreams of men, and not, as the Church affirms, facts of God? And therefore the Gospels, as we see, come mainly into consideration now; round them the combatants gather, the battle rages: they are felt to be the key of the position, which, as it is won or lost, will carry with it the issues of the day. Every one that would strike a blow at Christianity, strikes at them; criticizes the record or the fact recorded;—the record, that it is a loose and accidental aggregation of floating materials, of insecure traditions, which crumbles to pieces at any accurate handling—or the fact recorded, that a man who was God, and God who was man, is inconceivable, and carries its own contradiction on its front.

And as the Gospels are the point mainly assailed, so are they the citadel in which they must make themselves strong, from which they must issue, who would win in our day any signal victory for the Truth. First, the record itself must be vindicated, the glory and perfectness of its form, the mystery of those four Gospels in their subtle harmonies, in the manner wherein they complete one another, handing us on, the first to the second, and the second to the third, and the third to the last:—the wondrous laws of selection, and laws of rejection, which evidently presided at their construction, and do continually reveal themselves to the deeper inquirer, however the shallow may miss or deny them. And then, secondly, the facts, or, to speak more truly, the fact must be justified, which in those Gospels is recorded,—that it is the highest wisdom,—that a Son of God, who is also the Son of man, is the one, the divine fact, which alone explains either God or man,—is that which philosophy must end by accepting at the hands of Theology as the crowning Truth, and only in accepting which it will find its own completion, and the long and weary strife between the two obtain an end.

And as it was at the Reformation with the Pauline Epistles,—as it is now with the Gospels,—so, I cannot doubt, a day will come when all the significance of the Apocalypse for the church of God will be apparent, which hitherto it can scarcely be said to have been;—that a time will arrive when it will be plainly shown how costly a gift, yea rather, how necessary an armour was this for the Church of the redeemed. Then, when the last things are about to be, and the trumpet of the last Angel to sound, when the great drama is hastening with ever briefer pauses to its catastrophe,—then, in one unlooked for way or another, the veil will be lifted up from this wondrous Book, and it will be to the Church collectively, what, even partially understood, it has been already to tens of thousands of her children—strength in the fires, giving her "songs in the night," songs of joy and deliverance in that darkest night of her trial, which shall precede the break of her everlasting day; and enabling her, even when the triumph of Antichrist is at the highest, to look securely on to his near doom and her own perfect victory.

But we are dealing to-day with the *past* development of Scripture, not with the future—with what it has already unfolded, not with what it may have still in reserve. *That* may well occupy us hereafter; for the present, let us ask ourselves what is the great lesson which we should draw from this aspect of the subject which we have been this day contemplating. A lesson surely of the very deepest significance. For if other generations before us have had their especial task and work, so also must we; a work which none other have done for us, even as none other could; for just as each individual has some task which none other can fulfil so well as he, for it is *his* task, so every generation has its own appointed labour, and only can be at harmony with itself, when it has faithfully girded itself to that. Let us not then, under show of humility, flatter our indolence, and say that in this matter of the treasures of the knowledge of God all is searched out; that for us it remains only to live on the handed down, on that which others have already won from his Word. Let us not, in this manner, turn that into a standing pool or reservoir, which might be a spring of water springing up as freshly and newly to our lips as to the lips of any who have gone before us.

Shall we determine, for instance, to know no other Theology, no other results of Scripture, save those of the Church of the first ages? Are we thus honouring Christ's promise to His Church, when we imply, as so we do, that the Spirit of wisdom and understanding was given to her once, but is not given to her always? Shall all history, as an interpreter of God's Word, go for nothing with us—be assumed to stand in no relation to that Book, of which surely the very idea is, that as it casts light upon all, so it receives light from all? Or do we presume too far in believing that there are portions of its vast and goodly field, which we can cultivate with larger success than those who preceded us, to which we shall bring experience which they did not and could not bring, which will yield therefore to us ampler returns than they yielded to them?

Or, again, were it not as great a mistake, as partial a view upon another side, to require that the Theology of the Reformation should be the ultimate term and law to us,—to say that we would know nothing further, and to look, respectfully it may be, but still coldly, on any truths which were not at that day counted vital? Surely our loss were most real, refusing to take our part in cultivating this field which the Lord has blest, and which he has now delivered to us, that we in our turn might dress and keep, and enrich ourselves from it;—a loss we know not how great! for we too, had we been faithful and earnest, might have found hid in that field some treasure, for joy whereof we should have been ready to renounce all that we had, all our barren theories, and hungry speculations, and mutual suspicions, if only we might have made that treasure our own; so, reconciling, so evidently fitted would it have shown itself for all our actual needs.

We may purpose indeed to live on what others have done, the mighty men of the days which are past, the fathers or revivers of our faith; and we may count that their gains will as much enrich us as they enriched them. But this will not prove so indeed; for it is a just law of our being, one of the righteous compensations of toil, that what a man wins by his labour, be it inward truth, or only some outward suppliance of his need, is ever far more really his own, makes him far more truly rich, than aught which he receives or inherits ready made at the hands and from the toils of others. And they of whom we speak *earned* their truths, by toil and by struggle, by mighty wrestlings till the day broke; watering with the sweat of their brow, oftentimes with tears as of blood—yea, with the life-blood of their own hearts, the soil which yielded them in return a harvest so large. So was it, and so only, that they came again with joy, bearing their sheaves with them. And would we do the same, let us first indeed see that we let nothing go—that we forfeit no part of that which we inherit at their hands.

But also with a just confidence in that blessed Spirit, who is ever with His Church, who is ever leading it into the Truth which it needs,—let us labour, that through prayer and through study, through earnest knocking, through holy living, that inexhausted and inexhaustible Word may render up unto us *our* truth, —the truth by which we must live,—the truth, whatsoever that be, which, more than any other, will deliver *us* from the lies with which we in our time are beset, which will make *us* strong where we are weak, and heal us where we are divided, and enable us most effectually to do that work which our God would have done by us in this the day of our toil.

LECTURE VI.

THE INEXHAUSTIBILITY OF SCRIPTURE.

ISAIAH XII. 3.

With joy shall ye draw water out of the wells of salvation.

It was my endeavour in my last Lecture to bring before you the progressive unfolding of the Scripture for the Church—the manner in which for the company of faithful men in all ages, considered as one great organic body with one common life, there has been such a lifting up of veil after veil from the Word of God; they only gradually coming into the knowledge of all the riches which in that Word were their own. It were a worthy task for us to-day to consider, what no doubt all of us must often have felt, the way in which it has been ordained that the treasures of Holy Scripture should for the individual believer be inexhaustible also,—should be quarries in which he may always dig, yet which he can never dig out,—a world of wisdom in which the most zealous and successful searcher shall ever be the readiest to acknowledge that what remains to know is far more than what yet he has known.

For this is a most important need for a Book such as we affirm the Bible to be, a Book for the cultivating of humanity, for the developing, by the ministry of the Church, through the teaching of the Spirit, the higher life of every man in the world. It belongs to the very primal necessities of a Scripture which is ordained for such ends as these, that it should be thus inexhaustible;—that no man should ever come to its end, himself containing it, instead of being contained by it, as by something far larger than himself. The very idea of such a Book, which is for all men and for all the life of every man, is that it should have treasures which it does not give up at once, secrets which it yields slowly and only to those that are its intimates; with rich waving harvests on its surface, but with precious veins of metal hidden far below, and to be reached only by search and by labour. Nothing were so fatal to its lasting influence, to the high purposes which it is meant to serve, as for any with justice to feel that he had used it up, that he had worked it through, that henceforward it had no "fresh fields," nor "pastures new," in which to invite him for tomorrow. Even where this did not utterly repel him, where he maintained the study of this Book as a commanded duty, his chiefest delight and satisfaction in the handling of it would have departed; he no longer would draw water with joy from these wells of salvation, for they would be to him fresh springing wells no more.

It will be my purpose on the present occasion to trace, as far as I may, what there is in the structure and conformation of Scripture to constitute it this Book of unsearchable riches for each; and in so doing I shall not, as might perhaps at first sight appear, be going over again the subject which was treated last; for *that* was the organic unfolding of the Word for the Church considered as a whole; this the wealth which there is stored for each one of the faithful in particular, and which all, given to him in his Baptism, he yet only little by little can make his own, appropriating and transmuting it into the substance of his own life.

Now the first provision made for this by the grace and wisdom of God,—the first at least which I would note,—is one which by shallow or malignant objectors has been often turned into a charge against it, I mean the absence of a systematic arrangement; for such is the shape which the complaint generally assumes. But this complaint of the want of method in Scripture, what is it in fact but this, that it is not dead, but living? that it is no *herbarium*, no *hortus siccus*, but a garden? a wilderness, if men choose to call it so, but a wilderness of sweets, with its flowers upon their stalks—its plants freshly growing, the dew upon their leaves, the mould about their roots—with its lowly hyssops and its cedars of God. And when men say that there is want of *method* in it, they would speak more accurately if they said that there was want of *system;* for the highest method, even the method of the Spirit, may reign where system there is none. Method is divine, is inseparable from the ideas of God and of order; but system is of man, is a help to the weakness of his faculties, is the artificial arrangement by which he brings within his limited ken that which in no other way he would be able to grasp as a whole. That there should be books of systematic Theology—books with their plan and scheme thus lying on their very surface, and meeting us at once—this is most needful; but most needful also that Scripture should not be such a book. The dearest interests of all, of wise men equally as of women and children, demand this.

It is true that one of the latest assaults on Scripture by a living adversary of the faith, by one who, at first attacking only the historical accuracy of the Gospels, has since gone rapidly the downward way, till he has sunk at last, as his latest writings testify, into the bottomless pit of sheerest atheism,*—it is true that his assault is mainly directed against this very point. He demands of a book, which claims to be the appointed book for the guidance and teaching of humanity, that he should be able to lay his finger there upon a precept or a doctrine for each occurring need, —that he should be able to find in one place and under one head all which relates to one matter; and because he cannot find this in the Bible, he opens his mouth against it, and proclaims it insufficient for the ends which it professes to fulfil. But Holy Scripture is not this book for the slothful—is not this book which can be interpreted without, and apart from, and by the deniers of, that Holy Spirit by whom it came. Rather is it a field, upon the surface of which if sometimes we gather manna easily and without labour, and

---

* Strauss. Compare his *Leben Jesu* with his *Christliche Glaubenslehre*.

given, as it were, freely to our hands, yet of which also many portions are to be cultivated with pains and toil, ere they will yield food for the use of man. This bread of life also is to be often eaten in the wholesome sweat of our brow.

It is not a defect in Scripture, it is not something which is to be excused and explained away, but rather a glory and a prerogative, that there reigns in it the freedom and fulness of nature, and not the narrowness and strictness of art;—as one said of old who adorned this University, and is yet numbered among the honoured band of the Cambridge Platonists, when speaking of the delightful exercise of the highest faculties of the soul, which is thus secured: "All which gratulations of the soul in her successful pursuits of divine Truth would be utterly lost or prevented, if the Holy Scripture set down all things so fully and methodically that our reading and understanding would every where keep pace together. Wherefore that the mind of man may be worthily employed, and taken up with a kind of spiritual husbandry, God has not made the Scriptures like an artificial garden, wherein the walks are plain and regular, the plants sorted and set in order, the fruits ripe and the flowers blown, and all things fully exposed to our view; but rather like an uncultivated field, where indeed we have the ground and hidden seeds of all precious things, but nothing can be brought to any great beauty, order, fulness, or maturity, without our industry,—nor indeed with it, unless the dew of his grace descend upon it, without whose blessing this spiritual culture will thrive as little as the labour of the husbandman without showers of rain."*

But to pass to another branch of the subject;—it is part of this absence of system, with the presence in its stead of a higher method, of this constitution of Scripture as a Book which no man should ever search to the end, and then be tempted to lay aside as known and finished, that so much of it should be occupied with the history of lives. That which is to teach us to live, is itself life—not precepts, not rules alone, but these clothing themselves in the flesh and blood of action and of suffering. A system of faith and duty, however intricate, one might come to the end of at last. One might possess thoroughly a *Summa Theologiæ,* however massive and piled up; for after all, however vast, it yet has its defined bounds and limits. But life stretches out on every side, and on every side loses itself in the infinite. An Abraham, a David, a Paul—there is always something incomplete in the way in which we have hitherto realized their characters; they always abide greater than our conception of them, and at the same time always ready to reveal themselves in some new features to the

---

* Henry More, in his *Mystery of Godliness,* B. i., c. 2. Another in our own day has expressed himself in like manner: "Scripture cannot, as it were, be mapped, or its contents catalogued, but after all our diligence to the end of our lives and to the end of the Church, it must be an unexplored and unsubdued land, with heights and valleys, forests and streams, on the right and left of our path and close about us, full of concealed wonders and choice treasures."

loving and studious eye. Beheld in some new combination, in some new grouping with those by whom they are surrounded, they will yield some lesson of instruction which they have never yielded before. And if they, how much more He, whom we are bidden above all to consider, looking unto whom we are to run our course, and whose every turn and gesture and tone and word are significant for us. We might study out a system; but how can we ever study out a person? And our blessedness is, that Christ does not declare to us a system, and say, " This is the truth; " so doing he might have established a school: but he points to a person, even to himself, and says, " I am the Truth," and thus he founded, not a school, but a Church, a fellowship which stands in its faith upon a person, not in its tenure of a doctrine, or, at least, only mediately and in a secondary sense upon this.

But another reason why the Word of God should be for us this mine which shall never be worked out, is, no doubt, the following:—that our own life brings out in it such new and undreamt-of treasures. What an interpreter of Scripture is affliction! how many stars in its heaven shine out brightly in the night of sorrow or of pain, which were unperceived or overlooked in the garish day of our prosperity. What an enlarger of Scripture is any other outer or inner event, which stirs the deeps of our hearts, which touches us near to the core and centre of our lives. Trouble of spirit, condemnation of conscience, pain of body, sudden danger, strong temptation—when any of these overtake us, what veils do they take away, that we may see what hitherto we saw not; what new domains of God's word do they bring within our spiritual ken! How do promises, which once fell flat upon our ears, become precious now; psalms become our own, our heritage for ever, which before were aloof from us! How do we see things now with the eye, which before we knew only by the hearing of the ear; which, before, men had told us, but now we ourselves have found! How much, again, do we see in our riper age, which in youth we missed or passed over! And thus, on these accounts also, the Scripture is well fitted to be our companion, and to do us good, all the years of our life.*

Another provision which in it is made for awakening attention, and for summoning men to penetrate more deeply into its meaning, is to be found in its apparent, I need not say only *apparent*, contradictions. But it is not at pains to avoid the semblance of these. It is not careful to remove every handle of objection which any might take hold of. On the contrary, that saying, "Blessed is he whosoever shall not be offended in me," finds as true an application to Christ's Word

---

* Fuller. "The same man at several times may in his apprehension prefer several Scriptures as best, formerly most affected with one place, for the present more delighted with another; and afterwards conceiving comfort therein not so clear, choose other places as more pregnant and pertinent to his purpose. Thus God orders it that divers men, (and perhaps the same man at divers time) make use of all his gifts, gleaning and gathering comfort, as it is scattered through the whole field of the Scripture."

as to his person. For that Word goes on its way, not obviating every possible misconception, not giving anxious pains to show how this statement which it makes and that agree. It is satisfied that they *do* agree, and lets those that are watching for an offence take it. They whose hearts were already alienated from the Truth are suffered to stumble at this stone, which was set for this very fall and rise of many, that the thoughts of many hearts might be revealed, and that they who were longing for an excuse for unbelief might find one.

And with the same challenge to the false-hearted, the same fruitful supply of suggestive thought for the devout inquirer, these matters claiming reconciliation will meet us, not in the history only, but also in the doctrine. For it is ever the manner of that Word with which we have to do, now boldly to declare its truth upon this side, and then presently to declare it as boldly and fearlessly on the other—not painfully and nicely balancing, limiting, qualifying, till the whole strength of its statements had evaporated, not caring even though its truths should seem to jostle one another. Enough that they do not do so indeed. It is content to leave them to the Spirit to adjust and reconcile, and to show how the rights of each are compatible with the rights of the other—and not compatible only, but how most often the one requires that the other have its rights, before it can have truly its own. Thus how profitable for us that we have the divers statements of St. Paul and St. James—*divers*, but not *diverse*—each, in the words of St. Chrysostom, declaring the same truth, διαφορως, but not εναντιως—how do they summon us to a deeper entering into the doctrine than might otherwise have been ours, bidding us not to be satisfied till we reach that central point where we can evidently see how the two are at one, and do but present, from different points of view, the same truth. How useful to find in one place that God tempted Abraham, and in another, that God tempteth not any.* Should we have learned so well the significance of temptation, should we have been set to think about it so effectually by any other process? Or when the Lord sets before the pure-hearted, that they shall see God, that God whom his Apostle declares that no man hath seen nor can see,† how does this set us to meditate on that awful yet blessed vision of God, which in some sense shall be vouchsafed to his servants, even as in some it shall remain incommunicable even unto them.

If indeed these difficulties had been artificially contrived, if they had been puzzles and perplexities with which the Bible had been sown, that it might last us the longer, that in the explaining and reconciling of them we might find pleasant exercise for our faculties, they would be but of slightest value. But they grow out of a far deeper root than this; they have nothing thus forced and unnatural about them. Rather is it here as in the kingdom of nature. How often does nature seem to contradict herself, so beckoning us onward to deeper investigations, till we shall

---

* Compare Gen. xxii. 1, with Jam. i. 13.
† Compare Matt. v. 8, with 1 Tim. vi. 16.

have reached some higher and more comprehensive law, in which her seeming contradictions, those which lie upon her surface, are atoned. And this because she is infinite: for it is of the essence of manifold and endless life that it should at times thus present itself as at variance with its own self. It is the glory of Scripture that its harmonies lie deep, so deep, that to the careless or perverse ear they may be sometimes mistaken for discords. There might have been a consistency of its different parts—a poor and shallow thing—lying on the outside, traced easily and at once, which none could miss; but such had been of no value, had been charged with no deeper instruction for us.

To look, on another side, at the manner in which Holy Scripture presents itself as this inexhaustible treasure,—what riches are contained in its minutest portions! As it can bear to be looked at in its largest aspect, so it challenges the contemplation of its smallest details—in this again like nature, which shows more wonderful, the more microscopic the investigation to which it is submitted. Here truly are *maxima in minimis*—the sun reflecting itself as faithfully in the tiny dewdrop, as in the great mirror of the ocean. The most eminent illustrations of this widest wealth laid up in narrowest compass must naturally be found in single sayings of our Lord's. How do they shine, like finely polished diamonds, upon every face! how simple and yet how deep! apparent paradoxes, and yet profoundest truths! Every one can get something from them, and no one can get all. He that gathers little has enough, and he that gathers much has nothing over: every one gathers there according to his eating.* For example, "Whosoever will save his life shall lose it, and whosoever will lose his life for my sake shall find it;"—who sees not that in these words the keys of heaven and of hell are put into his hands? and yet who will venture to affirm that he has come to their end? that he has dived down into all their deeps, or that he ever expects to do so? that he has made altogether his own the mysteries of life and of death which are here? Or again, "Every one that exalteth himself shall be abased, and he that humbleth himself shall be exalted;"—what is all the history of the world, if read aright, but a comment on, and a confirmation of, these words? In the light of them what vast pages of men's destinies, of our own lives, become clear! Even the sceptic Bayle was compelled to call them an abridgment of all hu-

* Augustine (*Enarr. in Ps.* ciii) making spiritual application of the words, "*All* beasts of the field drink thereof," (Ps. civ. 11,) to the streams of Holy Scripture, beautifully says: Inde bibit lepus, inde onager: lepus parvus et onager magnus, lepus timidus, et onager ferus, uterque inde bibit, sed quisque *in sitim suam*. Non dicit aqua, Lepori sufficio et repellit onagrum · neque hoc dicit, Onager accedat, lepus si accesserit, rapietur. Tam fideliter et temperatè fluit, ut sic onagrum satiet ne leporem terreat. Sonat strepitus vocis Tullianæ, Cicero legitur, aliquis liber est, dialogus ejus est, sive ipsius sive Platonis, seu cujuscumque talium: audiunt imperiti, infirmi minoris cordis, quis audet illuc aspirare? Strepitus aquæ et fortè turbatæ, certè tamen tam rapaciter fluentis, ut animal timidum non audeat accedere et bibere. Cui sonuit, In principio fecit Deus cœlum et terram, et non ausus est bibere? Cui sonat Psalmus, et dicat, Multum est ad me?

man history; and such they are, setting us as they do at the very centre of the moral oscillation of the world. These examples of that, whereof hundreds might be adduced, must suffice.

Nor is it only what Scripture says, but its very silence which is instructive for us. It was said by one wise man of another, that more might be learned from his questions than from another man's answers. With yet higher truth might it be said that the silence of Scripture is oftentimes more instructive than the speech of other books; so that it has been likened to "a dial in which the shadow as well as the light informs us."* For example of this, how full of meaning to us that we have nothing told us of the life of our blessed Lord between the twelfth and the thirtieth years—how significant the absolute silence which the Gospels maintain concerning all that period; that those years in fact have no history, nothing for the sacred writers to record. How much is implied herein! the calm ripening of his human powers,—the contentedness to wait,—the long preparation in secret, before he began his open ministry. What a testimony is here, if we will note it aright, against all our striving and snatching at hasty results, our impatience, our desire to glitter before the world; against all which tempts so many to pluck the unripe fruits of their minds, and to turn that into the season of a

---

* Boyle (*Style of Holy Scripture:*) "There is such fulness in that book, that oftentimes it says much by saying nothing, and not only its expressions, but its silences are teaching, like a dial in which the shadow as well as the light informs us."

stunted and premature harvest, which should have been the season of patient sowing, of an earnest culture and a silent ripening of their powers.

How pregnant with meaning may that be which appears at first sight only an accidental omission! Such an accidental omission it might at first sight appear that the Prodigal, who while yet in a far country had determined, among other things which he would say to his father, to say, "Make me as one of thy hired servants," when he reaches his father's feet, when he hangs on his father's neck, says all the rest which he had determined, but says not this.* We might take this, at first, for a fortuitous omission; but indeed what deep things are taught us here! This desire to be made as a hired servant, this wish to be kept at a certain distance, this refusal to reclaim the fulness of a child's privileges, was the one turbid and troubled element in his repentance. How instructive then its omission;—that, saying all else which he had meditated, he yet says not this. What a lesson for every penitent,—in other words, for every man. We may learn from this wherein the true growth in faith and in humility consists—how he that has grown in these can endure to be fully and freely blest—to accept *all*, even when he most strongly feels that he has forfeited *all;* that only pride and the surviving workings of self-righteousness and evil stand in the way of a reclaiming of every blessing, which the sinner had lost, but which God is waiting and willing to restore.

* Compare in Luke xv. ver. 19 and 21.

Many other of the apparent accidents of Scripture, on what deep grounds do they rest! Thus, for example, in the history of Pharaoh's trial, that God should ten times be said to have hardened his heart, and he ten times to have hardened his own, or to have had it hardened, without any reference to other than himself. The least attentive reader will scarcely have failed to observe this hardening attributed sometimes to God, and, sometimes, more or less directly, traced to the king's own wilfulness and pride. But in the history of that great strife between the will of God and the will of his creature, in this the pattern history of that struggle, such exactly equal distribution of the language which assumes the freedom of man's will, and that which assumes the ultimate lordship of God over the course of the world—a lordship which even the resistance of the wicked does not derange or impugn—this exactly equal distribution of either language is surely most remarkable. The great, however mysterious, fact of the freedom of man's will going hand in hand with the sovereignty of God is not put in question by an exclusive use of a language resting on or assuming one of these truths or the other—nay rather, exactly equal rights are given to them both; for both are true, both of paramount importance to be affirmed. The sinner *does* harden his *own* heart; his resistance to God is most real; and yet there is a sense, a most true sense also, in which God hardens it; for, to use the old distinction, He who is not the *auctor* is yet the *dispositor malorum* —determines that the evil of the sinner shall break out in this form or in that, works even the dark threads of that resistance into the woof of providence which He is weaving; and as Solomon, in Jewish legend, compelled the wicked spirits to assist in the temple which he was building, so does God compel even his enemies, and *them*, when they are striving most fiercely against Him, to do his work, though they mean not so, and to contribute *their* stones to that heavenly temple of which He is the builder and the maker.

Neither let us leave out of sight, when we are taking into account the provision which Scripture makes for nourishing the faithful in all the stages of their spiritual life and growth, that infinite condescension, according to which, like the prophet who made himself small, that he might stretch himself, limb for limb, upon the dead child, it, in some sort, contracts itself to our littleness,* that we, in return, may become able to expand ourselves to *its* greatness. We see this gracious condescension in nothing more strongly than in that teaching by parables and similitudes, which there occupies so prominent a place. No one turns away from them in pride, as too childish; none retreat from them in despair, as too high. In the parable the Truth of God is not sought to be transplanted, as a full-grown tree, into our minds; for, as

---

* Or as one said in the middle ages: Tota sacra Scriptura loquitur nobis tanquam balbutiendo, sicut mater balbutiens cum filio suo parvulo, qui aliter non potest intelligere verba ejus.

such, it would never take root and flourish; we never could find room for it there. But it comes first as a seed, a germ—small to the small, but with capacities of indefinite expansion; it grows with our growth, enlarging the mind which receives it to something of its own dimensions. Little by little the image reveals itself more fully; some of its fitnesses are perceived at once, and more and more, as spiritual insight advances; all of them perhaps never, lying as they do so deep, and having their roots in the mind of God, who has constituted this outward world to be an exponent of the inner, a garment of mysterious texture which his creative thoughts have woven for themselves. But for this very reason, we come back again and again to these divinely chosen similitudes with fresh interest, with new delight, being continually rewarded with glimpses, unperceived before, of the strange and manifold relations, in which the visible and the invisible stand to one another.

Thus, brethren, have I endeavoured to present to you this day a few of the aspects under which this Word of the Scripture may be contemplated as one fitted evermore to provoke, and evermore to reward, our inquiries. As one said of old, *Habet Scriptura, Sacra haustus primos, habet secundos, habet tertios.* There is, indeed, a tone and temper of spirit, in which if we allow ourselves, all its wells will seem dry, and all its fields barren. The superficial dealer with this Word, he who reads, formally fulfilling an unwelcome task, he who feels in no living relation with the things which he reads, who consults the oracle, but expects no living answer from its lips, who has never known himself a pilgrim of eternity, to whom life has never, like that fabled Sphinx, presented riddles which either he must solve, or, not solving, must perish,—such a one may say, as in his heart he will say, What is this Word more than another? It may bring to him no other feelings but those of tedious monotony and inexpressible weariness. But with the loving and earnest seeker it will prove far otherwise: he will ever be making new discoveries in these spiritual heavens; ever to him will what seemed at first but a light vaporous cloud, upon closer gaze, to his armèd eye, resolve itself into a world of stars. The farther he advances, the more will he be aware that what lies before him is far more than what lies behind—the readier will he be to take up his hymn of praise and thanksgiving, and to wonder with the Apostle at "the depths of the riches both of the wisdom and knowledge of God" which are displayed at once in his works and in his Word.

LECTURE VII.

THE FRUITFULNESS OF SCRIPTURE.

EZEKIEL XLVII. 9.

And it shall come to pass, that every thing that liveth, which moveth, whithersoever the rivers shall come, shall live.

THE aspect of my subject, which I desire this day to bring under your notice is this, namely, the fruitfulness of Holy Scripture; in other words the manner in which it has shown itself a germ of life in all the noblest regions of man's activity; has with its productive energy impregnated the world; and how, to use the image suggested by my text, every thing has lived where these healing waters have come; so that in this way, too, this Word has attested itself that which in my preceding lectures I have endeavoured to prove that it was fitted for being, that which we might beforehand presume it would be, namely, the unfolder of all the nobler and higher life of the world. And these are considerations which will suit as well at a period of these discourses, when they are drawing nigh to their conclusion. For it were to little profit to have shown how the Scripture ought to have been all this, how it was fitted for being all this, unless it could be shown also that it had been; unless we could point to the world's history in evidence that it had done that, which we say it was adapted for doing. "The blind see, the lepers are cleansed, the dead are raised;"—it was to these mighty works that Christ appealed in answer to the question, "Art thou He that should come, or look we for another?" And this is the true answer to every misgiving question of a like kind. The real evidence for aught which comes claiming to be from God, is its power—the power which it is able to put forth for blessing and for healing. If the Scriptures manifested no such power, all other evidence for their divine origin, however convincing we might think it ought to be, yet practically it would fail to convince. Men will not live on the report that aught is great or true, unless they so see it and so find it themselves. But if they do, no assertion on the part of others that it is small, will prevail to make them count light of it. For a moment the confident assertions of gainsayers may perplex, or even seriously injure, their faith: but presently it will resume its hold and its empire again.

Thus it has been well and memorably said, that the great and standing evidence for Christianity is Christendom; and it was with good reason, and out of a true feeling of this, that Origen and other early apologists of the Faith, albeit they had not such a full-formed Christendom as we have to appeal to, did yet, when the adversaries boasted of their Apollonius and other such shadowy personages, and sought to set them up as rivals and competitors with the Lord of glory, make answer by demanding, "What became of these men? what significance had they for the world's after development? what have they bequeathed to show that they and their appearance lay deep in the mind and counsel of God? what society did they found? where is there a fellowship of living men gathered in their name? or where any mighty footmarks left upon the earth to witness that greater than mortals have trodden it?" And the same answer is good, when it is transferred to the books which at any time have made ungrounded claim to be divine records, and as such, to stand upon a level with the Canonical Scriptures; and which sometimes even in our day are brought forward in the hope of confounding the Canonical in a common discredit with them. We in the same way make answer, Is there not a difference? besides all other condemnation under which they lie, besides the absence of historic attestation, and the want of inward religious meaning and aim, are they not self-condemned, in their utter insignificance—in their barrenness—in the entire oblivion into which they have fallen—in the fact, in short, that nothing has come of them? What men have they moulded? what stamp or impress have they left of themselves upon the world? Where is there a society, or even a man, that appeals to them or lives by them?

Thus, let any one acquainted with the apocryphal gospels, compare them for an instant with the sacred Four which we recognise and receive. It is not merely that there is an inward difference between these and those, which would be characterized not too strongly as a difference like that which finds place between stately forest-trees and the low tangled brushwood which springs up under their shadow; it is not merely that those spurious gospels are evermore revolting to the religious sense, abandoning earth without soaring to heaven; robbing the person of Christ of its human features, without lending to it any truly divine; ever mistaking size for greatness, and the monstrous for the miraculous. It is not this only, but the contrast is at least as remarkable in this respect, that while the Canonical Gospels have been so fruitful, from those other nothing has sprung: while the Canonical have been as germs unfolding themselves endlessly; winged seeds endued with a vital energy, which, where they have lighted, have taken root downward and sprung upward; those other might be likened to the chaff borne about by the winds of chance, having no reproductive powers; owing their origin to obscure heretical sects, never extricating themselves from those narrow circles in which they first were born; and, save only as literary curiosities, with the perishing of those sects themselves perishing for ever. *They* have remained as dry sticks, as the barren rods which refused to blossom,—and as such not to abide in the sanctuary. (Numb. xvii.) But the Canonical Gospels have witnessed for themselves, as did Aaron's rod, when it budded and clothed itself with leaves and blossoms and almonds. They too, blossoming and budding, have borne witness to themselves, and to their right to be laid up in the very Ark of the Testimony for ever. For it is not the authority and decision of the Church which has made the Canonical Gospels potent, and the apocryphal impotent, those fruitful and these sterile; rather that decision is the formal acknowledgment of a fact, which was a fact before; a submission to authority, to the authority of the Spirit witnessing to and discerning that Word which is the Lord's; this, rather than any exercising of authority. That decision was the spiritual instinct of the Church recognising and setting her seal to a fact which was a fact before—namely, that these were false and those true; she distinguished thus the chaff from the corn, but it was not her decision which had any thing to do with making these to be chaff and those wheat.

It is the task which I propose to myself to-day, to consider a few aspects under which the Scriptures have thus shown themselves strong; have approved themselves quickeners of the spiritual and intellectual life of men; although here, in treating such a subject as this, one is tempted, as more than once has been my lot, to start back at the greatness of the theme, the vastness of knowledge of all kinds which to handle it worthily would require the fragmentary nature of aught which, even were the knowledge possessed, one could hope within the limits of a single discourse, to present. As the matter, however, may not be passed by, I will seek to present to you one or two reflections, in the hope that they may be only as the first thoughts of a more fruitful series which your own minds will suggest.

And, perhaps one of the first which suggests itself, is this, namely, how productive the Holy Scriptures have been, even in regions of inward life and activity, where, at first sight, one would least have expected it, where we should have been tempted, for many reasons, to anticipate exactly opposite effects. How many things Christianity might, at first sight, have threatened to leave out, to take no note of, or indeed utterly to suppress, which, so far from really warring against, it has raised to higher perfection than ever in the old world they had attained. With what despair, for example, a lover of art, one who at Athens or at Rome fondly had dwelt among the beautiful creations of poet and of painter, would have contemplated the rise of the new religion, and the authority which its doctrines were acquiring over the hearts and spirits of men. What a death-knell must he have heard in this to all in which his soul so greatly delighted. He might have been ready, perhaps, to acknowledge that our human life under this new teaching, would be more rigorously earnest, more severe, more pure: but all its grace and its beauty, all which it borrowed of these from the outward world, he would have concluded, had been laid under a ban, and must now vanish for ever. This was evidently, in great part, the cause of the unhappy Julian's mislike of the rising faith—of his alienation from it, as of that of many other heathens, like-minded with him. It is true, their hostility lay much deeper than this; that it grew out of a far bitterer root. But this was evidently one of their griefs against the doctrine of the Nazarene. They could not consent to lose the grace and beauty of the Hellenistic worship: all art seemed inextricably linked and bound up with the forms of the old religion, and, if that perished, inevitably doomed to perish with it: and so they resisted while they could; and when they could resist no longer, they sat down and made passionate lamentation at the grave of the old world, which all their lamentations could not call back to life; instead of rejoicing at the birth and by the cradle of the new, with which indeed all the hopes of the future were bound up.

And the Christian himself of those earliest ages might almost have consented to take the same view—even as we do find a Tertullian, and others of his temper, actually doing: nor in this was he at all to be wondered at, least of all did he deserve the sneers with which the infidel historian of the later empire has, on this account, visited him. His exaggerations were only those into which a man of strong moral earnestness might most naturally have fallen. So had all skill and device of poet and of painter engaged then in the service of the flesh, so did they do exclusive homage to the old idolatries, so deeply polluted, for the most part, were they, so far sunken with a sunken moral world, that the Christian neophyte, when he renounced, in his baptismal vow, all pomps of the devil, might easily have deemed that these were certainly included; and that to forego them wholly and for ever, was his one duty, his only safety.

How little, at any rate, could one or the other, could friend or foe of the nascent faith, have forecast that out of it,—that, nourished by the Christian books, by the great thoughts which Christ set stirring in humanity, and of which these books kept a lasting record, there should unfold itself a poetry infinitely greater, an art infinitely higher, than any which the old world had seen;—that this faith, which looked so rigid, so austere, even so forbidding, should clothe itself in forms of grace and loveliness, such as men had never dreamt of before? that poetry should not be henceforward the play of the spirit, but its holiest earnest; and those skilless Christian hymns, those hymns "to Christ as to God," of which Pliny speaks, so rude probably in regard of form, should yet be the preludes of strains higher than the world had listened to yet. Or, who would have supposed that those artless paintings of the catacombs had the prophecy in them of more wondrous compositions than men's eyes had ever seen—or that a day should arrive when, above many a dark vault and narrow crypt, where now the Christian worshippers gathered in secret, should arise domes and cathedrals, embodying loftier ideas, because ideas relating to the eternal and the infinite, than all those Grecian temples, which now stood so fair and so strong, but which yet aimed not to lift men's minds from the earth which they adorned.

How little would the one or other, would Christian or heathen have presaged such a future as this—that art was not to perish, but only to be purified and redeemed from the service of the flesh, and from whatever was clinging to and hindering it from realizing its true glory,—and that this book, which does not talk about such matters, which does not make beauty, but holiness, its end and aim—should yet be the truest nourisher of all out of which any genuine art ever has proceeded; the truest fosterer of beauty, in that it is the nourisher of the affections, the sustainer of the relations between God and men; which affections and which relations are indeed the only root out of which any poetry or art worthy of the name, ever have sprung. For these affections being laid waste, those relations being broken, art is first stricken with barrenness, and then, in a little while, withers and pines and dies—as that ancient art, which had been so fertile while faith survived, was, when the church was born, already withering and dying under the influence of the skepticism, the profligacy, the decay of family and national life, the extinction of religious faith, which so eminently marked the time: only having a name to live, resting merely on the traditions of an earlier age, and on the eve of utter dissolution. Such was its condition when Christ came, and cast in his Word, as that which should make all things new, into the midst of an old and decrepit and worn-out world.

Yet here it may be as well to observe, that when I use this language, it is not as assuming that the Bible, merely as a book apart, had done, or could have done, this, or aught else whereof presently there may be occasion to speak—not as though the book had been cast into the world and had leavened it, itself the sole and all-sufficient gift which Christ had bequeathed unto men. Rather, the Spirit, the Word, and the church are the three mighty factors which

THE FRUITFULNESS OF SCRIPTURE.   135

have wrought together for the great and glorious
issues of a Christendom such as that in the midst of
which we now stand. The church, taught and enlightened by the Spirit, unfolds and lays out the Word,
and only as it is informed and quickened by that
blessed Spirit of God, can lay it out for the healing
of the nations. We cannot think of this book by
itself doing the work, any more than we can think
of the church doing it without this book, or of the
two doing it together without the ever-present breath
of an Almighty Spirit.

But while this work is thus the result of a threefold energy; while we can never, so long as we think
correctly, separate one of its factors, save for distinction's sake, from the others; while therefore, speaking
of the Scripture and what it has wrought, we must
ever conceive of it as in the possession of a living
body of interpreters, the company of the faithful, and
of them as enlightened by the Holy Spirit to use it
aright; yet not the less may I ask you to contemplate
the mighty work of the world's regeneration in those
features upon which the influences of a Scripture are
mainly traceable, to note the part which this scripture
has borne in bringing about that new creation, wherein the old things of the world have passed away, and
all things have become new.

For, without running into the tempting error of
painting the old world black, for the purpose of bringing out, as by a dark back-ground, the brightness and
glory of the new; without denying to that old world
what it had of noble and true, or calling, as some have

done, its virtues merely showy and splendid sins; yet it is not easy to estimate how much was to be done, how much to be undone, ere a Christendom, even such as we behold it now, could emerge out of that world which alone yielded the materials out of which the new creation should be composed. The Word of the Cross had need, as a mighty leaven, to penetrate through every interstice of society, leavening language, and laws, and literature, and institutions, and manners. For it was not merely that at that change the world changed its religion, but in that change was implied the transformation, little by little, of every thing besides; every thing else had need to reconstruct itself afresh. And in this Word there resided a power equal to this need. The pattern of Christ, kept in the record of Scripture, ever clear in all its distinctness of outline before men's eyes, his work thus ever repeating itself for them over again, has given, as we ourselves see and feel, a new, inasmuch as it is an infinitely higher, standard of ideal goodness to the world —has cast down usurping pretenders to the name of virtues from their seats, has lifted up despised graces in their room. That Word has every where given to us graces for virtues, and martyrs for heroes; it has so reversed men's estimate of greatness, that a wreath of thorns is felt to be a far worthier ornament for a brow than a diadem of jewels—a Christ upon his cross to be a spectacle more glorious far than a Cæsar on his throne.

From that Word, too, we have derived such a sense of the duties of relation, of the debt of love which every man owes to every other, as was altogether strange to the heathen world. For when, in that well-known story, the poet awoke shouts of a tumultuous applause by declaring nothing human alien from himself who was a man, deep as was the feeling in men's hearts which was here appealed to, yet in those very shouts of applause, it was declared to be as new as it was deep. In those was the joyful recognition of a truth which lay deep in every man's bosom, but which had not taken form or shape or found utterance until then. Yet, with all our practical shortcomings in love to our brethren, how different is the condition marked by this little incident from ours, in which this noble utterance of the Roman poet is felt to be so true as hardly to escape from being a truism; and the love which men owe to one another on the score of their common stock, is so taken for granted, and the idea of it has so penetrated even into our common speech, that *kind* and *kinned*, *human* and *humane*, are, with us, but different pronunciations of the same words.

And, at least as wonderful, at least as fruitful, is the incoming of the Word of Christ, not into the midst of an old and corrupt civilization, but when it kindles for the first time a savage people into life. How does it seem to brood with a creative warmth and energy over all the rudiments of a higher life, which lay in that people's bosom, and yet but for this never could have come to the birth, rather were in danger of utterly dying out. How does it arrest at once that centrifugal progress of sin, which is ever drawing the men or the nations that have wandered out of the sphere of the divine attraction, farther and farther from God, the true centre of their being. Tribes which were in danger of letting go the last remnant of their spiritual heritage, nay, of utterly and literally perishing from the face of the earth, victims of their own vices, and of that uttermost degradation which had caused them at length to let go even those lowest arts by which animal existence is sustained, even these, that Word finds, even in these nurses up the dying embers of life; till the savage re-awakens to the consciousness of a man, and the horde begins, however feebly at first, to knit itself into the promise of a nation.

There may be spectacles which attract us more, there may be tidings to which we listen with a keener interest, but surely there can be no tidings worthier to be listened to, no spectacle upon which angels look down with a livelier sympathy, than those which such a land and time will often present; when, it may be, some gray-beard chief, stained in times past with a thousand crimes, but now having washed away them all in the waters of baptism, hangs upon the words of life, makes himself, perhaps, the humble and willing scholar of some little child, that he may learn to read with his own eyes of that Saviour who has pardoned even him. And ever, as he reads of "the gentleness of Christ," of his prayers for his crucifiers, of Him who, being first, made himself the last, who, being Lord of all, became servant of all, there dawns upon him more and more the glory of meekness, of overcoming evil with good, of serving others in love, instead of being himself served in fear: and he understands that this only is truly to live, and all which he has lived contrary to this, has been not life, but a hideous denial of life. Such sights other days have seen; such are to be seen in our own: for, blessed be God, it is not our fathers only who have told us of such things done in their times of old, but our own report the same. We, too, "see our tokens." In New Zealand, in the far islands of the Pacific, we have proof that this Word is yet mighty, through God, for casting down the strong holds of Satan and of sin.

Nor needs it to look thus far abroad to be reminded of what this Word has done. The Scripture itself is full of remembrancers of its own power. He who, tolerably acquainted with the past history of the Church, with the struggles which accompanied the unfolding, fixing, and vindicating of her dogma,—he who, furnished with this knowledge, passes over Scripture, may in some moods of his mind pass over it as over a succession of battle fields. He may be likened to a traveller journeying through some land, which, by the importance of its position or the greatness of its attractions, has drawn contending hosts to its soil, and been a battle ground for innumerable generations. Besides in all those pages which speak more directly to himself, they are eloquent to him with a thousand stirring recollections. For at every step which he advances, he recognises that which has been the motive of some mighty and long-drawn conflict, in which the keenest and brightest intellects, the kingliest spirits, the Bernards and the Abelards of their day, were engaged. Here, there, and every where, be it that he wanders among the extinguished volcanoes of controversies which have now burned themselves out, or among those which are flaming still, he meets with that, to maintain their conviction about which, men have been content to spend their lives, to make shipwreck of their worldly hopes, have dwelt in deserts, in caves, and in dungeons, yea, gladly have encountered all from which nature most, and most naturally shrinks. And whatever there may have been of earthly and of carnal mingling in the motives of the combatants, however in some of them he can recognise only the champions of error, yet in these mighty and passionate strivings, in these conflicts which generation has bequeathed to generation, he reads the confession which all past ages have borne, that this Word was worth contending for,—being felt by those worthiest to judge, dearer than life itself, and such that things else were cheap by comparison with it.

Strange, too, that even where there have not been these stirring excitements, where there has been no trumpet-peal sounding in men's ears, and summoning them to do battle for some perilled truth, that even here, too, multitudes of men should have been well-pleased to employ their lives in learning themselves better to understand, in seeking to make others understand better, this one Book—should have counted those lives worthily spent, and all other wisdom and knowledge than only to have found their true meaning and destination, when doing service as of handmaids unto it. For vast as is the apparatus of helps of al kinds which have accumulated round such other books as are signal monuments of human intellect and power; many as we find well satisfied to be nothing as independent labourers in the fields of knowledge, content to be only ministrant to the better understanding of this author or that book; yet are these taken altogether few and insignificant beside those that have thus felt in regard of the one Book with which we have to do. Surely the spectacle of any great library, and of the volumes there which stand in immediate relation to this one, with the certainty, that so long as the world stands, they will go on accumulating and multiplying, must to a thoughtful mind suggest many meditations of what the meaning and significance of that one must be, and the manner in which it must set in motion the minds of men. Nor will he, in estimating this, fail to call to mind that those which stand in *direct* relation to that Volume, which bear upon the front that they are thus connected with it, multitudinous past all count as they seem, are yet but a small fraction of those which owe to this one all which is most characteristic in them—their impulse, their motive, their form, their spirit; that all modern European literature is there as in its germ; that even the works which seem to stand remotest from it, least to own a fealty to it, do yet pay to it the unconscious, it may be the unwilling homage of being wholly different from what they would have been,—had they indeed at all existed,—without it.

Such, brethren, are a few aspects under which I

would ask you to consider how the Holy Scriptures have justified themselves by the effects which they have brought about, by the mighty deeds which they have done; showing themselves seeds of life, leaven of power in the world. And I should be untrue to my position here, did I conclude without asking you to make personal application of the things which you have heard to yourselves. This Word which has thus been fruitful every where, which has supplied what was lacking, and healed what was sick, and revived what was ready to die, will it be less effectual in us, if only we receive it aright? This, which has made so much else, like the dry rod of Aaron, to blossom and to bud, will it not be as potent in our hearts, till they too are clothed with foliage and fruits and flowers which are not naturally their own? Shall we say, "I am a dry tree," when we might be as trees planted by rivers of water, which should not fear the drought of the desert, nor see when the heat cometh? All things have lived whithersoever these waters which issue from the sanctuary have come. Shall not our hearts live also, until we too have like reason with the Psalmist for prizing these testimonies of God, even because with them He has quickened us?

LECTURE VIII.

THE FUTURE DEVELOPMENT OF SCRIPTURE.

REVELATION VI. 2.

Conquering and to conquer.

An earlier lecture in this present course was dedicated to the manner in which Holy Scripture had, little by little, laid bare its treasures to the Church; and in my very latest I had occasion to speak of the victories which the Truth had won and was winning still —the way in which the word of the Scripture was vindicating itself to be all that it claimed to be, showing itself mighty, through God, for doing its appointed work; how, like the personal Word, it had ridden forth, and was riding yet, a victorious conqueror over the earth. It remains to consider, and with this consideration we shall fitly conclude our subject, in what way it is likely to approve itself a conqueror to the end; what preparations we can trace in it for meeting the future evils of the world, the future needs of the Church; how far we may suppose that this Book, which has revealed so much, may yet have much more to reveal.

And this *is* our confidence, that as the Scripture has sufficed for the past, so also it will suffice for the time to come; that it has resources adequate to meet

all demands which may be made on it; that it has in
reserve whatsoever any new conditions of the world,
—any new shapes of evil, any new, if they be righteous, cravings of the spirits of men,—may require.
We believe that as the Scripture is an armory in which
the Church has found weapons for all past conflicts, so
will it find them there for all which are yet to come
—conflicts, which, it may be, we as little forecast or
dream of now, as we do of the weapons which are
ready wrought in this armory for bringing them to a
glorious termination; and the weapons, too, themselves
being oftentimes such, that they who were by God
employed to forge them, while they knew that they
would serve present needs, yet hardly knew, perhaps
knew not at all, what remote purposes they should
also serve, to what great ulterior purposes they should
one day be turned. Yet thus, no doubt, it shall be:
for just as in works of man's mind, *talent* knows all
which it means, but *genius*, which is nearer akin to
inspiration, means much more than it consciously
knows; even so wise men and prophets and evangelists, who were used for the uttering of this Word,
knowing much of that which they spake and recorded,
yet meant still more than they knew—the Holy
Ghost guiding and shaping their utterances, and
causing them oftentimes to declare deeper things, and
things of wider reach and of more manifold utility,
than even they themselves, enlarged and enlightened
by that Spirit as they were, were conscious of the
while. That which they spake being central Truth,
presented a front, not merely to the lies of their day,

not merely to the falsehood which they distinctly had in their mind to encounter, but presents a front to every later lie as well; and so we have entire confidence that the Truth being ever, in the language of Bacon, "a hill not to be commanded," the same those Scriptures, which are Scriptures of very truth, shall show themselves—a hill which shall never be commanded, but which rather shall itself command all other heights and eminences of the spiritual and intellectual world. However high these tower, this Word will always have heights which tower above them all; judging all things, it will be judged of none; itself the measure of all, no other thing will bring a measure unto it.

We can indeed guess but uncertainly what may be the future unrolling of the world's history—what antichristian forms of society may rise up for the moment seeming to keep their promise, consecrating the flesh, breaking down the walls of separation between the holy and profane, making all profane while they pretend to make all holy—what master-works of Satan, his latest and crowning forms of opposition to the Truth. Or, again, we can only uncertainly apprehend what heresies may appear, subtler and more attractive even than any which the world has yet beheld—coming with greater semblance of holiness, and well-nigh causing even the elect to fail. But our reliance in this Word and the revelation of the Name of God which is there, is this, that out of it the Church will be able to refute those heresies—by the help of its warnings and intimations to detect and to defy the attractions of Antichrist, even when he comes with all the lying wonders, and in all the false glory, of his kingdom.

For while it is hard for us to say what may be the exact forms of those future evils, while we cannot discern accurately beforehand the lineaments and proportions of these latest monstrous shapes which shall ascend from the pit,—as neither would this foreknowledge profit us much;—yet the hints which in God's prophetic word we have, the course of the mystery of iniquity as it is already working, seem alike to point to this, that as there has been an aping of the monarchy of the Father, in the absolute despotisms of the world, an aping of the economy of the Son, as though he already sat visibly on his throne, in its spiritual despotisms, and eminently in that of Rome; so there remains yet for the world, as the crowning delusion, a lying imitation of the kingdom and dispensation of the Spirit—such as in the lawless Communist sects of the middle ages, in the Familists of a later day, in the St. Simonians of our own, has attempted to come to the birth, though in each case the world was not ripe for it yet, and the thing was withdrawn for a time. Yet doubtless only for a time; to reappear in an after hour—full of false freedom, full of the promise of bringing all things into one; making war on the family, as something which separates between man and man, breaking down and obliterating all distinctions, the distinctions between nation and nation, between the man and the woman, between the flesh and the Spirit, between the Church and the world. So seems it; and when we translate St. Paul's words, with which he characterizes the final Antichrist, as though he had simply called him "that wicked one,"* we lose a confirmation of this view which his words more accurately rendered would have given us. He is not simply the *wicked* one, but ὁ ἄνομος the *lawless* one; and the mystery is not merely a mystery of iniquity but of lawlessness (ἀνομίας.) Law, in all its manifestations, is that which he shall rage against, making hideous misapplication of that great truth, that where the Spirit is, there is liberty.

Then, when this shall have come to pass, then at length the great anti-trinity of hell, the dragon, the beast, and the false prophet, will have been fully revealed in all deceivableness of unrighteousness;—and yet not so mighty to deceive, but that the Church of the redeemed, armed and forewarned by this Word of God, shall see in all this, only what it looked to see, only what it had been taught to expect; and in the might of the counter-truth, in the confession of the Father, the Son, and the Holy Ghost, shall be saved even in its weakest and simplest member, from that strong delusion, which shall be too much for every one besides.

And in thus speaking of Holy Scripture, I am but expressing a confidence which those who have searched the deepest into it have oftentimes expressed. Thus, to take but one name and another out of the noble catalogue of English worthies, Robert Boyle expresses

* 2 Thess. ii. 8.

himself thus: "I consider here that as the Bible was not written for any one particular time or people, but for the whole church militant diffused through all nations and ages, so that there are many passages very useful, which will not be found so these many ages; being possibly reserved by the prophetic Spirit that indited them, (and whose omniscience comprises and unites in one prospect all times and all events,) to quell some future foreseen heresy, which will not, perhaps, be born till we be dead, or resolve some yet unformed doubts, or confound some error that hath not yet a name." And Bishop Butler uses language well nigh the same: "Nor is it," he says, "at all incredible that a Book which has been so long in the possession of mankind should yet contain many truths as yet undiscovered. For all the same phenomena and the same faculties of investigation from which such great discoveries in natural knowledge have been made in the present and last age, were equally in the possession of mankind several thousand years before. And possibly it might be intended that events as they came to pass should open and ascertain the meaning of several parts of Scripture."

But, besides these mighty mischiefs which may hereafter arise, of which we can at most discern now only the dim beginnings, the obscure foreshadowings, there are also others which have already taken form and shape—some of them such as have stood strong and in the main unshaken for thousands of years; which yet we believe, which indeed yet we know, shall one day be overthrown by the greater power and prevalence of the Truth. For we are sure that the religion of Christ is as the rod of Moses, which did in the end swallow up every rod of the magicians—that the Church shall possess the earth—that "the field" in which the Son of Man sows his seed is not this land or that land, but "the world." And anticipating, or to speak more truly, being sure of this, it may not be unbecoming to see if we can at all discern in Scripture the preparations which have been there made, and the might which is there slumbering, against each of those closer conflicts, which the Church, by its help, must one day wage with those forms of untruth and error. Such inquiry will, at any rate, not be foreign to our subject; for that subject being the fitness of Holy Scripture for unfolding the spiritual life of men, a great part of that fitness must lie in its capacity to meet and overcome each deadlier form of superstition and error, which, under one name or another, cramps and confines, or wholly hinders, the true development of the spirits of men.

How profitable were it, in regard of the more effectual conducting of Christian missions, to be more conscious than generally we seek to be, of what is our peculiar strength, and what the peculiar weakness of each of those systems of error, which we seek, in love to the souls which are made prisoners by it, to overthrow;—so that we should not blindly run a tilt against it, with no other preparation save a confidence in the goodness of our cause, but wisdom and insight assail it there, where there were best hope of assailing with success. For every one of these, while their strength is in that fragment of Truth, which, however maimed and marred, with whatever contradictions and under whatever disguises, they hold, have also eminently their weak side, that on which they signally deny some great Truth which the spirit of man craves, which the Scriptures of God affirm—a side, therefore, on which, if assailed, they must sooner or later perish, or rather will not always continue at strife with their own blessedness. To know this, and to know, also, what engines out of the divine armory ought to be especially advanced against each of these strong-holds of confusion, to know not merely that we are strong and they weak, but where and why strong in regard of each, and where and why they are weak; this is surely a needful, as it is a much-neglected, discipline; this is a duty not indolently to be foregone by a Church like our own, a Church which God's providence and leading has so clearly marked out to do the work of an Evangelist on vast continents and in far islands of the sea.

To give such a training as this, was no doubt the meaning and purpose of the catechetical schools of Alexandria, so famous through all Christian antiquity; they were instituted to afford the highest culture to the evangelist, to give him the fullest understanding of what he was to oppose, and how he was to do it. And such an insight as this, could we have it clear, into Scripture and its adaptation for overcoming each shape of falsehood, how would it make us workmen that did not need to be ashamed. How would it enable us at once, and without beating the air, to address ourselves to the points really at issue between us on one side, and Jews, Mohammedans, and infidels, on the other. For the Truth which is still the same, which might not give up one jot or tittle of itself, though it had with this the certainty of winning a world, may yet of infinite love continually change its voice, and present itself ever differently, according to the different necessities of those whom it would fain make its own.

And on the other hand, we address ourselves but in a slight and inefficient manner to our work, when, without discrimination, without acquaintance with those systems which hold souls in bondage, which hinder them from coming to the light of life, we have but one method with them all—one language in which to describe them all—one common charge of belonging to the devil on which to arraign them; instead of recognising, as we ought, that each province of the dark kingdom of error is different from every other; instead of seeing that it is not a lie which can ever make any thing strong—that it is not certainly their lie which has ever made them strong, and enabled them to stand their ground so long, and some of them, saddest of all! to win ground for awhile from Christendom itself; but the truth which that lie perverts and denies. Handling them in that other way, we turn but to little advantage that manifold Word of wisdom with which God has enriched his Church, and which, containing as it does its own special antidote for every error, would allow, and indeed demands, a much more special dealing with each, and one which would get much more nearly to the heart of the matter.

Thus, the Mohammedan is strong in that he affirms God to be distinct from the creature, so that he may not without blasphemy be confused with it—a jealous God, who will not give his glory to another. In the might of this faith, in the conviction that God had raised him up to assert this truth in the face of all who were forgetting it, he overran half a world. But he is weak, and the moon of Islam, as it has waxed, so will it wane before the Sun of Righteousness, inasmuch as he makes the gulf which divides God and man to be a gulf which can never be bridged over, an impassable chasm, fixed for eternity; he is weak, because he knows not, and will not know, of one, the Son of Mary, the Son of God, in whom the human and divine were not confounded, nor lost one in the other, but united. He does not satisfy the longings of the human race, which was made for this union as its highest end and crowning perfection, which will be satisfied with nothing short of this; and therefore we are sure that the day will come, however little we may as yet discern its signs, when the fiery sword of Mohammed will grow pale before the ever-brightening lustre of the cross of the Son of Man; when the Scriptures will show themselves over all the dark places of the earth mightier than the Koran. We are sure of this, because those Scriptures maintain all which is there of truth—are as jealous and more jealous of the incommunicable name of God,—say, and say far more clearly, Our God is one God; but in addition to this, affirm that which is there denied, but which the spirit of man will never rest till it has found and known, a Son of God, and him also the Son of Man.

The Indian religions,—they, too, are not without their elements of an obscured truth—and in this mainly, that they declare it to be most worthy of God to reveal Himself as man—that this is the only true revelation of Him, that an incarnation is the fittest outcoming of the glory of God. But, not to urge that what they have to tell of such matters are only dreams of men, and not facts of God—besides this, they are comparatively worthless, in that they do not concentrate and gather up this revelation of God in one incarnation, but lose and scatter it through unnumbered. For while one incarnation is precious, a thousand are worth nothing; they become mere transient points of contact between God and man, momentary docetic apparitions of the divine under human forms. And the books which are the records of these, and the religion which rests on those books, must give way before that Book, which can say in holiest, yet soberest earnest, " The Word was made flesh "—and which knows not merely of an Incarnation, but of a Resurrection and an Ascension, in which the Son of God made manifest that he had wedded the humanity for ever, that he had not come merely into transient relation with it, but had made it his own for eternity; sitting down in it on the right hand of the Majesty on high.

And that other later birth of Hindooism, that other vast system of further Asia, which we are continually perplexed whether to call it a pantheism, or a gigantic atheism, that which in the end loses every thing in God, and makes absorption in Him the ultimate end of being, that, too, begins with fairer promises. For it starts with that which is so deeply true, that in God we live and move and have our being—that as man came from God, so he must return to God—that there is but one Spirit which moves through all things. But then, refusing to know aught but the Spirit, refusing to know the Father and the Son from whom that Spirit proceeds, so neither can it save its votaries from that gulf wherein all things, and man the first, are annihilated in an abysmal deep, which is not the less dreadful, because it calls itself God; that gulf which is ever yawning for every nobler and deeper speculator in theology, who has not the mystery of the ever-blessed Trinity, three Persons and one God, for his safeguard and his stay,—an ever-abiding witness to him for the distinctness of personal being. And we are sure that neither will this system stand before that Word which affirms, and only with far higher clearness, that " God is a Spirit; " but affirms also, that " there are *three* that bear record in heaven, the Father, the Word, and the Holy Ghost;" without which that other truth is only as a noble river presently to lose itself among the sands.

These, brethren, are the great rival religions to Christianity, which yet contend with it for the possession of the world—each of them, as you see, presenting points of contact for the absolute Truth; and at the same time all presenting points of weakness—

THE FUTURE DEVELOPMENT OF SCRIPTURE. 155

sides upon which they dumbly crave to be fulfilled by this Truth, even while they are striving the most fiercely against it; the Truth in Holy Scripture being at once the antagonist and the complement of them all.

Nor may I not observe that any other dealing with them than this, which, even while it wars against them, welcomes and honours the wreck and fragment of Truth which they still may retain—any ruder and less discriminating assault on that which men have hitherto believed, and which, however mixed up with falsehood and fraud, has yet been all whereby they have holden on to a higher world,—any such attack, even when it seems most successful, may be full of the utmost peril for them whom we thus coarsely seek to benefit, and with these unskilful hands to deliver. For, indeed, there is no office more delicate, no task needing greater wisdom and patience and love, than to set men free from their superstitions, and yet, with this, not to lay waste in their hearts the very soil in which the Truth should strike its roots—to disentangle the tree from the ivy which was strangling it, without, in the process and together with the strangling ivy, destroying also the very life of the tree itself, which we designed to save. Where this process of men's extrication from error has been rudely or unwisely carried out, either by their own fault or that of others, where they have been urged to rise up in scorn, and to trample upon their past selves, and all that in time past they have held in honour, how mournful frequently the final issue! Thus, how unable do we often prove to retain the converts from Romanism which we have won. They do not return to that which they have left, but they pass on, they pass *through* the Truth into error on the other side. They pass from darkness into the sunlight, and that sunlight scarcely gilds and brightens them for an instant, ere they glide into another and thicker darkness again; scarcely are they in the secure haven a moment, ere they put forth, as though incapable of enjoying its repose, among the shoals and eddies once more.

And so, too, the Hindoo children in our Indian schools, when we have gathered them there, and shown them in the light of modern philosophy, the utter absurdity and incoherence of their sacred books, and provoked them to throw uttermost scorn on these, we yet may not have brought them even into the vestibule of the Faith, rather may have set them at a greater distance than ever; for to have taught them to pour contempt on all with which hitherto they have linked feelings of sacredness and awe, is but a questionable preparation for making them humble and reverent scholars of Christ. Wiser surely was St. Paul's method, who ever sought a ground common to himself and him whom he would persuade, though it were but a handbreadth, upon which to take his stand— who taught men reverently to handle their past selves and their past beliefs,—who to the Athenians said, "Whom therefore ye ignorantly worship, Him declare I unto you," and spake of the Cretan poet as "a prophet of their own;" who re-adopted into the family of the Truth its lost and wandering children, however *they* might have forgotten their true descent, in whatever far land, under whatever unlikely disguises, he found them. Thus, and because he thus dealt, he became, in the language of a Greek father, which contains scarcely an exaggeration, the νυμφαγωγος της οικουμνεης, he who led up the world as a bride unto Christ.

But I must draw my subject to an end, and with a few general remarks on the aim and scope of what here I have been permitted to deliver, will conclude. My purpose has been, as I trust even they may have gathered who have heard but a part, and that the latest, of these discourses, to bring out an inner witness for Scripture from that which, to an earnest and devout examination, it shows itself as fitted for doing —from that which it has already done—from that which we may believe it will accomplish yet. And this subject I have chosen out of those which were before me, because truly there is great strength and comfort and assurance for us in these evidences for the things that we have believed, which are drawn, not from without, but from within—from their inner glory, their manifest fitness. Thus, for example, if gainsayers at any time should adduce apparent disagreements between one Gospel or one book of history and another, as between Matthew and Luke, Chronicles and Kings, and seek to trouble and perplex us with these, surely the true way to meet them were to bring first the whole question into a higher court. Let *us* put rather the question to be resolved as this, In what traceable connexion do these books, each by itself, each in relation to the whole of the other books, stand to the great purpose of God with humanity? Can they be shown evidently to form integral parts of a mightier whole? Do they reveal the Name of God? Do they yield *their* nourishment for the divine life of man? Have they yielded such for our own?

And then—not indeed to refuse entering into those lower and merely critical questions of detail; but if it has been found that the book satisfies higher needs, fulfils loftier requirements--claiming for it on the score of this, the entire, the trustful confidence of faith, that it will justify itself in all lesser matters, that it will come out as clear and clean in them, as in its greater purpose and aim. Here too that word will hold good, "He that believeth shall not make haste." He will be content to wait. For what weakness does it manifest, what inner mistrust of the things which we have believed, how feebly must we hold them, how little can they have blest us, when we raise a cry of fear at any new and startling results to which science or criticism may have, or may *seem* to have, arrived. These, too, will presently be shown what they are; if true, they will fall into their place, and that place a place of subjection to revealed Truth: if false, however noisy now, however threatening to carry the whole world before them, will vanish away in a little while. But to dread any thing, to wish that any thing which has been patiently sought or honestly won, should be ignored or kept back, betrays an extreme weakness; Christ has not laid his hand on us with power, or we should not be so easily persuaded to believe his cause tottering, or his Truth endangered.

And, indeed, as regards aught which may be brought forward with purposes hostile to the Faith, may not the past well give us confidence for the future? One and another adversary has risen up; for what has not the world beheld in this kind? Essays on the Miracles, Ages of Reason, Lives of Jesus, Theories of Creation. And then, in the first deceitful flush of a momentary success, oftentimes the cry has gone forth, It is finished; and the fortress of the Faith is held to be so fatally breached, as henceforward to be untenable, and its defenders to have nothing more to do than to lay down their arms, and surrender at discretion. And already those that dwell upon the earth begin to make merry over the slain witnesses; and already the new Diocletians rear their trophies and stamp their medals, the memorials of an extinguished Faith—they themselves being about to perish for ever, and that Faith to go forward to new victories. For anon the floods retreat; and temple and tower of God, round whose bases those waters raged and foamed and fretted for an instant, stand calmly and strongly as ever they did before. We, too, some of us have heard, and probably we shall hear again, such premature hymns of an imaginary triumph. And when such are confidently raised, the unstable are perplexed, and the waverers fall off, and seeds of doubt, to be reaped in a harvest of weakness, are sown in many minds. But let us, brethren, have a sanctuary to retreat to, till each such tyranny is overpast, as overpass it surely and shortly will. Let us have that immediate syllogism of the heart, against which no argument is good. Let us be able to say, These words, we have found them words of healing, words of eternal life. This is our sole security—to have tasted the good Word, to have known the powers of the world to come. And what if Theology may not be able, on the instant, to solve every difficulty, yet Faith will not therefore abandon one jot or tittle of that which she holds, for she has it on another and a surer tenure, she holds it directly from her God.

THE END OF THE LECTURES FOR 1845.

CHRIST THE DESIRE OF ALL NATIONS, OR,
THE UNCONSCIOUS PROPHECIES
OF HEATHENDOM:

BEING

THE HULSEAN LECTURES
FOR THE YEAR M.DCCC.XLVI.

CHRIST THE DESIRE OF ALL NATIONS, OR THE UNCONSCIOUS PROPHECIES OF HEATHENDOM.

LECTURE I.

INTRODUCTORY LECTURE.

HAGGAI II. 7.

The Desire of all nations shall come.

ALTHOUGH the Founder of these Lectures, which it is permitted me a second time to deliver in this place, did by no means offer a narrow range of subjects, from which the preacher should make his choice, but on the contrary, so expressed himself, that it would be quite possible to adhere to the letter of his injunctions, and still, at the same time, altogether to quit the region of Christian apology; yet I cannot but believe that in so doing I should be forsaking the spirit of these injunctions, and hardly fulfilling the intentions with which these Lectures were founded by him. Those who have gone before me in this honourable office, arguing, probably, from the subjects which he has placed in the foremost rank; from the purpose which kindred foundations, by him established among us, were evidently meant to serve; from the especial importance attached by good men in the age wherein he lived, to such defences of our holy faith, have generally concluded that they should best be fulfilling his intention, to which they felt a pious reverence was due, if they undertook the maintenance of some portion of the truth, which had been especially assailed or gainsayed. Nor do I purpose, on the present occasion, to depart from the practice which the example of my predecessors has sanctioned; having rather chosen for my argument a subject recommending itself to me, first, by a certain suitableness, as I trust will appear, to our present needs, and to controversies of our day, such as are approaching, if we were not actually in the midst of them as yet; and secondly, by an evident bearing which it has upon one of the two great branches of study cultivated among us in this University. *Christ the Desire of all Nations, or, The Unconscious Prophecies of Heathendom*—such appears to me the title which will best gather up and present at a single glance to you the subject, which it will be my aim in the following discourses, if God will, under successive aspects to unfold.

Leaving aside, as not belonging to my argument, what there was of positive divinely constituted preparation for the coming of Christ in the Jewish economy, I shall make it my task to trace what in my narrow limits I may, of the implicit expectations which there were in the heathen world—to contemplate, at least under a few leading aspects, the yearnings of the nations for a redeemer, and for all which the true Redeemer only could give,—for the great facts of his life, for the great truths of his teaching. Nor may this be all: for this, however interesting in itself, would yet scarcely come under the title of Christian apology; of which the idea is, that it is not merely the truth, but the truth asserting itself in the face of error. It will therefore be my endeavour further to rescue these dim prophetic anticipations of the heathen world from the abuse which has sometimes been made of them, to show that these dreams of the world, so far from helping to persuade us that all which we hold is a dream likewise, are rather exactly that which ought to have preceded the world's awaking: that these parhelions do not proclaim every thing else to be an optical illusion, but announce, and witness for, a sun that is travelling into sight; that these false *ancilia* of man's forging, tell of a true which has indeed come down from heaven. I would fain show that there ought to have been these; the transcending worth and dignity of the Christian revelation not being diminished by their existence, but rather enhanced; for its glory lies, not in its having relation to nothing which went before itself, but rather in its having relation to every thing, in its being the middle point to which all lines, some consciously, more unconsciously, were tending, and in which all centred at the last.

And this it is worth our while to show: for we do not here, as the charge has sometimes been made against us, first set up the opponent,—whom we afterwards easily overthrow, for he was but the phantom of our own brain. On the contrary, it has been at divers times from the very first, and is in our own day, a part, and a favourite part, of their tactics who would resist the Faith, to endeavour to rob it of its significance as the great epoch in the world's history, by the production of anterior parallels to it.

These may be parallels to its doctrines and ethical precepts; and *they* are brought forward with the purpose of showing that it is therefore no such wisdom of God, no such mystery that had been kept secret from the beginning of the world; that what it professed to give as a revelation from heaven, men had attained before by the light of reason, by the unassisted efforts of their own minds. The attempts to rob Christianity in this way of its significance are, as I observed, not new. If such objections have been zealously urged in modern times, they belong also to the very earliest. To take two examples, one old, one new. Celsus, in the second century, quoting words of our blessed Lord's, in which he exhorts to the forgiveness of enemies, remarks that he has found the identical precept in Plato,—with only the difference, as he dares to add, that it is by the Grecian sage better and more elegantly spoken.* And Gibbon,

---

* Origen, *Con. Cels*, l. 7, c. 58. In like manner Celsus affirmed that our Lord's words, Matt. xix. 23, were transferred from Plato, *De Legg.*, l. 5. 742. (*Con. Cels.*, l. 6, c. 16.) Augustine too (*De Doctr. Christ.*, l. 2, c. 28) makes mention of some in his own time, readers and lovers of Plato,—qui dicere ausi sunt omnes Domini nostri Jesu Christi sententias, quas mirari et prædicare coguntur, de Platonis libris eum didicisse. St. Ambrose also, as we learn from Augustine, (*Ep.* 31,) had found it necessary to write against such, which he

having occasion to speak of one of Christ's most memorable moral precepts, "Whatsoever ye would that men should do to you, do ye even so to them," cannot resist the temptation of adding—"a rule which I read in a moral treatise of Isocrates four hundred years before the publication of the Gospel." And in like manner we all probably remember, if not the contents, yet the title which the book of an English deist bore, one of the ablest of that unhappy band, "*Christianity as old as the Creation;*" a book which by that title at once indicated the quarter from which its author advanced to the assault of revealed religion.

And not seldom this charge appears in an aggravated form; and it has been sought to be proved, not merely that others had said the same before the Gospel, but that it had covertly borrowed from them —that so far from being more and higher than another birth of the human mind, it possessed so little vital and independent energy, as to have been compelled to go back to prior sources, and to build with the materials of others, and to adorn itself with their spoils. Urged by their desire to prove this, hoping to convict it thus of being in possession of things not its own, the adversaries of the Christian faith have gone

---

did in a work that now has perished. How excellent is Augustine's own answer (*Enarr. in Ps.* cxl. 6.) Dixit hoc Pythagoras, dixit hoc Plato ...Propterea si inventus fuerit aliquis eorum hoc dixisse quod dixit et Christus, gratulamur illi, non sequimur illum. Sed prior fuit ille quàm Christus. Si quis vera loquitur, prior est quàm ipsa Veritas? O homo, attende Christum non quando ad te venerit, sed quando te fecerit.

168   LECTURE I.

far to seek for the anticipations and sources of its doctrine. Thus, with Voltaire, India, and still more, China, were the favourite quarters from which he laboured to show that its wisdom had been drawn; although his almost incredible ignorance exposed him to the most ridiculous errors, and made him the dupe of poorest forgeries, palmed on him as works of the ancient wisdom of the East, and which by him were again confidently produced as such.* Somewhat later the Zend-Avesta and the religion of Zoroaster were triumphantly appealed to, as having been the true sun from which the borrowed light of Judaism and Christianity had proceeded. Then again, men said that our blessed Lord had been educated and initiated in the secret lore of the Essenes, and that he, the Wisdom of God, had first learned wisdom in these schools of

* There is a curious account of a fraud which was played off on him, in Von Bohlen's *Das Alte Indien*, v. 1, p. 136, connecting itself with a singular piece of literary forgery. A Jesuit missionary, whose zeal led him to assume the appearance of an Indian Fakir, in the beginning of last century forged a Veda, of which the purpose was, secretly to undermine the religion which it professed to support, and so to facilitate the introduction of Christianity—to advance, that is, the kingdom of truth with a lie. This forged Veda is full of every kind of error or ignorance in regard of the Indian religions. After lying, however, long in a Romanist missionary college at Pondicherry, it found its way to Europe, and a transcript of it came into the hands of Voltaire, who eagerly used it for the purpose of depreciating the Christian Books, and showing how many of their doctrines had been anticipated by the wisdom of the East. The book had thus an end worthy of its beginning.

men. Or by others, Rabbinical parallels to various sayings in the New Testament, to evangelical parables and doctrines, have been solemnly adduced, as solving the riddle of Christianity, as enough to dissipate that nimbus of glory with which it had been hitherto surrounded, to refute its loftier claims, and to prove its origin of earth, and not of heaven. So has falsehood travelled round the world, as inconsistent with itself as it is remote from the truth, each later birth of it devouring the preceding.

And they have wrought in the same spirit, and in reality with the same weapons to the same ends, who yet, somewhat shifting their ground, have not so much sought to turn our Christian faith into a doctrine which had been often taught before, as into a dream which has been often dreamed before; who have not therefore laboured to produce parallels to its isolated sayings or doctrines—to rob it here and there of a jewel in its crown; but have aspired to a completer victory, striking at the very person and acts of Him on whom it rests, and out of whom it has unfolded itself. And in this way;—they have ransacked all records of ancient religions for such parallels, nearer or more remote, as they could in them find, not now any more to the sayings, but rather to the doings, of his life; and having mustered and marshalled in threatening order as many of these as they could draw together, they have turned round and said to us—" In all times, and all the world through, men have been imagining for themselves, as you see, sons of God, expiations by sacrifice, direct communications with a higher world, oracles and prophecies, wielders of a power mightier than nature's, restorers of a lost Paradise, conquerors of Hades, ascensions into heaven. They have *imagined* them, and nothing more; for the things which they thus in spirit grasped at, never found an historic realization, however men may have enriched themselves, and we do not deny that they did so, with the thought that such things had been, or one day should be." And then it has been further asked us, What right had we to difference our hope from the hope of all others? They longed so earnestly, that at last their longing wove a garment, made even a body, for itself; what right have any to affirm that it is otherwise with the things which they believe?

And thus, because men have hoped for, and reached after, that which in Christ is given, and hoped so intensely, that they have sometimes imagined it to be actually theirs, so projecting their hope, as to give it at last an objective reality, we are bidden to believe that ours is but such an ardent desire, fashioning at length a body for itself. Parading a long line of shadows, these adversaries require us to acknowledge the substance we have embraced to be a shadow also; showing how much false money is in the world, and has at different times passed current, they demand of us, how we dare to assume that which we have accepted to be true;—when they *should* see that the shadows imply a substance somewhere, that the false money passes only under shelter of a true. Proving, as it is not hard to prove, those parallels to be groundless and mythical, to rest on no true historic basis, they hope that the great facts of the Christian's belief will be concluded to be as weak—that they will be involved in a common discredit*—and the faiths of which those other formed a part having come to nothing, or evidently hastening to decay, that this may be assumed to underlie the same judgment, and to be hastening to the same inevitable dissolution, however the signs of it as yet may not appear.

This scheme of attack has been so long and so vigorously plied, so much success has been expected from it, that in the works of the later assailants of revelation from this quarter, there speaks out a certain indignation, mingled with astonishment, at the resistance which it is still presuming to offer; as though it were not to be endured, that every other religion should have confessed itself a mythology, and that this should deny it still—that each other, like a startled ghost, should have vanished at the first cock-crowing of an intellectual morn, but that this should continue to affront, as boldly and as confidently as ever, even the light of the world's middle day—that each other should have crumbled into nothing at the first touch

* Tertullian (*Apol.* 47,) speaks of the way in which these parallels were played off against the Christian verities—Elysium not only having forfeited belief in itself, but having helped to destroy a belief in heaven—Minos and Rhadamanthus having rendered the judgment-seat of Christ a mockery;—though in his narrow fashion he sees in them nothing but the adulteria veritatis—the work of the jealous envy of evil spirits, quæ de similitudine fidem infirmarent veritatis. But if the truth was hard to receive with these, might it not have been impossible to receive without them?

of the wand of a critical philosophy, but that this should entirely refuse to obey its dissolving spell.

Now all charges against the truth, however destitute of any solid foundation, out of whatever perversity of heart or mind they may have sprung, yet, when continually re-appearing, when repeating themselves in different ages, and by the mouths of different objectors, and those independent of one another, have yet, we may be sure, something which has rendered them not merely possible, but plausible; which suggested them first, and, with the frivolous and thoughtless, with those that have been eager to believe them, and to be quit of the restraints of a positive faith, has given them currency and favour. Let me seek, then, as an important element of my subject, to consider what that something is, which has served to suggest, and afterwards to give a point to these charges; and, not pausing here, to show that the truth, which, however distorted, is at the bottom of these charges, is one which we may cheerfully and without any misgiving, recognise.

And this is not all: for I would fain also show that it would be a grievous deficiency, if that were absent from our Christian faith, which has been the motive and hint to these accusations—if that faith, as far as regards the whole anterior world except the Jewish, stood in relation to nothing which men had thought, or felt, or hoped, or believed; with no other coefficient but the Jewish, and resting on no broader historic basis than that would supply. It will be my purpose to inquire whether we may not contemplate the relations of the absolute truth to the anterior religions of the world, in an aspect in which we shall cease altogether from regarding with suspicion these apparent anticipations of good things given us in Christ, in which, instead of being secretly embarrassed by them, and hardly knowing exactly how to deal with, or where to range them, we shall joyfully accept these presentiments of the truth, so far as they are satisfactorily made out, as enhancing the greatness and glory of the truth itself; and as being, so far as they are allowed to have any weight, confirmations of it.

Nor will it be a small satisfaction,—if this be possible, as I believe it easy,—to make our adversaries do drudging work for us; to plough with their oxen; to enter, as we shall do then, upon their labours; and all that they have painfully gathered up with purposes hostile to the faith—to appropriate and make defensive of it; not so much anxiously defending our own position, as confidently turning theirs; wresting from them their own weapons, and then wielding them against themselves.

And first, in regard of the ethical anticipations of what is given to us in the gospel,—the goodly maxims, the striking precepts, the memorable sayings, which are gathered from the fields of heathen philosophy, and then sometimes used to depress the original worth of the teaching of Christ and his apostles,—I will not urge here, and I have no object in urging, though I may, in passing, remark, how many that are sometimes adduced of these are wholly deceptive, as parallels to Christian truths. How often in their organic connexion they would be very far from containing that echo or presentiment of truth which we deem we catch in them; how often they have indeed a very different significance from that which *we* first *put* in them, and only afterwards educe from them. Nor yet will I press how the goodliest maxim is indeed nothing, save in its coherence to a body of truth; how a world of such maxims, were they gotten together, would be only as ten thousand artificial lamps, failing altogether to constitute a day, and not in the remotest degree doing the work, or supplying to the world the place of a single sun.

Not to press this, and accepting fully and freely what has been said wisely and well before the gospel and apart from the gospel, and allowing to the full that it has many times touched the heart of the matter, yet still is there nothing here which we need wish we could deny, which we should not rather desire to find. Indeed, so far from there having been, in time past, a shunning or ignoring of these heathen parallels, the early apologists perhaps only admitted them too freely: yet thus at any rate they testified that to acknowledge them they felt to be no confession of a weakness in their position. Thus more than one has likened the faithful delivered from an evil world to the children of Israel brought out of Egypt, who borrowed and carried forth from thence vessels of gold and vessels of silver, the same which probably afterwards furnished the precious metals which they dedicated to the holier uses of the sanctuary. In like manner, they said, there was much which the faithful, delivered out of the spiritual Egypt, would leave behind him, as all its abominable idolatries; but something also which he would carry forth, and which he had a right to carry forth, for it was not truly the riches of that land. This silver and this gold had been originally dug from mines of divine truth, and bearing it with him, he only reclaimed to its noblest purposes that which had been more or less alienated and perverted from them.*

Nor need *we* deal more timidly with these parallels than they did. So long, indeed, as we regard God's

---

* Thus Augustine (*De Doctr. Christ.*, l. 2, c. 40·) Philosophi autem qui vocantur, si qua forte vera et fidei nostræ accommodata dixerunt maximè Platonici, non solùm formidanda non sunt, sed ab eis etiam tanquam injustis possessoribus in usum nostrum vindicanda. Sicut enim Ægyptii non solùm idola habebant et onera gravia, quæ populus Israel detestaretur et fugeret, sed etiam vasa atque ornamenta de auro et argento, et vestem, quæ ille populus exiens de Ægypto sibi potius tanquam ad usum meliorem clanculo vindicavit, non auctoritate propriâ, sed præcepto Dei, ipsis Ægyptiis nescienter commodantibus ea, quibus non bene utebantur, sic doctrinæ omnes Gentilium non solùm simulata et superstitiosa figmenta gravesque sarcinas supervacui laboris habent, ... sed etiam liberales disciplinas usui veritatis aptiores, . . quod eorum tamquam aurum et argentum, quod non ipsi instituerunt, sed de quibusdam quasi metallis divinæ providentiæ, quæ ubíque infusa sunt, eruerunt, ... debet ab eis auferre Christianus ad usum justum prædicandi Evangelii. Origen (*Ep. ad Gregor.*, t. 1, p. 30,) uses the same illustration, observing, however, that, according to his experience, the gold which is brought out of Egypt is oftener used for the fashioning of an idol, a golden calf, the work of men's own hands, which they worship, than for the adorning of the tabernacle of God.

revelation of Himself in Christ, as a revelation merely of certain moral truths, it may be startling to find aught that is therein anticipated in any other quarter. But when we more rightly contemplate it as the manifesting of life, that the Life was manifested, and dwelt among us, then we feel that they who gave, and could give, precepts and maxims only, however precious these were, whatever witness they bore to a light shining in the darkness, to a divine spark not trodden out in man, to a God nurturing the heathen, with all this yet gave not that, which, for man, is the gift of gifts and blessing of blessings. And this is the true way in which to contemplate it. That which differences Christianity from all other religions, is not its theory of morals; this is a most real, yet at the same time, only a relative difference, for there were ethics before there were Christian ethics.* But its difference is, that it is life and power, that it transforms, that it

* Grotius, indeed, says, (*De Verit. Rel. Christ.*, l. 4, c. 12.) Ejus [scil. religionis Christianæ] partes singulæ tantæ sunt honestatis, ut suapte luce animos quasi convincant, ita ut inter paganos non defuerint qui dixerint singula, quæ nostra religio habet universa. Lactantius expresses himself more cautiously, and is careful to add how none but a teacher sent from God could have knit these scattered limbs into a body. He says, *Inst. Div.*, l. 7, c. 7: Nullam sectam fuisse tam deviam, nec philosophorum quendam tam inanem, qui non viderit aliquid e vero. Quodsi extitisset aliquis, qui veritatem, sparsam per singulos, per sectasque diffusam, colligeret in unum, et redigeret *in corpus*, is profectò non dissentiret à nobis. Sed hoc nemo facere, nisi veri peritus ac sciens, potest: verum autem non nisi ejus scire est, qui sit doctus à Deo.

transfigures, that it makes new creatures, that it does for all what others only promised to do for a few. Herein the essential difference resides. Men, for instance, before it came, could speak worthy things, and could really feel them, about the beauty of overcoming their desires, of forgiving their enemies, of repaying injuries with kindness, of coming to God with clean hands and a clean heart. Such sayings abound in every code of morals:* but the unhappiness was, that they who uttered these sayings and they who admired them, did little more than this. It was not that there was any falseness in their admiration: they delighted in them after the inner man, but in the actual struggle with evil, they were ever weak to bring them to effect. There was a great gulf between the saying and the doing, which never till in Christ, was effectually bridged over; so that the Christian speaker in that beautiful dialogue, the *Octavius* of Minucius Felix, exactly hit the mark, when, to characterize the practical of Christian life as distinguished from the speculative of heathen philosophy, he exclaimed of that sect every where spoken against, to which he belonged, *Non eloquimur magna, sed vivimus*.

And yet, brethren, when we thus trace the miserable contradiction that ever existed in a world out of Christ, between the good seen and the evil done, the vast chasm between the two, let this be with no pur-

---

* See, for instance, in Von Bohlen, (*Das Alte Indien,* v. 1, p 364,) a beautiful collection of Indian sayings of this kind, on the love of our neighbour, and the forgiveness of injuries.

pose of laying bare their sores, with no thought of glorying in their infirmities, to whom in a less favoured time the only fountain of effectual strength and healing had not yet been opened. For indeed, brethren, may there not be many a one among ourselves to whom, with far less excuse, all this explains itself, alas! only too easily? many a one, it may be, who remembers times of his own life, before his moral convictions had been gathered up and found their middle point in Christ—and in those times repeated falls under temptation, which explain to him only too vividly the condition in which this ever-recurring infidelity of men to their moral convictions found place—in which they were thus able to trace the outlines of a righteousness, but impotent to fill them up, and so ever leaving it in outline still—well skilled to draw a ground-plan, but weak to build any superstructure thereon—the virtue loved, till the opportunity came for practising it; the sin hated, till the moment for testifying that hatred had arrived.

But to pass on to the other charge, to the resemblances to the great facts on which our faith reposes, to the great events of our Lord's life, which are adduced from other quarters, with the requirement, because those have proved weak to stand, that we should acknowledge these to be weak also;—they only will consent to such a conclusion, who have failed to perceive that according to the very highest idea of Christianity, such there needs must have been. For what do we affirm of Christ? when do we conceive worthily of Him? When we conceive of Him, in the prophet's words, as "the Desire of all nations"—the fulfiller of the world's hopes—the stiller of creation's groans—the great birth of time, unto which all the unspeakable throes of a suffering humanity had been tending from the first. These resemblances disturb us not at all,—they are rather most welcome; for we do not believe the peculiar glory of what in Christ we possess to consist in this, that it is unlike every thing else, "the cold denial and contradiction of all that men have been dreaming of through the different ages of the world, but rather the sweet reconciliation and exquisite harmony of all past thoughts, anticipations, revelations." Its prerogative is, that all whereof men had a troubled dream before, did in Him become a waking reality; that what men were devising, and most inadequately, for themselves, God has perfectly given us in his Son; that in the room of shifting cloud-palaces, with their mockery of temple and tower, stands for us a city, which hath come down from heaven, but whose foundations rest upon this earth of ours;—that we have divine *facts*—facts no doubt which are ideal, in that they are the vehicle of everlasting truths; history indeed which is far more than history, for it embodies the largest and most continually recurring thoughts which have stirred the bosom of humanity from the beginning. We say that the divine ideas which had wandered up and down the world, till oftentimes they had well nigh forgotten themselves and their own origin, did at length clothe themselves in flesh and blood; they became incarnate with the Incarnation of the Son of God. In his life and person the idea and the fact at length kissed each other, and were henceforward wedded for evermore.

If these things be so, and it will be my desire in this place, and in these lectures, to trace how they are, one or two considerations will lie very near to us; and with the pressing of these on your thoughts and hearts I will this day conclude. And first, the general consideration, that what there may have been in the world obscurely struggling to be Christian before Christ and his Church, so far from suggesting to us poorer thoughts of what in Him we possess, under how far more glorious aspect does it present that to us! All which men before could conceive, but could not realize, could feel after, but could not grasp, could dream of, but ever when they awoke found nothing in their hands,—it is here; "the body is of Christ." And the Church which he has founded, we behold it as sitting upon many waters, upon the great ocean of truth, from whence every stream that has at all or at any time refreshed the earth was originally drawn, and to which it duteously brings its waters again.* We may contemplate that Church as having, in that it has the Word and Spirit of its Lord, the measure of all partial truth in itself; receiving the homage of all human systems, meekly, and yet, like a queen, as her right; understanding them far better than they ever understood themselves; disallowing their false,

---

* Clement of Alexandria on this very matter (*Strom.*, l. 1, c. 5) Μια μεν ουν της αληθειας οδος· αλλ' εις αυτην καθαπερ εις αεινναον ποταμον, εκρεουσι τα ρειθρα αλλα αλλοθεν.

and what of true they have, setting her-seal upon that true, and issuing it with a brighter image, and a sharper outline, and a more paramount authority, from her own mint.

Again, if the more excellent glory of that which we possess in Christ is, that it is not shadow but substance, not anticipation but possession—not the idea, but the fact, or rather the fact and the idea in one,— how are we letting go our most precious gains, when we at all let go, or when we even slight, our historic faith, resting on and finding its object in the person of the Saviour! What a miserable exchange, to give up this, and to accept the largest, the most vaunted theories concerning the godlike and the true in its room and as its adequate substitute, the most magnificent ideas in the place of the humblest affiance on the Son of God—soon to find that we have gotten pebbles for jewels, words for things, that we are in a world peopled only with ghosts and phantoms! Oh, loss unutterable, if we allow any to strip off for us the historic realization of the truth in the person of Jesus of Nazareth, as though it were not of the essence of the matter, as though it were a thing indifferent, useful perhaps for the simpler members of the Church, but for others hindering rather than helping the contemplation of the pure idea, which they would persuade us it is alone needful to retain. They promise, it is true, who invite to this sacrifice, that if only we will destroy this temple of our historic faith, in three days, yea, in an instant, as by a magic wand, they will raise up for us a goodlier and more gorgeous fabric in its room. Let it be our wisdom to give no credence to their words; knowing this, that it was the very blessedness which the coming of the Son of God in the flesh brought us, that it brought us that, which these would fain persuade us to relinquish and renounce, that it lifted men out of and above that condition into which these deceivers would willingly persuade them to return.

No doubt there is a temptation to give in to this, a temptation working in each one of us—to take up, that is, with a religion which shall consist in the contemplating of great and ennobling ideas, instead of in the serving with a straightforward and downright obedience a personal God. Those ideas we feel that we can deal with them as we like; they exert no constraining power upon us; we are their masters, and not they ours: or if we have allowed them any rule over us, when the stress comes, we can withdraw it again; allowing them just as much authority as is convenient to us. There is no " Be thou holy, for I am holy," in them—no pointing to the rugged way of the Cross, with a Forerunner walking there, and a command that we follow him in it. Let us watch earnestly against so subtle a temptation, showing as it does so fair, and finding so much in our slothful and sinful hearts that makes them only too ready to embrace it.

And surely, brethren, at this season the Church suggests and presents to us mighty helps against all this. What help so effectual as to enter truly and deeply into the Passion of our Lord—to carry at no cold and careless distance from that cross to which each day of this lenten season is now bringing us nigher? but to seek to draw forth the riches of grace which are laid up for us in it, and in the considering of Him that hanged thereon. Let us determine, brethren, that in this coming week, the beginning it may be of a more holy life, we will bring ourselves continually within the sphere of those mighty, those transforming influences, which are ever going forth from thence. Let us make proof how it can open for us the fountain of purifying tears, sealed it may be for long—how a burden can be laid down at its foot which is crushing us to the earth, and from which nowhere else is deliverance. Let us seek to enter into nearer fellowship with the Man of sorrows, with our crucified God. And then, when we have proved how this fellowship can bless us, how it can cleanse us from our impurities, how it can strehgthen us for our tasks, can enable us to tread under foot our enemies, we shall not readily exchange such a fellowship as this with a living Lord, so full fraught with blessings, for that of mere notions and phantoms; which, however much they may promise, will desert us in the hour of need, and prove utterly helpless, whensoever the real stress of life's trial comes.

LECTURE II.

THE VANQUISHER OF HADES.

(*Preached on Easter Sunday.*)

MARK XVI. 3.

Who shall roll us away the stone from the door of the sepulchre?

THE heathen expectations of a deliverer I ventured in my preceding lecture to characterize as "the unconscious prophecies of heathendom;"—prophecies indeed which knew not at what they pointed, of which the lines were most wavering and indistinct when set beside the clear outlines of Jewish hope—yet in a wider and laxer sense prophecies still; or, if we will not make that word common, but reserve it for the highest of all, we may call them the world's divination at the least. For in these expectations of a world, which, though deeply fallen, remained God's world still, it was divining what it needed, and obscurely feeling after it. And this divination, these guesses at, and reachings out after, the truth, so far from shunning and keeping out of sight, we may use, I said, not of course putting them in the forefront of our array, yet may we use them still, as arguments for that Faith, to which all has thus tended from the first, which the world was craving for before it received, and short of which it never found its perfect satisfaction or rest.

It is the same argument, applied in a different region, of Christianity as evidently the complement of all that went before, which the early apologists were wont to use in their conflict with Gnostic and Manichæan. They urged the manner in which the Christian revelation as the Church received it, rooted itself deeply in an anterior constitution, was evidently not a sudden improvisation, but the culminating fact of an idea which had been realizing itself through all the sacred history of the past, was as the perfect flower, of which all genuine Judaism had been the stalk and stem. And they founded on this traceable connexion the superiority of its claims to those of all rival systems, which could produce no such accordance of their new with pre-existing and pre-established harmonies in the spiritual world; but had rather abruptly and violently to force a place for themselves, than to fit into one already prepared for their reception, which rested on an undoing and denying of the past, rather than a sanctioning and perfecting of it.* And as there was, no doubt, a most real force in their argument, exactly so has it for the thoughtful mind a deep

---

* See especially Tertullian, *Adv. Marcion.*, l. 3 and 4, passim, in which this is his ever-recurring thought, re-appearing in an infinite variety of forms. Oh Christum et in novis veterem! he exclaims, having shown how the rudiments of almost all Christ's miracles are to be found in the Old Testament.

significance, that Christ should have met and satisfied all nobler longings of the heathen world—that all deeper and better impulses which were any where at work, should have been tending toward *Him*. The worth of the unspeakable gift which in Christ is ours, is wonderfully testified by the fact that all should have been in one way or another either asking for that gift, or fancying that they had gotten it, or mourning its departure, or providing substitutes for it. For, however in the one elect people, as the bearers of the divine promises,—the beating heart of the spiritual world,—the appointed interpreters to the rest of their blind desires, this longing after a Redeemer came out in greater clearness and in greater strength, and with no troubling disturbing elements,—*their* education being far more directly from God, and being expressly aimed at the quickening of these longings to the highest,—yet were those longings themselves not exclusively theirs. They, indeed, yearned, and knew what they yearned for: the nations yearned, and knew not for what. But still they yearned: for as the earth in its long polar night seeks to supply the absence of the day by the generation of the northern lights, so does each people in the long night of its heathen darkness bring forth in its yearning after the life of Christ, a faint and glimmering substitute for the same. From these dreamy longings after the break of day have proceeded oracles, priests, sacrifices, lawgivers, and the like. Men have no where given up hoping; nor acquiesced in the world's evil as the world's law. Every where they have had a tradition of a time when they were nearer to God than now, a confident hope of a time when they should be brought nearer again.

No thoughtful student of the past records of mankind can refuse to acknowledge that through all its history there has run the hope of a redemption from the evil which oppresses it; nor of this only, but that this hope has continually linked itself on to some single man. The help that is coming to the world, it has ever seen incorporated in a person. The generations of men, weak and helpless in themselves, have evermore been looking after one in whom they may find all which they seek vainly in themselves and in those around them—redressers of the world's wrong, deliverers from the world's yoke, vindicators of the honour of the race, souls of heroic stature, in which all the features of greatness that are imparted with niggard hand unto others shall be found gloriously and prodigally combined. Such in almost every religion men have learned to look back to, as having already come: such we find that they are every where expecting as yet to appear.

As little can one deny that there is that in men, which prepares them to welcome these at their appearing. There is a natural gravitation of souls, which attracts them to mighty personalities; an instinct in man, which tells him that he is never so great as when looking up to one greater than himself—that he is made for this looking upward—to find, and, finding to rejoice and to be ennobled in, a nobler than himself. And doubtless this instinct in itself is divine. It is the natural basis on which the devotion of mankind to

Christ is by the Spirit to be built; it is an instinct which, being perfectly purified of each baser admixture, is intended to find its entire satisfaction in Him. True, it may stop short of Him; true, it may turn utterly away from Him. It may stop short of Him, resting in human heroes, in men glorious for their gifts, eminent for their services to their kind; and we have then the worship of genius instead of the worship of God. Or it may turn utterly away from Christ, and then, being in itself inextinguishable, and therefore surviving even in those who have wholly forsaken Him, it will, thus perverted and depraved, lay them open to all the delusions of false prophets and of antichrists.

For it is this, this attraction of men to a mightier than themselves, which, being thus perverted, has filled the world with deceivers and deceived; which has gathered round the hunters of men the ready instruments which have executed their will. It is this which has drawn souls, as moths to the candle, to rush into and to be scorched and to be consumed in the flame, which some wielder of heavenly gifts for hellish aims has kindled. It is this which swells the train round some conqueror's car, as he urges his destructive course through the world. What, for instance, to take a near illustration, was the devotedness of the French soldiery to their great leader but this? Who does not feel that this devotion, out of which thousands and tens of thousands were ready to meet, and did joyfully meet, dangers and fatigues and agonies and deaths, only for the hope of one word of approbation, one smile from him, counting all more than repaid by this—who does not feel that this was the inverted side of something in itself most true and most noble, to which even in its degeneracy it bore witness; and only had now run wild and lost its appointed destination? It is this, this craving of men passionately to devote themselves to some one, which makes an Antichrist possible, which will make him so terrible when he appears—men by a just judgment of God being permitted to dedicate all which they ought to have dedicated to Christ, to his opposite, to him who comes in his own name,—because they refused to give it, because they refused to give themselves, to Him who came in the name of his Father. It will then be fearfully seen that there can be an enthusiasm of hell, no less than an enthusiasm of heaven.

And as on the one side there is a preparedness to acknowledge these kings of men, these spiritual and intellectual chiefs of our race, so soon as they show themselves; thus too, upon the other hand, such have never been wanting to claim the reverence and the homage of their fellows, to seat themselves on these prepared thrones of the world. Certainly there is nothing in the study of the past which fills one with more awe and wonder than the infinite significance of single men in the development of the world's history. That history lies out before our eyes no Tartarian steppe, no Indian savannah, stretching out at one vast level, or with only slight elevations or depressions; but with marvellous inequalities, and here and there with ravines deep almost as hell itself, and again with mountain summits towering well nigh unto heaven.

Every where we encounter those that bring to their brethren a new blessing or a new curse, that gather as at a centre the world's light or the world's darkness; from whom that light or that darkness diffuses itself anew and with a new energy—beneficent lords or baleful tyrants in the spiritual kingdom of men's thoughts and feelings—each one for weal or for wo, in narrower and wider circles, for longer or shorter spaces, wielding his sceptre over the hearts and spirits of his fellows; helping to make them slaves or to make them free, to exalt or to cast them down. On the one side august lawgivers, founders of stable polities, bringers in of some new element of civilization, restorers, even amid heathen darkness, of some purer knowledge of God; on the other side, destroyers that have known how to knit to them as with magic bands multitudes of their brethren, and to make them the passionate servants of their evil will; proclaimers of sensual philosophies, that have assisted to make our life cheaper than beasts', to empty it of its loftier hopes and its faith in a higher destination; seducers after whom the world has wondered; stars whose name has been Wormwood, that, falling from heaven, have made the waters of earth bitter, so that the men died who drank of them.

Thus has it been, brethren, that the world has been ever opening wide its arms to welcome its redeemers,—oftentimes cruelly deceived, counting oftentimes, like Eve, that it had gotten a man from the Lord, even him who should comfort it under the curse, when indeed it was thus welcoming only the deepener of the curse, and it may be the author of some new mischief;—yet hoping ever, with hopes that even at the best were only most imperfectly and inadequately fulfilled. Thus have the multitudes of men still gathered and grouped themselves round central figures in history, giving testimony even by an oftentimes fatal readiness for this, that mankind was made for a Christ, for a divine leader in whom it should be set free, by the mightier and holier magic of his will, by the prevalence of a divine attraction which he should exercise upon them, from all the potent spells of seducing spirits and seducing men— that humanity was made for one to whom it should be able to deliver itself perfectly and without reserve, and to be blest in so delivering itself. For he being identical with righteousness, and wisdom, and love, they who lose themselves in Him, only lose to find themselves again for ever.

So much, brethren, we may say generally concerning the hope which the world has cherished of redeemers and saviours—a hope which at length was fulfilled so perfectly in Him, and only in Him, who bears both these titles, that we well nigh feel as if the titles themselves, to say nothing of any deeper homage or devotion, cannot, without wrong to Him, and encroachment upon his due honour, be lent to any other. And upon this day, brethren, upon this resurrection morn, it will fall in well with the joyful solemnities of the time, with the current in which our thoughts must needs be running, and from which it would only be a loss if the discourse you heard in this place should awhile divert them, to address ourselves to a part of the subject, which, had not this high day come upon us, might perhaps have been more conveniently reserved to a later occasion; but which if now, moved by the fitnesses of the season, I a little anticipate, you will pardon me this wrong. The aspect of the subject which I mean is this,—the world's hope of its deliverers as conquerors of death, its expectation of One who should lead captivity captive, in whom mortality should be swallowed up in life, who should be a vanquisher of hell, a bringer back of souls, and first and chiefly of his own, from the prison-house of the grave.

Such expectations in abundance there were; for nowhere have men sat down content under the heavy laws of death which bound them. They have ever been imagining a reversal of the curse, a breach or a repeal of those inexorable laws. The old world was ever feeling after " Jesus and the Resurrection." And being full of this thought, it traced it every where. Thus, in the cycle of the natural seasons, when the earth in spring starts up from its long winter sleep, men saw a symbol and a never-failing prophecy of life rising out of death: that winter was as the world's death, this spring as the world's resurrection. The enthusiasm which the spring woke up, the rapture with which the outbursting of bud and blossom, the signs of the reviving year, were hailed—the way in which the chiefest and joyfulest feasts of almost all religions were coincident with, and evidently celebrated, this time, being full of this spring gladness,—

all this was not an evidence, as some would have us to believe, that those religions were merely physical, did merely commemorate the revolutions of the natural year. But this rapture and delight with which the outer tokens of renovation and revival were hailed, had their root in a profound and instinctive sense of the connexion between man and nature, in a most true feeling that the symbols of renovation in nature could not be aimless and unmeaning, symbols of nothing, but must needs point to deeper realities in the life of man.* The spring time suggested such joyful

* I may quote, though long, the sublime passage in Tertullian on the vestiges of a resurrection which we may trace every where in nature (*De Resurr. Carnis*, c. 12) Dies moritur in noctem, et tenebris usquequaque sepelitur. Funestatur mundi honor; omnis substantia denigratur. Sordent, silent, stupent cuncta: ubique justitium est Ita lux amissa lugetur: et tamen rursus cum suo cultu, cum dote, cum sole, eadem et integra et tota universo orbi reviviscit; interficiens mortem suam, noctem, rescindens sepulturam suam tenebras, heres sibimet existens, donec et nox reviviscat, cum suo et illà suggestu. Redaccenduntur enim et stellarum radii, quos matutina succensio extinxerat: reducuntur et siderum absentiæ, quos temporalis distinctio exemerat: redornantur et specula lunæ, quæ menstruus numerus attriverat: revolvuntur hyemes et æstates, verna et autumna, cum suis viribus, moribus, fructibus. Quippe etiam terræ de cœlo disciplina est arbores vestire post spolia, flores denuo colorare, herbas rursus imponere, exhibere eadem quæ absumpta sunt semina, nec prius exhibere, quàm absumpta. Mira ratio! de fraudatrice servatrix: ut reddat, intercipit, ut custodiat, perdit, ut integret, vitiat, ut etiam ampliat, prius decoquit ..Nihil deperit, nisi in salutem. Totus igitur hic ordo revolubilis rerum, testatio est resurrectionis mortuorum. Operibus eam præscripsit Deus antequàm literis;

solemnities, because it was felt to be in some sort the Easter of nature, and obscurely to give pledge, or at least intimation, of a higher Easter in store for man.

And if it may be permitted me to take a little wider range, and to gather proofs and confirmations of what I am affirming, of the manner in which human nature has claimed a resurrection as its own, not from the heathen world only, but wherever in popular faith or tradition I can find them, I would then adduce, as a remarkable illustration of this, the exceeding difficulty with which the world has ever persuaded itself of the death of any who have mightily blest it, or with whom it has confidently garnered up its dearest hopes—the eagerness with which it snatches at the thought, that such a one has not truly died, making much of the slightest hint that seems to give a colour to this hope; so congenial is it to the heart of man. It was said of Moses, "No man knoweth his sepulchre unto this day," (Deut. xxxiv. 6,) and these words, despite the plain declaration that went before, were sufficient provocation for a whole family of Jewish legends, to the effect that he had not really paid the debt appointed to every man living. In like manner we know how that word of the Lord concerning the beloved apostle, "If I will that he tarry till I come, what is that to thee?" this was enough to

---

viribus prædicavit antequàm vocibus. Præmisit tibi naturam magistram, submissurus et prophetiam, quo facilius credas prophetiæ, discipulus naturæ, quo statim admittas, cùm audieris quod ubique jam videris, nec dubites Deum carnis etiam resuscitatorem, quem omnium noris restitutorem.

cause the report to go forth that he should not die; and not the express denial by St. John himself of any such significance in the words, was able to extinguish this belief, which continued to propagate itself from age to age.*

In like manner we sometimes see a whole nation which has found it impossible to believe that he on whom its hopes were fondly built, whom it had trusted should at length have delivered it, and with whose death those hopes have all fallen to the ground, —that he indeed has come, like other men, under the law of mortality,—has passed away, and left his work, as it seems, unconcluded. How long Britain was waiting for her Arthur; how long did the legends that told of him as surviving yet in the far valley of Avalon live on the lips and in the hearts of a people. And exactly in the same manner, in a later and more historic age, Portugal waited for her youthful king, looking fondly and with aching expectation for his return—and this, for many a weary year after he had perished, not obscurely, but in open fight, among the sands of Africa.†

* See Augustine, *In Ev. Joh.*, Tract. 124· Tertullian, *De Animâ*, c 50, Hilary, *De Trinit.* l. 6, c. 39, Jerome, *Adv. Jovin.*, l. 1, c. 26, Neander's *Kirch. Gesch.*, v. 5, p. 1117

† Thus Michelet (*Hist. de France*, l. 17,) having told the death of the last Duke of Burgundy: "Il n'était pas facile de persuader au peuple que celui dont on avait tant parlé était bien vraiment mort. Il était caché, disait on, il était tenu enfermé, il s'était fait moine, des pélerins l'avaient vu, en Allemagne, à Rome, à Jerusalem, il devait reparaître tôt ou tard; comme le roi Arthur ou Frédéric Barberousse, on était sûr

And may not some of us have known, brethren, in our own experience, something that quite explains to us this difficulty of believing in death? Have we not found this difficulty ourselves? and how, when the loved are gone, when they have left their places empty, it is only by repeated efforts that we can realize to ourselves that it indeed is so—how we have to say again and again to hearts half incredulous still, that it will never again in this world be otherwise—that so much truth and faith and love have indeed been withdrawn from hence and for ever. Thus earnestly does the spirit of man protest even against that semblance of annihilation, which death seems to wear.

Nor need it of necessity be the loved or hoped in, those in whom the expectations of others have intensely centred: let it be only some terrible man, one that has curdled the life-blood of the world with fear; and even such a one as this, having once been so much to men, though only so much to their fears, they will hardly be persuaded to have indeed passed away from the earth which so quaked and shuddered at his tread. How long after the death of Nero did the firm persuasion survive, that he was only hidden for a season, and that the earth should once more be cursed with his presence—the Christians of the Ro-

---

qu'il reviendrait. Il se trouvait des marchands, qui vendraient à crédit pour être payés au double, alors que reviendrait ce grand duc De Bourgogne. It is well known how many obscure rumours have in like manner found favour with the common people in different parts of Europe, that Napoleon is yet alive.

man Empire giving this expectation a colouring natural to them, and conceiving of him as the personal Antichrist, who should make presently his terrible re-appearance from the East, to carry forward against them the work of blood which he had commenced.*

But to return to the sphere more directly marked out for me by my subject, and to look there for evidences of the manner in which the spirit of man is incredulous of death, witnesses, protests against it, as by a second sight sees what shall be in the fulness of time, and prematurely grasps at it,—what frequent mention in the Greek fable we meet of visiters of Hades, of those that have descended and held intercourse with the spirits there, those who have in a sense " preached to the spirits in prison," and then returned from the kingdom of night—or it may be burst for others, as well as for themselves, the gates and barriers of the grave, rescuing and bringing back from that dark region to the glad light of life some delivered soul. I may spare any great details in proof of this; time would not allow them; such might scarcely seem in place; and to a congregation like that which I address they would be evidently superfluous. By one example only I would indicate that which I mean, but that example the most illustrious which ancient fable supplies. It is familiar to us all how the great cycle of the labours of Hercules was not finished till he had done battle with Death.

---

* Tacitus, *Hist.*, l. 2, c. 8, Suetonius, *Nero*, c. 57; Augustine, *De Civ. Dei*, l. 20, c. 19, Lactantius, *De Mort. Pers.*, 2.

Earthly exploits, even the mightiest and most marvellous of these, were not sufficient. It was felt, and most truly, that to complete even the idea of the hero-champion of men, something more was needed, a greater victory was demanded at his hands: he must wrestle with, and in personal conflict overcome, foes mightier than those of flesh and blood—even the last enemy, death and the grave. Nor even then had his own life attained its perfect consummation; since for this it was needed that all which was of earth in himself should be burned out, that the dregs of mortality should be cleansed away in the purifying flames of a funeral pyre, willingly ascended—and this being done, that he himself, in sign that he could not die any more, that he was indeed made partaker of immortality, that death could have no more dominion over him, should be wedded to eternal Youth amid the blissful mansions of the immortal gods.*

* In Buttmann's *Mythologus*, v. 1, p. 252 seq., the higher significance of the whole mythus of Herakles is unfolded with an exquisite tact and beauty. Without entering into the merits or demerits of other parts of the book, it may yet be as well to say that it is only this single treatise which I wish to speak of in this language of admiration. If K. O. Muller is right in his conjecture that Αδμητος-Αδάμαστος (*Il.* 9, 158,) the indomitable, a name belonging to Hades, and that Apollo's service of Admetus is his passing down to the infernal world in consequence of having slain the earth-born Python, if this be true, and he brings much that is curious in confirmation of this view, we may then add one more, and that not the least remarkable, to the Greek mythic narrations of this description. (See his *Scientific Mythology*, p. 243—246 Engl. Transl.)

THE VANQUISHER OF HADES. 199

Such, no doubt, is the interpretation of this pregnant symbol; and thus, brethren, by a thousand voices, in a thousand ways, the world has been declaring that it was not made for death, for that dread and alien thing, which, notwithstanding, it found in the midst of it. Thus has it looked round for one who should roll away the stone from the door of that sepulchre, to which it had seen its sons one after another unreturningly descend; and eking out the weakness of its arguments for immortality by the strength of its desires, it has been forward to believe that for this one and that the stone had been actually rolled away. But yet presently again, it has felt only too surely that it had but the shadow, and not the very substance, of the things hoped for: and in doubt and perplexity, in despondency and fear, has made the words of the Psalmist its own: "Dost thou show wonders among the dead? Shall the dead rise up and praise thee?" but, unlike to him, it has not known what answer to give to its own question.

And so it went on, until at length, after many a false dawn, the world's Easter morning indeed broke, and from beside an empty tomb they went forth, the witnesses of Jesus, preaching Him and the resurrection; men able to declare things which they had seen, — that there was indeed a risen Head of our race, one who had tasted death for every man, who, not in poet's dreams, or in legend of olden time, but in very truth, had burst its bands, because it was impossible He should be holden by them; that there was one for whom death was what men had so often, and so fondly and significantly called it—even a sleep; for He had laid Him down and slept, and after his three days' rest in the grave, risen up again, because the Lord had sustained Him. The day at length arrived, when men were able to go forth, preaching Him who had shown himself alive by many infallible proofs; in whom too, being risen, mortality *was* swallowed up in life; and who was now seated at the right hand of the Majesty on high, angels and principalities and powers being made subject unto Him.

Such was the word of their message—that the stone *was* rolled away, that the riddle of death *was* solved; and hearts unnumbered welcomed the tidings, and expanded themselves to it, as flowers, shut through some long dreary night, unfold themselves to the warmth and the light of the returning day. And shall not we, brethren, bear our part in the great jubilee which that message of theirs has summoned the world to keep, in the glory and gladness of this day and of this day's mystery, before which all phantoms and shadows of the night flee away, before which all sadness and despair are weak to stand? Truly, with a deep insight into the mystery of this Easter morn, did the great poet of our modern world make the Easter hymn—the glad voices which said *Christ is risen*, these, caught by accident, of potency sufficient to wrest the poison-cup untasted from the hand of the despairing one, who had already raised it to his lips.*

And how, brethren, fares it with ourselves? Is

---

* See Goethe's *Faust*, Scene 1.

that word for us a scatterer of sadnesses, a quickener of joys? Does it enable us to put off the sackcloth of our spirits, and to gird ourselves with gladness? Let us earnestly ask ourselves this question; for surely it is a sign that all is not right with us, when other things make us glad, but not this—when the natural spring fills our hearts with a natural joy, but this with no spiritual—when we stand aloof, cold and unsympathizing, as the wondrous cycle of the Christian year goes round, as the great events of our Lord's life and death and resurrection and glory succeed one another in a marvellous order; not humbling ourselves in the humiliations of that life, and therefore not exulting in its triumph; never having stood beside the cross of Jesus, and therefore having no right and no desire to stand beside that open tomb, where he reared his first, his everlasting trophy over death. If we feel not this gladness, let us take shame to our dull hearts, and claim it as a gift from our God, which he will not deny us. Let us ask that we too may be borne upward and borne onward on the great stream of the Church's exultation. Let us ask this earnestly; let us ask it as something which we ought not to be without. For of this let us be sure, that now, after eighteen hundred years, that announcement of the angel, "He is not here, but risen," *should be* as fresh and new, as full of an unutterable joy to us, as it was to those weeping women, who came to pay the last sad honours to their dead Lord, but found only his empty and forsaken grave.

LECTURE III.

THE SON OF GOD.

ACTS XIV. 11.

And when the people saw what Paul had done, they lifted up their voices, saying, in the speech of Lycaonia, The gods are come down to us in the likeness of men.

It was my endeavour when we last met, to trace out the manner in which humanity has ever been looking in one quarter or another for its redeemers and saviours—for deliverers from physical, deliverers from moral evil. Carrying forward my subject a step, it will be now my aim to show how it has not merely been *heroic* men, men who triumphed over all, even death itself, but *divine* men, for whom the world has been craving; in whom it has felt deeply that its help must lie—a most true voice of man's spirit ever telling him that only from heaven the true deliverance of the earth could proceed. We shall see how men have been ever cherishing the conviction of a real fellowship between earth and heaven, and *that* not merely an outward one, but an inward; a conviction that the two worlds truly *met*, not by external contact only, but in the deeps of personal life, in persons that most really belonged and held on to both worlds. We shall see how the world, with all its discords, has had also its preludes to the great harmonies of redemption; has had its incarnations—sons of God, that have come down to live a human life, to undertake human toils, to die a human death: its ascensions—sons of men, that have been lifted up to heaven, and made partakers of divine attributes: we shall see how men have never conceived of this world around us as totally dissevered from that world above us, with an impassable gulf between them, but always as in living intercommunion the one with the other.

And to this subject the words of my text will form a fitting introduction, yielding, as they do, a signal testimony to a wide-spread faith through the heathen world in these living relations between heaven and earth; for no sooner did those men of Lystra see in Paul and Barnabas, beneficent healing presences, with power to chase away the sicknesses of men, than at once they leaped to the conclusion, "The gods are come down to us in the likeness of men," and could hardly be restrained from offering them divine honours. The words themselves are a noticeable evidence of the world's preparedness, even in that day, when so much of an earlier and more childlike faith had perished, to welcome its deliverer from heaven. Nor are we without a parallel evidence to the same in that exclamation of the awe-struck heathen centurion, who, at sight of nature suffering with her suffering Lord and setting her seal to the awful meaning of his death, could come to no other than a like conclusion, and exclaimed, "Truly this was the Son of God."

For indeed this, which is peculiar to our Christian

faith, namely, that in it at length, and in it only, a real meeting-place between heaven and earth has been established in the person of Jesus of Nazareth—that the divine was born into the human, and so, not by transient and external contact, but in very deed, heaven came down to earth, and the earth was lifted up into heaven, God became a man, and man God—this, which is the peculiar prerogative and glory of our Christian faith, is yet not so peculiarly ours, but that every religion has, in some shape or other, made pretension to the same. It was claimed of all, though fulfilled only in one. "The tabernacle of God is with men, and he will be their God, and dwell among them"—this in positive fulfilment did only in the Only-begotten come true; yet, as far as the idea reaches, is the essence and centre, not of one religion, but of all. Men may conceive it under different aspects, may imagine it to be brought about in various ways; some of these ways will approach nearer to the heart of the matter than others; but this idea, in one shape or another, must constitute the central one of every religion.

I will endeavour to trace a few proofs of this, as in the heathen religions of antiquity they meet us every where,—to hold up before you a few forms in which, with more or less distinctness, men expressed their desire after, or embodied their belief in, this fellowship,—and more than fellowship, this union between God and man; and then to show how far short, even in idea, not to speak of the realization of that idea, all which men ever conceived in this way fell of the actual fact upon which the Church is founded.

And first, would we trace what is nearest to a nation's heart, we should turn to its poetry; there we shall find not what it has, but what it is reaching after—not its actual work-day world, but that ideal world after which it is longing. If, then, we turn to the oldest, the epic, poetry of Greece, we behold heroes and gods and men mingling familiarly together. In this free intercourse, in this beaten and well-trodden way between earth and heaven, we have what we might venture to call the heathen counterpart to the heavenly ladder seen by Jacob in dream, on which angels were ascending and descending, with the Lord himself at the summit; even as that was but the weak intimation of a closer union between earth and heaven to be effected in the person of the Son of Man—a union wherein God should no longer appear at the summit of the ladder, but at its foot—no longer a God far off, but near;—men now at last beholding the "heaven open, and the angels of God ascending and descending upon the Son of Man."

We may select one instance more, which Greek art will supply, of the sense of so intimate relations between God and man, as only the Incarnation could at length adequately express. We oftentimes take it as a matter of course, one which therefore excites in us no reflection or surprise, that the statues of the Grecian gods should be in human forms, in the perfection of human grace and beauty—the highest which the skill of artist could attain. And yet, what a wonderful thing was this,—to have arrived at the conviction that the human was the most adequate expression for the divine—that if God did reveal himself, it would be as man—that the nearest approximation to the ideal of humanity was the worthiest type of the Godhead. These too in their kind we must regard as prophecies of the Incarnation; not, indeed, of the deeps of that mystery, but weak prophecies of it still.

Not, however, in the ideal world of art only did this faith find utterance, but in the actual world as well. The whole scheme of an Oriental court, and eminently that of the Great King, was laid out on the idea that it was the visible representation of the court of heaven, and the king himself a visible incarnation of the highest God. The sense of this speaks out in every arrangement, in the least as in the greatest, and is the key to them all. Thus, the laws of that kingdom, when once uttered, could not be reversed or changed, (Dan. vi. 8,) because the king who gave them was the incarnation of God, and God cannot repent, or alter the thing which has gone out from his lips.*

---

* God is ἀτρεπτος, his counsels ἀμετομελητα, and he not a man that he should repent, and even such his visible representative on earth must be. It was on this unchangeableness of what had once gone forth from the lips of the king, which itself was thus no capricious state rule, but grew out of the very idea on which the Persian monarchy rested, that the enemies of Daniel founded their confident expectations of success in their conspiracy against him. (Dan. vi. 8, 15.) So, too, when then the purposes of Ahasuerus the king were altered concerning the Jews, he yet could not reverse the edict which permitted them to be attacked by their enemies he could only give another edict, allowing them to stand upon their defence. (Esth. viii. 10, 11.)

None, as again we learn from the Book of Esther (iv. 11,) might come into the king's presence unbidden and live, save by a distinct act of grace. They must die, unless the golden sceptre, in token of this grace, was held out to them; because none but the pardoned can behold the countenance of God and not perish at its intolerable brightness. So, as that same book teaches us, it was forbidden to one clothed in sackcloth to enter within the palace; (iv. 2;) and this, because heaven, of which that palace was the image, is the region of life and gladness, not of sorrow or of death; which, therefore, as they might not enter there, so neither might these things, which are their visible signs and symbols, enter into the palace of the king. The seven princes that stood nearest to the throne, and saw the king's face, (i. 14,) corresponded to the seven highest angels that were supposed to stand before, and nearest to the throne of God. Nor was the adoration offered to the Persian king a mere act of homage or sign of fealty, but was most truly, and in the highest sense, a *worshipping;* and exactly because felt as such, was so earnestly resisted, though from different motives, by the Greek alike and the Jew—by the Greek, as dishonouring to himself, by the Jew, as dishonouring to his God. It was a worshipping of the king's person for the presence of God, which was supposed to dwell singularly in him.

Again, when the foremost place in all the earth had passed into the possession of another, what was the apotheosis of a Roman Cæsar, in life, or after death, but a troubled speaking out of men's sense, that he who stood in the forefront of humanity, the chiefest of the sons of men, should also be more than man? This, in itself most true, did only become the fearful blasphemy it was, when the worship was misapplied, and the object to which it was due had been mistaken. It was indeed an irony of the heathen world, and of its magnificent pretensions, worthy of the great author of mischief, when the honour that it owed to Christ the Lord, being diverted on the way, was rendered to a Nero or a Tiberius. The prince of this world was herein mocking his votaries, exactly as he mocked the Jews, when they too were led to incorporate their rejection of all that was best, and their choice of all which was worst, in an outward fact, in that cry of theirs—" Not this man, but Barabbas."

And I may perhaps be permitted to observe as not alien to our present argument, but as another striking proof of this craving of men for that which is given to them in Christ and in his incarnation, for such a bridal of two worlds as was celebrated therein, that whenever, even in Christendom, men have lost their faith in this gift, or have suffered that faith to grow weak, then they have not rested till they have created for themselves a substitute for that truth which thus they have let go. Thus, no sooner had men's faith in a present, though invisible, Head of his Church waxed feeble—no sooner did the God-man, because he could not be seen, or touched, or handled, appear far off to carnal and sense-bound generations, than they began to yearn for a substitute, who should give them in palpable form all which they no longer felt that they possessed in Him. And thus men began to lend questionable honours and ambiguous titles to a pope; and ever as they more let go their sense of the reality of Christ's headship, they lent more of his glories, of his names, his honours, his divine attributes, to the man who had placed himself in his seat, and offered them in a gross and visible way that connexion between earth and heaven, which they were intended to have found in Him of whom it is written, "The Head of every man is Christ."

Exactly in the same manner, a thoughtful observer of the progress of Unitarianism in our own day, will not have failed to note that a system which shrinks from saying "Christ is God," yet finds it impossible to rest in that denial, and is rapidly and inevitably hastening to say, even as it has already said plainly enough by the lips of its most forward votaries, "Man is God," giving, in the end, to every man, that which it started with affirming it was blasphemy to give to any, even to the Son himself. And were that, or any other yet barrener form of unbelief, to succeed for a time in emptying the throne in men's hearts wherein the Son of God is sitting, on the instant we should behold impious and frantic enthusiasts springing up on every side, claiming the vacant seat, and obtaining, too, the homage which was withholden from Him. For truly, our deliverance from superstition lies not in unbelief but in faith. In holding fast the truth, and only in that, are we delivered from its distorted counterfeit. Thus the Holy Eucharist, satisfying, as it does, the solemn and mysterious cravings of the human soul, delivers the Christian world from hateful mysteries and dark orgies. Thus, again, faith in the sacrifice once offered upon Calvary hinders and cuts off those hideous attempts at expiation, which, but for that, the sin-laden heart of man would inevitably devise for itself. And thus, too, an exalted Saviour preserves us from blasphemous usurpers of divine honours, the truth of God from the lie of the devil.

But let us see, brethren, what nearer to the heart of the matter the old world had, of incarnations and ascensions; let us see the highest form in which it presented these truths to itself. And, contemplating that highest, let us still take note how the Christian truth of the Word made flesh, *even as a doctrine*, was original—not to say that alone in Christ it passed from a speculation, and became a fact. It will be instructive to mark how all other systems not merely did not give what they professed to give, (for that of course,) but how even what they professed to give, fell short of, and was only an approximation to, the actual needs of humanity.

Thus the Greek mind could conceive of a much-suffering man lifted up for his toils' and virtues' sake into the highest heaven. Their pantheon is full of such,—of heroes after the toils and conflicts of a life worthily spent for their fellow-men, made free of heaven, and admitted even into the circle of the immortal gods; and so far they had in their popular belief anticipations of Him, the man Christ Jesus, whom, because He humbled Himself, and for our sakes became obedient to the death of the cross, therefore God greatly exalted Him, setting Him at his own right hand.

But yet how little was there here any true blending of the human and divine, and how truly men felt this; as is wonderfully testified by the fact that this exalted and glorified man, however many divine attributes were added to him, yet did not get the name of God; he was but a δαίμων after all; he was not, to use language which has been well used of the Son, *Deus ex radice.* They felt with a right instinct that a deified man did not thereby, and that indeed he could not, become God — that no accumulation of divine honours could make one truly God, who was not such already; even as the church, in a later day, was not to be deceived into accepting the Arian theory concerning the Son of God as an adequate substitute for her own, by the utmost prodigality of divine names, and titles, and honours which were proposed to be lavished upon Him. She felt rightly that all these would not in the least fill up the chasm that divided, and must divide for ever, God from that which was not God. So was it with the apotheosis of heroic men: the divine glory did but gild and play upon the surface of their being; if a man was to be also God, if there was to be any perfect union of the two, it must be by other means, by a process which must reach deeper and much farther back than this.

But, moreover, the other half, the other factor,

even of the idea of such a person as this, was altogether strange to the Greek mind. A God coming down from heaven, emptying himself of his glory, and in a noble suffering undertaking a human life, and, that he might be the helper and deliverer of men, enduring all, even the hardest, for them, tasting death itself,—all this, a God thus stooping, and suffering, and dying, was wholly alien to every conception of theirs. The very idea of the gods with them was of beings free from all care, untouched by any sorrow, living ever joyful, and ever at ease: or, if they sojourned for awhile in this toilsome and tearful world, yet sojourning as visiters only—not touching the burden of its wo with the tip of their finger—undertaking it might be human tasks, yet undertaking them in sport, not really coming under, or feeling their weight. True, indeed, that this conception of a suffering God, which was so strange to all western habits of thought, was familiar to the mythologies of the East. They have their Osiris,—and not him alone, though in him these sufferings of a divine nature come the most prominently and gloriously out—who, in the fulness of his beneficent purposes for the race of men, and in mighty and earnest conflict with the prince of evil, endures all things, going down even to the deeps of death: and thus, no doubt, the Eastern religions were not without their anticipations of Him, who, though He was rich, yet made Himself poor, even the poorest, for us, that we through his poverty might be rich.

And yet how imperfect, even as regards the idea,

was this too. Humanity, however it craved a God for its deliverer, yet craved just as earnestly a man; it wanted a redeemer out of its own bosom, one in whose every triumph over moral or physical evil it could rejoice that "God had given such power *unto men.*" It felt, and truly, that no other would serve its turn—that, forasmuch as the children are partakers of flesh and blood, he also, if he would be every man's brother, and thus able to be every man's redeemer, must be partaker of the same; "fairer than the children of men," and yet himself a child of man—that from the midst of itself, from the depths of its own life, its redeemer must proceed. A God who was *only* God, might conquer for himself, but there was no pledge or proof in his conquest, that man could conquer; a God who overcame death and rose from the dead, gave no assurance thereby of a resurrection for the race of man.

And thus each of the great divisions of the Gentile world had but a fragment, even in thought and desire, of the truth: the Greek world, the exaltation of manhood—the Oriental, the glorious humiliations of Godhead; and thus it came to pass that each of these, even as a speculation, was maimed and imperfect. These systems, so far from providing what man needed, had not satisfactorily and on every side even contemplated what he needed; much less had they given it.

And how indeed could it be given? This was the riddle which He alone whose counsels were from everlasting, who knew all the true needs of man, and meant to satisfy them all, could solve. It seemed indeed that the world, craving one who should be man no less than God for its deliverer, put its demands in irreconcilable contradiction with themselves; and, again, that demanding for its redeemer one in whom the human and divine should not slightly and transiently touch one another, but should be brought into innermost union, it here too required that which it was impossible that it ever should receive. And yet the same wonder-stroke of God solved both these problems.

The first difficulty was this, If the world needed a man, yet where should it find the man that it needed? It had often put forth its champions, but there was ever found an attainder of blood in every man's descent, a blot on every man's scutcheon, a flaw in every man's armour. If no helper of humanity but one born out of its bosom would do, and yet every one born from thence partook in its sin, was one needing to be healed, and who could not therefore be himself the healer, was a sharer in the diseased organism, and could not therefore expel its poison from others, whence was such a one to come? The answer was at length given in the Virgin-born. Men had long before had an obscure apprehension that only so could the difficulty be solved. The birth from a pure virgin had been attributed to many.* For there was that in men's hearts which told them that for one to be an effectual Saviour he must be a new beginning, a new

* Especially to founders of religions, as Buddha, Zoroaster.

head of the race; not a mere link in the chain of sinful humanity, since of the sinful the sinless could never come; but by such marvellous means as that miraculous conception he must be exempted from the corruption transmitted from generation to generation of the children of men.

But this was not all; this Virgin-born was also Immanuel, was that which men had asked for, "God with us." He had, indeed, a Father, but that Father was God; and thus in the deepest deep, in the innermost core and centre of his life, this man was also God. In the cradle of Bethlehem, when a pure Virgin had been touched with fire from heaven, and had borne a Son, in Him, at length, the world found all its longings fulfilled, its seemingly irreconcilable desires all satisfied and atoned.

Thus, brethren, I have sought to trace out before you, to-day, that which was perhaps the worthiest element in the religions of the heathen world—that which, indeed, entitled them to the character of religions at all—their recognition, with all shortcomings and deficiencies, of a real bond between earth and heaven, their sense that the Divine could reveal itself no way so fitly as in the forms of the human, that the human could be lifted up to, and made to bear the weight of, the Divine—that man was God's offspring, of the blood royal of creation. The pervading sense of this was indeed what mainly constituted them, in God's providence, preparations and predispositions for the absolute truth which should in fulness of time be revealed. For that there were upon these points certain predispositions for the reception of the truth in heathendom, which did not exist among the Jews, no one, I think, can deny. None can thoughtfully read the early history of the church, and mark how hard the Jewish Christians found it to make their own the true idea of a Son of God, as indeed is witnessed by the whole Epistle to the Hebrews—how comparatively easy the Gentile converts; how the Hebrew Christians were continually in danger of sinking back into Ebionite heresies, making Christ but a man as other men, refusing to go on unto perfection, or to realize the truth of his higher nature;—no one can mark this, and contrast it with the genial promptness of the Gentile church to embrace the offered truth, "God manifest in the flesh," without feeling that there must have been effectual preparations in the latter which wrought its greater readiness for receiving and heartily embracing this truth when it arrived. And what other preparations could they have been, but these which we have been tracing?*

It is true that there was with this, infinitely too feeble a sense, too feeble even in the best, of the manner in which sin had cast them down from the

---

* The Christian apologists often find help here. Thus Arnobius, (*Adv. Gen.*, l. 1 c. 37.) Natum hominem colimus. Quid enim, vos hominem nullum colitis natum? Non unum et alium, non innumeros alios, quinimmo non omnes quos jam templis habetis vestris, mortalium sustulistis ex numero, et cœlo sideribusque donâstis? He could appeal to such passages as that of Cicero, (*Tusc Quæst*, l 1, c. 13.) Totum prope cœlum nonne humano genere completum est?

high places of their birth—a confession far too weak and wavering, (for only the Holy Ghost could have wrought a right confession,) of that attainder that was in their blood, the utter forfeiture of their inheritance which their sin had brought about. It was not seen how man had ceased to be a son of God, could never, but by a new adoption, a regeneration, become such again. But man's divine original, his first creation in the image of God, was so firmly held fast to by all nobler spirits, that St. Paul, upon the hill of Mars, could at once take his stand on this as a great meeting point between himself and his Athenian hearers—as the ground which was common to them and him: "Certain also of your own poets have said, For we are also his offspring." (Acts xvii. 28.) Here at least, they were at one.

And, brethren, it is possible that we may learn a lesson which we need, or at least remind ourselves of truths which we are in danger of suffering to fall too far back in our minds, by the contemplation of those, who, amid all their errors and darkness and confusion and evil, had yet a sense so deeply imprinted, a faith so lively, that man was *from* God, as well as *to* God; capable of the divine, only because himself of a divine race. Oftentimes it would seem as if our theology of the present day had almost lost sight of this, or at least held it with only too feeble a grasp; beginning, as it so often does, from the fall, from the corruption of human nature, instead of beginning a step higher up—beginning with man a liar, when it ought to have begun with man the true image and the glory of God.

And then, as a consequence, the dignity of Christ's Incarnation, of his taking of humanity, is only imperfectly apprehended. That is considered in the main as a make-shift for bringing God in contact with man; and not to have been grounded on the perfect fitness of man, as the image of God, of man's organs, his affections, his life, to be the utterers and exponents of all the life, yea, of all the heart of God. It is oftentimes considered the chief purpose of Christ's Incarnation, that it made his death possible, that it provided him a body in which to do that which merely as God he could not do, namely to suffer and to die; while some of the profoundest teachers of the past, so far from contemplating the Incarnation in this light, have rather affirmed that the Son of God would equally have taken man's nature, though of course under very different conditions, even if he had not fallen—that it lay in the everlasting purposes of God, quite irrespective of the fall, that the stem and stalk of humanity should at length bear its perfect flower in Him, who should thus at once be its root and its crown. But the Incarnation being thus slighted, it follows of necessity, that man as man is thought meanly of, though indeed it is only man as fallen man, as separated by a wilful act of his own from God, to whom this shame and dishonour belong. In his first perfection, in the truth of his nature, he is the glory of God, the image of his Son, as the Son is the image of the Father, declaring the Son as the Son declared the Father:—surely a thought, brethren, which if we duly lay to heart, will make us strive that our lives may be holy, that our lives may be noble, worthy of Him who made us after his image, and when we had marred that and defaced it, renewed us after the same in his Son.

LECTURE IV.

THE PERFECT SACRIFICE.

MICAH VI. 6, 7.

Wherewith shall I come before the Lord, and how myself before the high God? shall I come before him with burnt-offerings, with calves of a year old? Will the Lord be pleased with thousands of rams, or with ten thousands of rivers of oil? shall I give my first-born for my transgression, the fruit of my body for the sin of my soul?

THERE are few facts more mysterious, brethren, than the prevalence of the rite of sacrifice through the world. Nations which it is impossible could have learned it of one another, nations the most diverse in culture, the highest in the scale, and well nigh the lowest, differing in every thing besides, have yet agreed in this one thing, namely, in the offering of things which have life to God,—or when the idea of the one God has been lost,—to the gods many, of heathenism —the essential of that offering in every case being that the life of the victim was rendered up. And they have all agreed in considering that this act of theirs had a value, that it did place upon a new and better footing the relations in which they stood to the heavenly powers; that by these sacrifices they might more or less re-constitute the relations between themselves and God, which by any cause had been disturbed, bringing themselves nigher to Him, and rendering Him more favourable to them.

Now there are few or none in our day who would count that they had explained the prevalence of these convictions, in the conspiracy of the more artful few to hold the simpler many in bondage. These convictions were too wide-spread, too universal; moreover, men were too direfully earnest in carrying them out, to allow us to accept any such explanation as this. Sacraments they might be, and often were, of the devil, and not of God, but yet dreadful sacraments still—bonds and bands by which men knit themselves to one another, and knit themselves also to a spiritual world,—if not to heaven, yet to hell. Those who explain them into artful contrivances, may so give witness for their own shallow insight into the past history of the world, for the absence of any deeper needs at work in their own hearts, since if there had been such, they would have suggested a profounder explanation: but the time is past when they will find any number of persons to accept their explanation as sufficient.

As little can *their* theory be historically justified, who trace up the existence of sacrifice to the rude notions about God which belonged to an early age; for then we should see a people, as it attained worthier views about Him, gradually outliving and renouncing the practice of this rite. But, contrary to this, we find in the most cultivated nations the theory of sacrifice only the more elaborately worked out, the sacrifices themselves only multiplied the more. Here and there there might be found in some obscure corner of the earth, a savage tribe or horde, which had sunk below the idea and practice of sacrifice; though one in which, in one form or another, it did not survive, it would be difficult to point out; but nowhere a people that had risen above it. Here and there a philosopher may have set himself against the popular belief, but nowhere has he been able to change it; he has ever stood single and alone, and has as little carried with him the more thoughtful and deeper spirits of his time as the common multitude. He may have eloquently declaimed on the absurdity of supposing the gods would be pleased with the death-struggles of animals, with the blood of bulls and of goats; but there was ever something in men, though they might not be able to explain it to themselves, which told them that sacrifice had a significance and a meaning, which a few plausible words could not get rid of or destroy.

Such, brethren, I think you will admit are the facts, for I speak to those capable of judging. Whether we turn to those pages of Greek and Roman literature, brought by our studies in this place especially before us, or whether we take a wider range within our ken, every where alike we encounter a consciousness upon man's part, that the relations between him and the powers in whose hand he is, have been interrupted and disturbed. The fact might be sometimes overlooked and forgotten by him in times of prosperity, but we see it evermore mightily emerging from the deep of his heart, when the judgments of offended heaven were evidently abroad. Everywhere, too, we encounter the effort by certain specific and definite acts of expiation and atonement to restore those disturbed relations again. "Without blood is no remission of sin," was a truth as deeply graven on the heart and conscience of heathen as of Jew.

For vast and complex as is the Jewish system of offering, yet it is not a greater body of sacrifice than we meet almost everywhere else, when we turn to the ritual of heathenism. That Levitical system is of course in every way more complete: it is an organic whole; excluding all individual caprice, all too into which the true idea of sacrifice, when escaping from God's control, would inevitably degenerate. Moreover it was no will-worship, but the appointed way in which God was to be sought, and not that in which men out of their own hearts imagined that they would seek Him. But with all this, it does not, I think, run into greater detail, nor take more entire possession of the whole life of man, nor demand a more continual recognition of a distance and separation from God which has need to be removed, than did the heathen systems of sacrifice with which it was surrounded, when we take them in their sum total, when we count up all their infinite forms and varieties. For doubtless it was meant that they too, by this their multitude and repetition, should give testimony against themselves, should witness as plainly as did the Jewish in the same way, for their own weakness and unprofitableness; since of them, too, we may say, that had they been effectual to do what they professed to do, "would they not have ceased to be offered, because the worshippers once purged would have had no more conscience of sin?" But thus, by their endless multiplication, and by the confession of weakness contained therein, they pointed, though not with prophetic explicitness, yet still in their degree, away from themselves, and *to* that one all-sufficient sacrifice once offered upon Calvary.

Nor need we, when we look a little deeper into the matter, when we come to apprehend what was the central idea of sacrifice, be so much surprised, as at first we are, to find it this rite of an almost universal character. For then we perceive that it was no arbitrary invention, for which a thousand others might have been substituted as well; but rather that the essence of all religion lies in that of which sacrifice was the symbol—namely, in the offering up of self, in the rendering up of our will to the will of God, the yielding of our life to Him as something which had been rebellious in time past, and therefore worthy to die, but of which we desire that the rebellion may cease, that so we may of his mercy receive it back a life pardoned and forgiven. The blood is the seat of the life, the seat therefore of the επιθυμια, the desire, which in fallen man is a desire at variance with the will of God. In sacrifice, in the pouring out of the blood, is the symbolic rendering up of this rebellious principle; a confession that it is only worthy to die; that as the thing offered died, so the offerer might justly die—the act having of course only its true significance when the offerer did realize to himself what he did—rested not in the outward work, but said to himself and to God, "I stand in living communion with this which I offer; even as this blood, so I offer myself; dying that I may live; giving myself to Thee, that I may receive my true life back again at thy hands; losing my life that I may find it." Of course, it is not to be supposed that each worshipper so distinctly gave to himself an account of what he was doing; but this lay more or less obscurely in the background of his mind, and gave a meaning to his act. Our ordinary use of the word *sacrifice*, shows how truly we have gotten to the innermost heart of its meaning; for it is ever used to signify the giving up of something dear. And what so dear as our self-will? The giving up of that is indeed the giving up of all.

But when we speak of the idea of sacrifice as being this giving up of the self-will, there may seem a difficulty in applying this, when we come to the great and only perfect sacrifice offered by Christ on the cross. Of course it was not there—no one would dare to suppose it was—the offering up of a *rebellious* will; we hardly dare speak of such a thing, though it be but to deny it. But it was the giving up of *his own* will*—that will which had the liberty of choosing for

---

* And therefore the controversy of the Church with the Monothelites in the seventh century, a conflict in which commonly so little interest is taken even by Students of Church History, was one for life and death. The denial of a human will in Christ was in fact a denial of his sacrifice.

itself what the Father had not chosen for it, but in the entire rendering up of which he realized the very central idea of all sacrifice, which all that had gone before had only pointed at weakly: "Sacrifice and burnt-offering Thou wouldst not; then said I, Lo! I come to do thy will, O God." In other words, sacrifice and burnt-offering God was weary of—those shadows of the true; and Christ came to give the substance; and his actual pouring out of his soul to death was the outer embodiment of the inward truth, that this yielding of his will to his Father's reached to the uttermost, did not shrink from or stop short of the last and most searching proof to which it was put.

In sacrifice, then, was the confession of a life forfeited, and this confession incorporating itself in an act, wherein the forfeiture was actually carried out. This however is but half the idea of sacrifice: for it is ever this confession made in another. If a man had given himself to death, because he felt that he was worthy to die, he would but have involved his already confused relations to God in deeper confusion. He might be unworthy to live, but was not therefore at his own choice to die. If as a sinner, he owed God a death, yet as God's creature, made to serve Him, he equally owed Him a life. The premises are right, that man's life is forfeited; but the conclusion fearfully wrong, when he carries out himself and in his own person the forfeiture. Such false conclusions from right premises they draw, the miserable victims that in our day fling their bodies to be crushed beneath the wheels of some idol car; the same they have drawn, who, in despair at the greatness of their sins, have lifted up their hands against their own life; for even self-murder, that most hideous perversion of the idea of sacrifice, yet grounds itself on a sense of life being the only worthy offering. Thus a Judas goes and hangs himself, because he feels his sin so great that it cannot be left without an atonement, and in the darkness and unbelief of his heart, he has put back the one atonement which would have been sufficient even for a sin so great as his; and this too is the thought of each other, who by a like fearful act of self-violence has denied the love, though he cannot deny the righteousness, of God.

Never then in himself, never by means of his own life, could man's acknowledgment that that life was forfeited rightly be carried out. It must needs be in another. And the same reason exists against making that other some fellow-man. His life too is a sacred thing, is itself an end. It could not therefore be used as this means to some other end. In human sacrifices, in the offering of other men's lives, there appear the same false consequences from right grounds as in men's offering of their own. It remained that, if sacrifice was to be, the sphere of animal life must be that of which it should take possession, and in which it must move—the life of animals being the nearest akin to, and the noblest after, man's—and therefore fitter than any meaner for the setting forth his oblation of himself. And man thus taking possession of this, either at God's express command, or moved by his own religious instincts, was indeed taking possession of that over which he had entire right, of that which having been given him for the use of his body, was much more given him for the spiritual needs of his soul.

Such, I think, we may venture to say was the normal unfolding of the idea of sacrifice; the abnormal appears in those revolting caricatures of the true idea, on which we have lightly touched—in human sacrifices—in dreadful self-oblations—in Baal priests cutting themselves with knives, and so pouring out, if not all, yet a part of their life—in the self-inflicted tortures and living death of Indian Fakirs—in the blind despair of mighty sinners, who with profane hand have broken in upon and laid waste the awful temple of their own lives.

Wonderful indeed, brethren, is the manner in which, armed with the truth, we may look upon past pages of the religious history of man, some of the most soiled and blotted, and decypher there an original writing of God, which all those stains and blots have not availed to render illegible altogether.* If only we have an ear to hear, marvellous voices will reach us, and from quarters most unexpected, which shall speak *to us* of Calvary and of the Cross, though they little mean it themselves—such voices for instance as his, who, accounting for the human sacrifices of the Gauls, observed, that they were deeply persuaded that only the

---

* Tertullian (*De Animâ*, c. 41,) Quod enim à Deo est non tam extinguitur quàm obumbratur. Potest enim obumbrari, quia non est Deus, extingui non potest, quia à Deo est.

THE PERFECT SACRIFICE. 229

life of man was a fit redemption for man.* What was this conviction of theirs but the dark side of that truth which the apostle to the Hebrews proclaimed, when he said that the blood of bulls and of goats could not take away sin, but that it must be purged away by better sacrifices than these?† Nor do I think that it will otherwise than repay us well to follow a little into detail the convictions of the world concerning that which constituted a sacrifice of worth, and trace how every thing here pointed whether, it meant it or not,

---

* Cæsar (*De B. G.*, l. 6, c. 16:) Pro vitâ hominis nisi hominis vita reddatur, non posse aliter deorum immortalium numen placari arbitrantur. Cf. Muller's *Dorians*, b. 2, c. 8. § 2. Out of a sense of this arose the extreme difficulty of eradicating human sacrifices in the Roman empire, and the long survival of some of them. Thus Tertullian (*Apol.* 9.) Infantes penes Africam Saturno immolabantur palam usque ad proconsulatum Tiberii. Cf. Scorp., c. 7, Minucius Felix, p 199, Ouzel's Edit., Pliny, *H. N*, l. 30, c. 3, 4, Eusebius, *Præp. Evang.*, l. 4, c. 17.

† Thus there was an obscured truth in those abject and crouching superstitions which Plutarch paints with such a masterly hand in his exquisite little treatise, Περι Δεισιδαιμονιας —a truth which *he* misses—a recognition, that is, of sin, of a great gulf fixed between the sinner, and the offended power of heaven, which the δεισιδαιμων, however vainly, was seeking to bridge over. His terror and his trouble had a true ground, and one which would hinder him from accepting as sufficient such attempts to pacify his fears, as those which Plutarch offers him, namely that the gods were kind (μειλιχιοι.) There was something else besides this which he was craving to know, before he could dare to believe that they were other than enemies to him.

yea, when it seemed most to point away from Him, to the central figure in the world's spiritual history, to the immaculate Lamb, which taketh away the sins of the world.

Thus it is hardly needful to observe, that it lay ever in the deepest convictions of men that an offering, to be acceptable, must be an offering of value, not something which cost the bringer nothing,—that, while all was poor by comparison with Him to whom it was offered, or considered in relation to that for which it was offered, yet must it be the best which the offerer had;—not the lame and the blind, not the scanty gifts of a niggard hand;—he thus giving token, that if he had aught worthier he would bring it. Therefore must the selected victim be pure of fault and of blemish, or, having such, was unfit for the altar—the sense of this required perfection being as lively in heathen sacrifice as in Jewish. Therefore was the bullock brought which had never yet submitted its neck to the yoke, the horse which had known no rider, or, in Hindoo ritual, no touch even of man; in other words, that was brought which had not been already used and in part worn out in the service of the world, but which was thus wholly and from the first consecrated to heaven. Hence, too, as the offering must not be a niggard one, the prodigality in sacrifice which startles us at times: the hecatombs of victims, the rivers of oil, the cattle from a thousand hills.

Herein, too, lay the explanation of yet direr sacrifice—as of their sons and daughters in the Moloch-worship of the Phenicians—the fruit of their body for the sin of their soul;—such offering, for instance, as we read of at Carthage, when, instead of the cheaper substitutes with which they had satisfied themselves for long, they sought out, in the mighty peril of the city, the dearest things which they had, the choicest children of the noblest houses, and cast them into the glowing arms of that merciless idol, which their sin-darkened hearts had devised for their god.* Out of this same sense that an offering grew in worth with the worth of that which was offered, sprang the rejoicing among the worshippers of Odin, when the lot of the yearly sacrifice fell upon no meaner man than the king—the pledge of a future felicity to the nation which was esteemed herein to lie.† To what did all this reaching out after the worthiest, the purest, the choicest, the best, point, even in its dreadfullest perversions, but to Him who was the fairest of the children of men, the choicest which the earth had borne, the one among ten thousand, who yet, being such, did by the eternal Spirit offer Himself without spot to God—who being the anointed King of the world, was

---

* Diodorus Siculus, l. 20, c. 14. Cf. 2 Kin. iii 27, Eusebius, *Præp. Evang*, l. 4, c. 16.

† Witsius (*De Theol. Gent*, p 683:) De Septentrionalibus populis refert Dithmarus primo anni mense nonaginta novem sortitò eligi solitos qui diis immolarentur, idque durâsse usque ad Henrici I Germaniæ regis, tempora. Faustissimum vero id regno litamen existimatum, *si sors regem tetigisset;* quam victimam totius populi multitudo summâ cum gratulatione et applausu prosecuta sit.

thus in a condition to make acceptable atonement for all men?

Nor less significant was the sense of a more prevailing atonement, of an added value which was imparted to an offering, when one, not thrust on by necessity, not compelled to die, but willingly, offered himself; the feeling of which was so strong, that if not the reality, yet at least the appearance, of this willingness, was often by singular devices sought to be obtained.* When, for example, the foremost man of a nation gathered upon his sole devoted head all the curses which impended on his people, all the anger of the immortal powers,† and with that upon him gave himself to a willing death for all, so turning, it might be, into victory the tide of disastrous battle, what have we here but in its kind a reaching out after Him, the chief and champion of the race of men, whose life no man took from him, for He might have asked of his Father more than twelve legions of angels against his enemies—but who sanctified Himself, freely pouring out his soul unto death—and who, not that He might deliver some single people, but all the world, became the piacular expiation of that world, drew upon his own head the penalties which would else

---

* Thus Tertullian, of the parents that offered their children to the Phenician Moloch (*Apol.* 9) Libentes respondebant, et infantibus blandiebantur, *ne lacrimantes immolarentur.* Cf. Plutarch, Περι Δεισιδαιμονιας, c. 13.

† Thus Livy, of Decius, (*Hist*, l. 9) Omnes minas periculaque ab Deis superis inferisque in se unum vertit —On this whole subject of men as φαρμακοί, καθαρματα, περιψήματα, ἀποτρόπαιοι, see Lomeier, *De Lustrat Vet. Gent.*, c. 22.

have alighted upon all, became a curse for man; and, when all was at the worst, when all seemed for ever lost, changed by his accepted death the certain defeat into the glorious victory of our race?

We may not refuse, brethren, to recognise these references to the cross of Christ: we shall read the history and mythology of the old world with little profit if we do. Nor need we fear the recognition; for it is the marvellous, and at the same time most natural prerogative of Christianity, that, being the absolute truth, it *has,* or rather itself *is,* the touchstone to discover all true and all false, detects the truth which is hidden in every lie, finds witness for itself in that which oftentimes seems, and indeed is, most opposed to itself, is able to recognise in the tares of earth the degenerate wheat of heaven;—in the world's harshest discords, the wreck and ruin of God's fairest harmonies;—and in Satan himself, the lineaments of the fallen angel of God.

But besides the witness for the great coming sacrifice, which was contained in the sacrifices of heathenism, how mighty a sense of the cross of Christ, and of its significance, do we meet in other regions of ancient life. What a boding of it, for instance, forms the background of the Greek tragedy. How mysterious is the manner there in which, from some far back transgression, some $\pi\rho\omega\tau\alpha\rho\chi o\varsigma$ $\alpha\tau\eta$,* the curse clings to a family, passes on from generation to generation, an ever-increasing load of transgression; until at

* Æschylus, *Agamemnon,* 1163

length the great calamity, the headed-up guilt of all, lights *not* on the most, but on the *least* guilty head, on the head of one that by comparison is innocent. What an unconscious symbol this of the curse cleaving to the Adamic race! For as in each lesser circle of that race we most often see the burden of the cross resting with the heaviest weight on the truest heart in that circle, so in the great circle of humanity we behold Him of the truest heart of all, the only unguilty One, bearing on the accursed tree the accumulated curse of the whole Adamic family, which had come down through long ages; and not bearing only, but bearing it *away*. For as in those solemn and stately works of ancient art to which I alluded, mild breaths of reconciliation seem to make themselves felt, when once the curse has lighted, the expiation has been made,—not otherwise, and only far more gloriously, does the deep inner connexion between the judgment of the world and the forgiveness of the world appear in that death of Christ, which was at once judgment and forgiveness, in which the world was condemned, and in which, being condemned, the world was also forgiven.

But another evidence of the sacrifice of Christ, as that to which the world had been tending, lay in the endeavour of those who, after that sacrifice had been finished, would not accept it, to substitute something else of the same kind in its room. They felt that only so could they stand their ground, could they recover or maintain any hold upon the hearts of men. With what monstrous exaggerations the idea and practice of sacrifice re-appeared in the final struggle of Paganism with the Christian faith, is abundantly known to every student of Church history. The apostate Julian, for instance, of whose life the revival of Paganism was the ruling passion, ran here into extremes which earned him the ridicule of the more lukewarm adherents of the old superstition themselves;* and he, the same who had trod under foot the cross of Christ, and counted the blood with which he was sanctified a common thing, did yet submit himself to loathsome rites,† seeking in the blood of bulls profusely poured on him, as in a cleansing bath, that purifying which he had refused to find in the precious blood-sprinkling of the Lamb of God, slain from the foundation of the world.

Again, the inner necessity of having somewhere a sacrifice to rest on, the certainty that if men have not the true, they will generate a substitute in its room, was signally proved by the manner in which the doctrine concerning the mass grew up in the Christian Church itself. No sooner did men's faith in a finished sacrifice, one lying at the ground of every prayer, every act of self-oblation, every acceptable work, grow weak, than the feeling that they must have a sacrifice somewhere, produced, or, so to speak, by instinct de-

---

* See the manner in which the heathen Ammianus Marcellinus (l. 22, c. 12,) speaks of the prodigality of his sacrifices. *Victimarius* was the title which was given him at Antioch, not apparently by the Christians alone.

† Those of the taurobolıad. Prudentius (*Peristeph.* 10, 1006—1050,) gives a description at large of this revolting rite.

veloped, a doctrine to answer their needs—turning that Holy Eucharist, which is the ever-present witness in the Church of a sacrifice once completed on the cross, and continually pleaded in heaven,—turning that *itself* into the sacrifice, and seeking to supply by these poor but continual repetitions, the weakness of their faith in the one priceless offering, upon the acceptance of which, as upon an unchangeable basis, the Church everlastingly reposes.

And now, brethren, by way of practical conclusion from all this on which we have been entering to-day—what a witness is there here against that shallow view of the truth which should bless us, that would leave it a bare doctrine, a system of morals, lopping away as superfluous and mystical, as a remnant of Judaism, all which speaks of atonement, of propitiation, of blood-sprinkling, of sacrifice. The contemplation of the benefits of Christ's death under aspects suggested by these words, so far from being this shred of Judaism, which a more perfect knowledge must strip off, finds on the contrary as many anticipations every where besides as there. They are as busy about sacrifice in the outer court of the Gentiles as in the holier place of the Jew; and as little there as here is it a separable accident, the garniture and fringe of something else, but in either case itself constituting the core and middle point of worship, recognised in a thousand ways as that which must lie at the ground of all approaches unto God.

And these things being so, how can we escape from

THE PERFECT SACRIFICE. 237

owning that some of the deepest, the most universal needs of the human heart have not yet been awakened in us, if we have never yet desired to stand under the cross, nor ever claimed our part in the great oblation which was made thereon, as on the holiest altar ever reared upon the earth—needs which that transcendent offering on Calvary was meant for ever and perfectly to satisfy? It is plain, brethren, that we are leading an outside life, playing but with the surfaces of things, never having brought ourselves in contact with inmost realities, that there never yet has risen upon our souls the awful vision of a holy God, that we have wholly shrunk from looking down into the abysmal deeps of our own corruption, if as yet we have never cried, "Purge me with hyssop, and I shall be clean; wash me, and I shall be whiter than snow." For when once we have learned aught of this, we then surely feel that not amendment of life, that not tears of sorrow, that not the most perfect baptism of repentance, that not all these together, would of themselves reach our needs, or remove our stains, or give peace for the past, or confidence for the future; that only in the Lamb slain is there purity, or pardon, or peace.

Oh then, brethren, let us hasten there, where we may make that precious blood-sprinkling our own; let us hasten there, lest they rise up against us in the last day—those heathens, who set such a price on their sacrifices, which were at best but shadows of the true; who made by them such continual acknowledgment of guilt which they had contracted, of punishment which they deserved, of reconciliation which they desired; lest they rise up, condemning *us*, who shall have counted the blood with which we were sanctified a common thing, and brought into the awful presence of the Judge a conscience stained and defiled, which yet might have been purged and for ever perfected by far better sacrifices than theirs.

LECTURE V.

THE RESTORER OF PARADISE.

GENESIS V. 29.

And he called his name Noah, saying, This same shall comfort us concerning our work and toil of our hands, because of the ground which the Lord hath cursed.

A WORD or two may be needful on commencing again these lectures, which, after the lapse of some months, I am permitted to resume; I may thus hope to remind such among my present hearers as have heard the earlier discourses, and inform such as have not, what has been their course, and what the road we hitherto have travelled over. I have undertaken, then, to trace in a few leading lines the yearnings of the world which was before Christ, or which, though subsequent to Him, has yet lain without the limits of Christendom, and beyond the mighty influences of his word and Spirit,—a world to which He was still therefore a Saviour to come—to trace, I say, the yearnings of this world after its Redeemer, and the presentiments of Him which it cherished. I have sought to show that if there was much in the world, as in a fallen world there needs must have been, ready to resist and oppose the coming in of the Truth, prompt to take up arms against it at its appearing, so also, on the other hand, in that it was a world which came first from God, and which had never been abandoned by Him, but which all along He had been in highest wisdom and highest love preparing for and leading to this glorious consummation, there were in it certain predispositions for the Truth, there was that which was ready to range itself under the banners of that Truth, so soon as once they were openly set up. I have endeavoured, too, to prove that the existence of unconscious prophecies of the truth, resemblances in lower spheres of the spiritual life to all which at last was perfectly manifested in the highest, is only that which we should have expected: so that it is not the presence of these resemblances which need perplex us, but rather their absence which would have been justly surprising, which would have been indeed most difficult to account for.

I take up my subject at this point, and go forward to another branch of it, seeking to show that in another aspect beside those already contemplated by us, we have in Christ our Lord "the Desire of all nations," inasmuch, that is, as we have in Him one who was at perfect understanding with nature, wielded it at his will, declared that He was come to restore it, to bring back the lost Paradise; and did not merely declare this in word, but by first fruits of power exercised upon it, by the mighty works that He did, gave manifest tokens that He was come, at once to set *it* free from the bondage of corruption, and to set free the race of which He appeared as the Head from the blind tyranny which it exercised upon them—to give to his people something more than the Stoic freedom of opposing an intrepid and obdurate heart to the assaults of fortune, or the accidents of nature. For though that in its place was well, which should enable a man to say, amid a falling world, *Impavidum ferient ruinæ*, yet better still his work, who should so bear up and strengthen and establish the shaken pillars of the universe, that wreck and ruin should find place in it no more.

But why, it may be asked, should this deliverance of nature have been, upon one side, part of the world's expectation? or why, which is in fact the same question on its other side, should the giving of this deliverance cohere so intimately, as we shall see it does, with Christ's redemptive work, as to be in fact one aspect of that work itself? For this reason—because of the closest connexion in which the disorder from which the redemption was expected, stood related to the sin of man. That disorder was felt truly to be the echo in nature of the deeper discords in man's spiritual being. When man sinned, then in the profound and not exaggerated language of our great poet, "All nature felt the wound." Man was as the highest note in the scale of creation, and, when he descended, through all nature there followed a corresponding reduction. It became subject to vanity, not willingly, not by an act of its own will, but by reason of another, by reason of him who subjected the same, by reason of man. (Rom. viii. 20.) We behold the fact itself on all sides acknowledged, the fact, I mean, of a primal perfection, of a present disorder. Of the sense of primal perfection we have singular witness in the language, (and there is no such witness as the unconscious one which language supplies,) of two the most highly cultivated nations of the ancient world, whom all the present confusions of nature could not hinder from using words signifying *order* and *elegance** to designate the world which they beheld around them;—for so to them did this grace and beauty gleam through its present disorders, so instinctively did they feel these to belong to the true idea of the universe, grievously as that was now defaced and marred.† While with all this, on the other hand, its present disorders appeared so great, its discords so harsh, that the Epicurean poet found, as he thought, warrant and ground enough in these for his atheist conclusion, that no hand of Eternal Wisdom presided at its planning, that no final causes could be traced throughout it, but that all was the work of a blind chance.‡ That conclusion of his was indeed most false, yet this much was true,

---

* Κόσμος and *mundus*. Pliny (*H. N*, l. 2, c 3·) Quem κόσμον Græci, nomine *ornamenti* appellaverunt, eum nos à perfectâ absolutâque *elegantiâ* mundum. Pythagoras is said to have been the first who applied the word κόσμος to the material universe—a word which was in its way almost as great an acquisition for natural philosophy, as was Plato's ιδέα for intellectual and spiritual.

† Compare the *De Naturâ Deorum*, b. 2.

‡ Lucretius:

    Nequicquam nobis divinitus esse paratam
    Naturam rerum, *tantâ stat prædita culpâ*.

that Paradise *had* disappeared from the earth; and man, the appointed prince of creation, did stand among the rebel powers of nature; which had cast off *his* yoke, at the moment when he cast off the yoke of his superior Lord, practising *upon* him, by a just judgment, the disobedience and the contumacy which it had learned *from* him; and which did now, with its thorns and its briers, its wastes and its wildernesses, its earthquakes and its storms, present him too faithful a reflex of the sin and evil, the desolation and barrenness of his own heart.

Yet nevertheless, though Paradise was gone, he kept in his soul the memory of that which once had been, and with the memory the hope and the confidence that it would yet be again—that perhaps, though *his* eyes could see it nowhere, it yet had not wholly vanished from the earth. If there bloomed no Paradise in the present, at least there lay one before him and behind. If it lay not near him, yet in the distance,—in the happy Iran,—among the remote Hyperboreans,*—in the far land of the blameless Ethiopians. He felt, indeed, that he was himself weak to win it back, but he could not resign the trust that a champion would raise, and accomplish for him that which he was unequal to accomplish for himself. Nor was it only when the son of Lamech was born that men said in a joyful expectation, "This same shall comfort us because of the ground which the Lord hath cursed." Of many more the same hope was fondly conceived.

* See Muller's *Dorians*, b. 2, c. 4.

The world could hardly picture to itself any one of its leading spirits, of the great benefactors of the past, the mighty deliverers in the future, without thinking of the curse upon the earth as more or less lightened in his time and by his aid. For it truly understood that however the resistance which we find in nature, a resistance so stubborn that only with long labour and toil we make it subject to our will, may be part of the needful discipline of the present time—may be, though good in itself, yet good for our present condition, and something which we could not be without—still that release from all this, from this resistance and contradiction of the outward world, is a portion of the blessedness in store, not indeed so much for its own sake, as because it will go hand in hand with, and be the outward expression of, another and greater healing and deliverance in the inner domain of men's spirits.

This yearning after a lost paradise, this belief that it should some day or other be restored, we find existing every where, and, as was to be expected, in the worthier religions the most vividly. Thus it comes out with a remarkable strength and distinctness in that which has so many noble elements in it, which is in many respects so remarkably free from the more debasing admixtures of most other worships of heathendom—I mean the religion of the ancient Persians. Through that all, there runs the liveliest expectation of a time when every poison and poisonous weed should be expelled from the earth, when there should be no more ravening beast, nor fiery simoon, when streams should break forth in every desert, when the bodies of men should cast no shadows, when they should need no food to sustain their life, when there should be no more poverty, nor sickness, nor old age, nor death.

And, what is most remarkable, and makes these expectations to belong to our argument is, that not in Jewish prophecy alone were these hopes, and the fulfilment of these hopes, linked with, and consequent upon, the coming of a righteous king, one of whom, righteousness should be the girdle of his loins, and faithfulness the girdle of his reins, who should reprove with equity for the meek of the earth, (Isai. xi. 4, 5;) but in *all* the anticipations upon all sides of these blessings to men, they were thus connected with the expectation of a king reigning in righteousness. In his time, and because of his presence, these blessings should accrue: he should be himself the middle point of blessing, from which all should flow out. For there was a just sense in men, which hindered them from ever looking for, or conceiving of, any blessings apart from a person with whom they were linked, and from whom they were diffused. Even in the *Pollio* of the great Latin poet, however little interpreters are at one concerning the wondrous child, the kindler of such joyful expectations, however unsatisfying the common explanations must be confessed to be, yet this much is certain, that the poet could not conceive or dream of a mere natural golden age. It must centre in and unfold itself from a living person: it must stand in a real relation to his appearing, being the outcoming and reflection of his righteousness. The world's history can have no sentimental and idyllic, it must needs have an epic and heroic, close.

But, it may be asked, Are we justified in looking at this expectation as the expectation of something which is to be indeed made ours in Him that is true? All will, I think, allow that the prospect of a restored paradise,—in other words, of a world lightened from its curse, does belong to the very essence of our Christian hope—that there was a truth in the ancient Chiliasm, which all its sensual exaggerations should not induce us to slight or to put aside in so far, that is, as it was a protest against the dishonour which would have been put upon a part of God's creation, or rather upon the completeness of the redemption of that part, if it had been regarded as so utterly and irrecoverably spoiled, that now it could only be destroyed, and not renewed. Assuredly, the hope of this recovery forms part of the anticipation of prophets. The waste places of the world, those outward signs of sin, impressed visibly on nature, shall disappear; "the wilderness and the solitary place shall be glad." What glory the world yet keeps shall be enhanced and infinitely multiplied; "The light of the moon shall be as the light of the sun, and the light of the sun shall be sevenfold, as the light of seven days, in the day that the Lord bindeth up the breach of his people, and healeth the stroke of their wound."* (Isai. xxx. 26.)

---

* For the way in which the Jewish commentators under-

All the discords which have followed hard upon the fall shall be hushed to peace; "The wolf also shall dwell with the lamb, and the leopard shall lie down with the kid." (Isai. xi. 10.) And apostles take up the strain: they too declare how "the whole creation groaneth and travaileth in pain together until now;" how "the earnest expectation of the creature waiteth for the manifestation of the sons of God." (Rom. viii. 19.) They see, in ecstatic vision, not merely a new heaven, but a new earth, and One sitting upon his throne who says, "Behold, I make *all* things new." (Rev. xxi. 5.)

And we have, not lying thus on the surface of Scripture, other obscurer yet not less significant indications of the intimate connexion between the restoration of man and the restoration of the outward world, —as, for instance, in the use of the same word in the New Testament to signify the one and the other. There is a *regeneration* of man, but the same word (παλιγγενεσία,) is most significantly applied to nature also, and expresses that great and transcendent change which for it also is in store. (Matt. xix. 28.) There is for it also a new birth, for so much this word thus applied tells us, no less than for man,—a casting off of its old and wrinkled skin,—a resurrection morn, when it too shall put on its Easter garments; when, as some foster-nurse, it shall share in the glory of the

---

stood such passages as these, see Schoettgen, *Hor. Heb.*, v. 2, pp. 62, 171, and Eisenmenger's *Entdeckt Judenthum*, v. 2, p. 826.

royal child whom it has reared; and who, at length, ascending the throne of his kingdom, is mindful of her in whose lap in time past he has been nurtured.*
Man's regeneration is indeed a present one, and nature's, in the main, a future; yet are they but workings, in narrower and wider spheres, of the same almighty power, and so may thus justly be called by the same name.

Nor by word alone, but also by pregnant symbol, it was declared that this redemption was a part of that work which the Son of man came to effect. For I cannot doubt that there was a symbolic pointing at what had been lost, and what was to be won back, in the fact of the temptation of our blessed Lord finding place *in the wilderness.* The garden and the wilderness are thus set forth to us as the two opposite poles. By sin the first Adam lost the garden, which henceforward disappeared from the earth, so that the very site of it has since been vainly sought; and from that day forth the wilderness was man's appointed home. Christ, therefore, the second Adam, taking up the conflict exactly at the point where the first Adam had left it, and inheriting, so to speak, all the consequences of his defeat, did, in the wilderness, do battle with the foe, and triumphing in righteousness, won back the garden for man—which, though we see it not yet, will in due time unfold itself from Him and as one of

---

* Chrysostom Καθάπερ γὰρ τιθήνη, παιδίον τρέφοισα βασιλικόν, επι τῆς ἀρχῆς εκεινου γινομένου τῆς πατρικῆς, και αυτὴ συναπολαυει τῶν ἀγαθῶν, οὕτω καὶ ἡ κτίσις

THE RESTORER OF PARADISE. 249

the fruits of his victory; for the centre being won, the circumference will be won also. We recognise a slight hint of the meaning that lay in making the wilderness the scene of this great conflict, in that which one evangelist alone records, and which might at first sight seem but as a stroke added to enhance the desolate savageness of his abode: " He was with the wild beasts." (Mark i. 13.) But surely it means that in Him, the ideal man, the paradise prerogatives were given back; the fear of Him and the dread of Him were over all the beasts of the field: " He was with them," and they harmed him not, but did rather own Him as their rightful Lord.

Nor may we confine to that single act of our Lord's life, the tokens which He gave that He should be this deliverer of nature; nor may we say that the glory of a redeemed nature is a glory which as yet *altogether* waits to be revealed. Rather is it already and most truly begun. In his miracles we see the germs and beginnings of its liberation. In them nature is no longer stiff but fluent: its laws, so stubborn to others, become elastic in his hands: before Him each of its mountains becomes a plain: it listens for, and hears, and obeys the lightest intimation of his will.

That all this had need so to be in the presence of one claiming to be all which He claimed, that it all stood in vital and intimate connexion with his work, was most truly felt by a world which evermore adorned its champions with like powers, which evermore conceived of them as workers of wonders, as bringers back, in like manner, of the lost harmonies of creation, and conceived of nature as plastic in their hands and obedient to their will. It was a true instinct, however mistaken in the persons to whom the wondrous works were ascribed, out of which the world concluded that he who professed to deliver his fellows, must not be bound upon any side with the same heavy yoke as they were—that the very idea of a champion of mankind was that of one in whom should be found again all the lost prerogatives of every man.

And when we thus say that the miracles which Christ wrought were these signs and tokens of a redemption, let us not pause here, nor contemplate them as insulated facts, once and once only having been, but rather as facts pregnant with ulterior consequences, as the earliest steps of a series, as first fruits of a gracious power which did not stop with them, but has ever since continued to unfold itself more and more. What Christ once, and in them, wrought in *intensive* power, he works evermore in *extensive*. Once or twice He multiplied the bread, but evermore in Christian lands, famine is become a stranger, a more startling, because a more unusual, thing—the culture of the earth proceeding with surer success and with a larger return. A few times he healed the sick, but in the reverence for man's body which his gospel teaches, in the sympathy for all forms of suffering which flows out of it, in the sure advance of all worthier science which it implies and ensures, in and by aid of all this, these miraculous cures unfold themselves into the whole art of Christian medicine, into all the alleviations and removements of pain and disease, which are so rare in other, and so frequent in Christian lands. Once he quelled the storm; but in the clear dominion of man's spirit over the material universe which Christianity gives, in the calm courage which it inspires, a lordship over the winds and waves and over all the blind uproar of nature, is secured, which only can again be lost with the loss of all the spiritual gifts with which he has endued his people. Already Paul was *de facto* admiral in that great tempest upon the Adrian sea.

Thus, then, brethren, we see that the world's expectation upon this side also has an answering fact. There is One who does truly give what the hearts of men have desired. Their longing after a redeemed creation was no delusive dream, however the ways in which they realized that longing, and gave it an outward shape, were premature and vain. And here you will bear with me, even though I repeat an admonition once made already, but the importance of which will abundantly justify its repetition. Let us then for ourselves take care that we view aright these askings after the true, and understand what they mean: let us see that they be not, by the fraud of men, used against us, to undermine, or, at least, to embarrass, the faith which they ought to help to establish. We have spoken already of the way in which they might be so used. The slight upon the miracles of Scripture, and all other God's mighty gifts to the world by his Son, through the adducing of other works, seemingly of a like kind, other similar pretensions made by, or on behalf of, others,—the mingling, and so losing sight of the divine facts amid a multitude of phenomena apparently similar,—this opposition to the truth has been often attempted, but is probably now working itself out into a more consistent theory, and one more conscious of itself, and what it means, and what advantages it possesses, than ever in times past it has done.

The evading of the stress of Christ's works by the reply, that such have been the accompaniment of every heroic personage, glories and ornaments which the imagination of his fellows has inevitably lent him, the halo with which it has clothed him,—for instance, that it has evermore been presumed that the outer world will obey him, no reluctant slave to his material force, but a ready servant to his spiritual will;—this manner of dealing with the marvellous works of Christ, is likely to find great favour in our time. Nor is it hard to see the reason. It falls in remarkably with the tendencies of our age. It retains, and is consistent with a certain measure of respect toward the records of revelation. For it does not presume those parts of them which affirm supernatural facts to be a fraud or forgery, nor yet to be the record of deceptions and sleights of hand, but only that the men to whom we owe these accounts lay under the same laws, were subject to the same optical illusions in the spiritual world as all their fellows, as belong to the very essence of man's nature: it fared with them but as with others, that the mighty desire became father to the belief.

This theory offers a way of dealing with a great multitude of statements presented as historic, which men are unwilling to brand outright as falsehoods, and yet as little willing to accept as truths. It offers a middle course, decently respectful to Christianity, and at the same time effectually escaping from its authority: and presenting, as it seems to do, a calm and philosophical explanation, both for its more perplexing phenomena, and also for very much beyond it, it will be strange if, in our age, which rejoices so much in large and inclusive points of view, it does not find a ready and a wide acceptance.

But in truth, brethren, this universal imagination, these consenting expectations upon all sides, in so many thousands and thousands of hearts, these, if we believe in a divine origin and destination of man, if we believe that this man or that may be deceived, but that all men cannot—since whatever there may be of false at the surface, the foundations of his being are laid in the truth, being laid in God—if we believe that this or that generation may be dreaming fantastic and merely feverish dreams, which have no counterparts whatever in the actual world of realities, but not all generations—if there is that in us which, prior to all argument, solemnly binds us to believe that no such cruel falsehood would be played off upon man as a great longing laid deep in his heart, without a corresponding object—then to us believing so, these wide-spread, or say rather these universal expectations, will themselves give testimony to a truth corresponding to them. We shall not indeed look for a truth answering to them in all their accidents, for of these many will be local, temporary, varying: and the truth, when it comes to pass, must more or less depart and differ from that form in which it clothed itself to them who waited for it. So of necessity it must be; for that form perforce was more or less injuriously affected, distorted, and obscured by that sinful element, which in the mind of each would mingle with, and in part debase and degrade it. But there will be a testimony in these consenting expectations for that which lies at the root of, and after the merely accidental is stripped off, remains common to, and so constitutes the essence of, them all.

And when we are deeply convinced of this, then in all those in whom the world has greatly hoped—workers, as it has been thought, of wondrous works—bringers back of a golden age—utterers, as has been fondly deemed, of the forgotten spell of power—graspers anew of the sceptre over nature which had fallen from the hand of every one beside—readers backward of the primal curse—in the mighty acts attributed to each one of these, we shall trace proofs of the exceeding fitness which there was, that He who indeed came in the fulness of the time, should come furnished with signs and wonders and mighty works, so that even the winds and the sea obeyed Him, and the bread multiplied in his hands, and the wild beasts knew him for their lord, and in the desert Paradise bloomed anew at his presence. In legend and in tale utterly worthless as history we shall yet read prophetic intimations, which indeed understood not themselves, of Him who, in the days of his flesh, by first-fruits of power, declared Himself the promised Seed of the woman who should comfort us for the earth which God had cursed, and at length bring about its perfect redemption from that curse, making it, thus redeemed, a fit dwelling-place for his redeemed people.

LECTURE VI.

THE REDEEMER FROM SIN.

ROMANS VII. 21, 23.

I find then a law, that, when I would do good, evil is present with me. For I delight in the law of God after the inward man: but I see another law in my members, warring against the law of my mind, and bringing me into captivity to the law of sin which is in my members.

WE were occupied, when last we met together, with the world's expectation of one who should deliver all outward nature from its curse, of one in whom the Adamic prerogatives should re-appear. To-day I shall be led, as by a natural transition, to speak of a yet nearer deliverance, and one which it imported to man yet more that he should win, or that another should win for him—a harmony which he demanded with a yet more earnest longing than this harmony of nature with itself, or of nature with him—an inner harmony, a deliverance from his own evil, from that in himself which was threatening his true being with destruction, from the lusts which embraced his soul, but while they embraced, strangled and destroyed. For sin has never reigned so undisputed a lord in his heart, but that there were voices there protesting against its lordship.

His will was enslaved; but he knew that it was enslaved, that freedom was its birthright; and that bondage, however it might be its miserable necessity now, yet was not its true condition from the first.

It was the sense of this, of such an inner contradiction in his life, which made one to exclaim that he felt as if two souls were lodged within him;* and another to set forth the soul of man as a chariot, which two horses, one white and one black, were drawing—†so did the wondrous fact present itself to him, of the flesh lusting against the spirit, and the spirit against the flesh, so had he learned that if there is that in every man which is drawing him up to God and to the finding of his true freedom in God, there is also that which would fain drag him downward, till he utterly lose himself and his own true life in the mire of sensual and worldly lusts, till the divine in him be wholly obscured, and the bestial predominant altogether.‡ It was the sense of this, which made the image of the two ways, a downward and an upward—one easy and strewn with flowers, but a way of death;

---

* Xenophon, *Cyropæd*, l. 6, c. 1, § 41   Cf. Seneca (*Ep*. 52:) Quid est hoc, Lucili, quod nos alio tendentes alio trahit et eò unde recedere cupimus, impellit? quid colluctatur cum animo nostro, nec permittit nobis quidquam semel velle?

† Plato, *Phædrus*, c 25.

‡ This sense of the latent beast, or the more latent beasts than one, in every man, which may be fed and pampered, and roused to fiercest activity, while the true man in him perishes with hunger, supplies the groundwork of that famous and often imitated passage in Plato, *Rep*, l. 9, c. 12

one hard and steep and sharp set with thorns, but a way of life, as familiar to heathen moralists* as to us who hear of the broad and the narrow way, the wide and the straight gate, from the lips of the Lord himself.

And thus the problem which each nobler system proposed to itself was the delivering from this evil, the bringing of a harmony into the inner life—its end to make man a king, so that he should have dominion over himself, and over all of his nature which was not truly himself—that which was appointed to rule in him, ruling, and that which was appointed to serve, serving—the charioteer charioting, and not dragged in the dust at the heels of his horses. The promise which it held out of giving this, was that which to every more earnest spirit each system had of attractive, and only as it promised this, had it an attraction for them. They *only* felt drawn to it, as it undertook to give them this liberty, and harmoniously to re-adjust the disturbed relations of their inward life.

I know that when we undertake to speak of these things, and would fain show in how wonderful a de-

---

* Hesiod, *Op.* 289—292, cebes, *Tab.*, c. 12, Xenophon, *Memorab.*, l 2, c. 1, § 21 seq., in regard to which last passage there is a very interesting discussion in Buttmann's admirable elucidation of the mythus of Herakles. (*Mythol.*, v. 1, p 252.) He there shows that, according to all likelihood, the "temptation" of Herakles belonged to the original legend, and was not the mere poetical invention of Prodicus. Lactantius (*Inst. Div.*, l. 6, c. 3) notes how heathen poet and philosopher had already used this image of the two ways.

gree the ancient world was engaged with the same moral and spiritual problems as are engaging ourselves, there is a caution which we must take home to ourselves, if we would not trace entirely delusive resemblances, and be led away by merely accidental likenesses in expression, which yet point to no real likeness at the root; this caution, I mean—that since there are points of apparent contact in almost all systems, it follows that before we can find any significance in these, or conclude one because of them to stand in any real affinity to another, we must strictly ask ourselves, how deep these resemblances go, whether they lie merely on the surface, or reach down to the central heart of the matter, to that which determines the nature of each; whether we have been caught by words and phrases which have a similar sound, but which, looked into more nearly, will be found to conceal under language which sounds nearly the same, statements which are really and essentially most diverse. This mistake no doubt has often been made; phrases have been snatched at and claimed as ours, as anticipating and bearing witness to Christian truths, without waiting to inquire what place they really hold in the complex of the system from which they are taken. Thus a Latin Father* has spoken of Seneca as "one of us" on the score of certain showy maxims which sound, at first hearing, and till they are adjusted into their place, like great Christian truths; and this, though perhaps there could not have been two schemes

---

* Jerome (*Adv. Jovin.*, l. 1, in fine.) *Noster* Seneca.

more opposite at the heart to one another than that Stoic, which in its pride would teach us to seek all in ourselves, and the Christian, which bids us with an humbler yet truer wisdom to seek all out of ourselves and in God.

But at the same time, and owning our liability to be thus deceived, we must yet keep far from that other course, which, shunning the faults and exaggerations of this, refuses to see stirring at all in the heathen world the same riddles of life and of death which are perplexing ourselves. Into this extreme they run, who will give any explanation rather than a moral one, and the more trivial the better, to the legend and the tale of antiquity, obstinately refusing to hear in the most earnest voices which reach them from the past cries after the same deliverance for which we yearn. The tendency to this is in truth at its root antichristian; for it grows, whether it owns it or not, out of a conviction that all with which Christianity deals is in fact accidental, and does not belong to the essential stuff of humanity—that this revelation of which we boast, has no claim to be considered as an answer to the deepest and most universal needs of men—that echoes of it therefore are nowhere to be listened for, or being caught, are in no wise to be accounted more than accidental reverberations of the air.

Keeping then that caution in view, but as a caution only, and resisting, as we are bound to do, the endeavour to rob the whole heathen world, its philosophy and mythology alike, of all moral significance for us, on the score that significance has sometimes been found where truly there was none, we may boldly say that the highest philosophy of the old world did concern itself with a redemption—not of course with a Redeemer, for of such it knew not: but it did avowedly set before itself as its aim and purpose the helping of souls to a birth out of a world of shows and appearances into the world of realities, out of a world of falsehood into one of truth, turning them from darkness to light, from the contemplation of shadows to the contemplation of substance.* That favourite saying of Socrates that he exercised still the craft of his mother, that his task and work, his mission in the world, was such a helping of souls to the birth, by the helping to a birth the conceptions which were struggling there,† this rested on no other thought,— was in its kind and however remotely a prelude to far mightier truth, the earthly anticipation of a heavenly word, of *his* word who said, "Ye must be born again." It pointed, although at an infinite distance, to the possibility of a birth into a kingdom, not merely of reality as opposed to semblance, but of holiness as opposed to sin.‡

* The great passage in the *Republic* of Plato, l. 7, c. 1, 2, will at once suggest itself to many.

† Plato's *Theætetus*, c. 6. Stallbaum's edit., p. 63. See Van Heusde's *Initia Philosophiæ Platonicæ*, v. 2, p. 52 seq.

‡ And so, too, there are counterparts, weak and pale ones they must needs be, of the Christian idea of *conversion*, which find place in the same philosophy. How remarkable are the very terms, μεταστροφὴ ἀπὸ τῶν σκιων ἐπὶ τὸ φῶς (*Rep.* l. 7, c. 13,)

What again is "Know thyself," that great saying of the heathen philosophy, in which, when it turned from being merely physical, and a speculation about natural appearances, the sun the moon and the stars, to the making of man and man's being the region in which it moved, the riddles of humanity, the riddles which it sought to solve*—what was that "Know thyself," that great word in which it embodied and expressed so well its own character and aim, and all that it proposed to effect, but a preparation afar off for a higher word, the "Repent ye," of the Gospel? Since let that precept only be faithfully carried out, and in what else could it issue but repentance? or at least in what else but in an earnest longing after this great change of heart and life? For out of this self-knowledge nothing else but self-loathing could grow—so that men being once come, as they presently must, to a consciousness of their error and their departure from goodness and truth, should hate themselves, and flee from themselves to whatever higher guide was offered them; to the end that they might become different men, and not remain the same which before they were.† What could any man behold himself, if

περιστροφὴ, ψυχῆς περιαγωγή, (*Rep.* l. 7, c. 6,) with which we may compare the ἐπιστρέφεσθαι of the New Testament, 2 Cor. iii. 16, 1 Thess. i 9, Acts xviii 18.

* Cicero, *Tusc. Quæst.*, l. 5, c 4.

† See the affecting words, which Plato (*Synops.*, c. 32,) puts into the mouth of Alcibiades, concerning the mysterious and magical power of the truth, even as partially embodied in the words and person of a Socrates, to convince of sin, un-

only he beheld himself aright, but, to use the wonderful comparison of Plato,* as that sea-god, in whom the pristine form was now scarcely to be recognised, so were some limbs of his body broken off, and some marred and battered by the violence of the waves, while to the rest shells and stones and sea-weed had clung and overgrown them, till he bore a resemblance rather to some monster than to that which by nature he was? What was man but such a wreck of his nobler self, what but such a monster could he show in his own eyes, if only he could be prevailed to fix those eyes steadfastly upon himself?

And when men, thus learning their fall, and how great it was, learned also to long for their restoration, very interesting and instructive is it to observe how Christ realized for yearning souls not only the very

---

til, as the young man owned, it seemed to him that it were far better not to live than to live the man he was. (ὥστε μοι δόξαι μὴ βιωτὸν εἶναι ἔχοντι ὡς ἔχω.)

* *De Rep*, l. 10, c. 11: 'Ὥσπερ οἱ τὸν θαλάττιον Γλαῦκον ὁρῶντες, οὐκ ἂν ἔτι ῥᾳδίως αὐτοῦ ἴδοιεν τὴν ἀρχαίαν φύσιν, ὑπὸ τοῦ τά τε παλαιὰ τοῦ σώματος μέρη τὰ μὲν ἐκκεκλάσθαι, τὰ δὲ συντετρίφθαι καὶ πάντως λελωβῆσθαι ὑπὸ τῶν κυμάτων, ἄλλα δὲ προσπεφυκέναι ὄστρεά τε καὶ φύκια καὶ πέτρας, ὥστε παντὶ μᾶλλον θηρίῳ ἐοικέναι ἢ οἷος ἦν φύσει. οὕτω καὶ τὴν ψυχὴν ἡμεῖς θεώμεθα διακειμένην ὑπὸ μυρίων κακῶν. This Glaucus, as the Socialist tells us, discovered the fountain of immortality, of which he drank; but not being able to show it to others, was by them hurled into the deep of the sea. From time to time, the fishermen catch sight of him, or hear him bewailing his immortality. The way in which this mythus is used by Plato, is a testimony for the profound meaning which he found in it.

thing which they asked for, but that in the very forms under which they had asked it; most instructive to observe how the very language of Scripture, in which it sets forth the gifts which a Saviour brings, was a language which more or less had been used already to set forth the blessings which men wanted, or which from others they had most imperfectly obtained—the Gospel of Christ falling in not only with the wants of souls, but with the very language in which those wants had found utterance.

Thus there had continually spoken out in men, a sense of that which they needed to be done for them, as a *healing*, as a binding up of hurts, a stanching of wounds. The art of the physician did but image forth a higher cure and care, which should concern itself not with the bodies, but with the souls, of men. They were but the branches of one and the same discipline, so much so, that the same god who was conceived master in one, the soother of passions, was master also in the other, the healer of diseases. It was conceived of sins as of stripes and wounds, which would leave their livid marks, their enduring scars, on the miserable souls which had committed them, and which carried these evidences of their guilt, visibly impressed on them for ever, into that dark world, and before those awful judgment-seats, whither after death they were bound.*

---

* Plato, *Gorgias*, c. 80, Stallbaum's edit. p. 314. Tacitus (*Annal.* 6) has a fierce delight in applying these words to Tiberius.

How deep the corresponding image of Christ's work as a work of healing, reaches in Scripture, I need not remind you. His ministry of grace had been set forth in language borrowed from this art, by prophets who went before; He should be anointed to heal the broken-hearted, to bind up the bruised; and when he began that ministry, He claimed these prophecies for Himself, laying his finger on the most signal among them, and saying, "This day is this Scripture fulfilled in your ears." (Luke iv. 21.) And then, too, we shall all remember how in another place He spake of sinners as being sick, and Himself as their physician, (Matt. ix. 12;) and by the good Samaritan it has been often thought more than likely, that He shadowed forth Himself, the despised of his own people, and yet the true binder up of the bleeding hurts of humanity. But what need of more proof, when we use the very word *health** as equivalent for salvation. That fearful saying of the heathen sage remains most true, that every sin *is* a wound, that it leaves behind it its scar, invisible now,—for it is a scar not on the body, but the soul,—which will yet be only too plainly visible in the day of the revelation of all things. Yet He so heals them whom He takes in hand, He makes so perfect a cure, that not even the scars of their hurts shall remain; "by whose stripes

---

* Thus Plato (*De Rep.*, l. 4, c. 18, Stallbaum's edit. p. 324:) Ἀρετὴ μὲν ἄρα ὡς ἔοικεν, ὑγίειά τέ τις ἂν εἴη καὶ κάλλος καὶ εὐεξία ψυχῆς, κακία δὲ ὅσος τε καὶ αἶσχος καὶ ἀσθένεια.

ye are healed." He only waited till there was an earnest desire awakened in men that they might find themselves in an hospital of souls—till these desires came to a head,—till it was felt that all which was offered elsewhere reached not to an effectual binding up of hurts, was but a healing of them slightly, presently to break out anew, or a covering of them over with purple and with gold, leaving them the while to fester unhindered beneath. He only waited till it was owned that a divine Physician, and none other, could take the great sufferer in hand, and then straightway He stood by the sufferer's side, and proffered him all that he had asked for, but had now despaired of finding, even help and healing, and these in the very forms under which he had asked them.*

Nor was it otherwise with the idea of *freedom*—an idea which lies so close to the very heart and centre of the Gospel, that its benefits and blessings are perhaps oftener set forth by a word borrowed from this circle of images than by any other, oftener described as a *redemption* or a purchase out of slavery, and Christ as a Redeemer or purchaser, and thus a setter free, than by any other language. It is true that we have come to use these words with so little earnestness, have taken them so much in vain, we have so lightly passed them backward and forward

* Augustine (*Serm.* 87, c. 10:) Jacet toto orbe terrarum ab oriente usque in occidentem grandis ægrotus. Ad sanandum grandem ægrotum descendit omnipotens medicus. Humiliavit se usque ad mortalem carnem, tamquam usque ad lectum ægrotantis.

from hand to hand, that the sharpness and distinctness of their first outline has been for us almost lost and worn away, so that they scarcely, or only now and then, with any vividness, bring to our minds the truths which they affirm—the awful truth of that slavery *out* of which we were delivered, the glorious truth of that liberty *into* which we have been brought. But still these words, though we may forget it, do evermore proclaim this; and they are words by which oftener perhaps than by any other, the Holy Spirit in the Scripture declares the benefits whereof Christ has made us partakers.

And being this Redeemer or setter free, He was in this regard also "the Desire of all nations." For He, when He said "Whosoever committeth sin, is the servant of sin," (John viii. 34,) when his apostle characterized himself in his natural state as a slave "sold under sin," (Rom. vii. 14;) when another of his apostles spoke of evil men as "servants of corruption," (2 Pet. ii. 19,) He and they, using this language, were but affirming the same which had been found out and felt by every sinner that ever lived, of which the confession had been wrung out, too, from the lips of thousands. When, too, he offered freedom, a victory over all which was bringing into bondage, an overcoming of the world; as the issue of obedience unto Him, He was but offering that, which in one shape or another, each guide and teacher of his fellows had offered before,—with indeed the mighty difference, that He could make good his offer, and they not. I need not remind you with what frequency we meet, sometimes almost to satiety, declarations of this kind,—of wisdom being the only freedom,—the wise man, the only free man, the only king,—of the soul of the sinner as a tyrant-ridden city,*—of lusts as evil mistresses which enslave the soul and bring it into bondage; how the promise of liberty is on the lips of each who would gather disciples round him. All this is strewn too thickly over the pages of heathen literature to need any proof in particular. And meeting these statements thus frequently and thus earnestly expressed as we often do meet them there, we must see how they bear testimony that men continually envisaged the highest benefits which their souls could attain, under the aspect of freedom, of redemption—that the attaining of this freedom was the object of their lives and hopes, however little they could make it their own, however they discovered and were meant to discover, through their fruitless struggles and toils, that only when the Son made them free, they could be free indeed.

Again, a pointing at the crowning gift which was at length given unto the world in Him, may be traced in the idea of *music* which was so frequently and so fondly used as the best outward expression of inner life-harmony. This indeed was felt to have so singular and profound a fitness, that a term borrowed from this art, was, we may say, formally adopted as the aptest for setting forth that whole discipline which occupied itself with the right composure of the higher

* Plato, *Rep*, l. 9, c 5.

powers, with the bringing into one concent the threefold nature of man;—he in whom this language comes most prominently forward, finding no worthier terms in which to describe that wisdom with which he was enamoured, than as the fairest and mightiest of the harmonies;* while sin, on the contrary, presented itself to him and to many more, as a deep inner disharmony, as a discord which had forced itself into the innermost centre of man's life, and only through the expulsion of which he could again make it what it ought to be, rhythmic, numerous, and harmonious. All these thoughts, which, though first expressed by one or two, yet found echoes in the bosoms of all, how did they in their weakness to realize themselves, in the fact that discords ever made themselves too plainly felt in the lives, not of the taught only, but of the teachers as well—how did they ask for One, the mighty master of all spiritual melodies: whose own life, free from one jarring note, should make perfect music in the ears of God; and not this alone, but who should attune once more that marvellous instrument which had lain silent so long, or from which discords only had proceeded, even the soul of man, and draw from it again sounds which should be sweet even in the ears accustomed to the symphonies of heaven.

Surely all their language, though they knew it not, pointed to such a mighty master of heavenly harmonies as this. For if it be true of Him, that as He

---

* Plato (*De Legg*, l. 3) Καλλίστην καὶ μεγίστην τῶν συμφωνιῶν.

emptied the golden seats of Olympus, and swept their long line of heroes and demi-gods and gods into the darkness and corruption of the tomb, He gathered from each idol as it fell its pretended majesty and dominion and power, claiming all rightfully for his own, and weaving all the scattered rays of light into one crown of glory for his own head; then of none of these could this be more truly spoken than of him whom men feigned to be the god of harmony, to have potency thereby over the spirits of men, with power to exalt, to purify, and to soothe, whose music acted as a charm to tranquillize the passions and attune the spirit to a peace with itself, and with all which was around it.* For Christian peace, the peace which Christ gives, the peace which He sheds abroad in the heart, is it aught else than such a glorified harmony— the expelling from man's life of all that was causing disturbance there, all that was hindering him from chiming in with the music of heaven, all that would have made him a jarring and a dissonant note, left out from the great dance and minstrelsy of the spheres, in which mingle the consenting songs of redeemed men and elect angels?†

---

* Müller's *Dorians*, b. 2, c. 8, § 11.

† It is remarkable enough that although Christian art shrunk, and, so long as there was a heathenism rampant round it, rightly shrunk, from any large use of symbols borrowed from heathen mythology, yet pictures of Christ as Orpheus taming the wild beasts with his lyre, are probably as old as the third century (*Christl. Kunst-Symbolik*, p 134, and Piper's *Mythologie der Christl. Kunst*, p. 121.) Compare the opening of

Thus did the Son of God at his coming in the flesh, take up the unfulfilled promises of all human systems. For they *were* unfulfilled; those systems had wrought no deliverance worthy of the name in the earth. How scanty was the number of those whom they would even undertake to save,—a few highly favoured or greatly gifted spirits of the world—not the poor, the ignorant, the weak; in this how different from that Gospel which is preached to the poor, and whose tidings are good because they are these,—that the Lord hath founded Zion, and the poor of his people shall put their trust therein! But theirs was essentially an aristocratic salvation,* which should help a few, setting them apart from their fellows, on pinnacles from whence they were in danger of looking down far more with gratulation at their own deliverance, than with any inward and bleeding compassion for the multitudes which were toiling and vainly seeking for a path below. And indeed often it was not a salvation at all, even in the very lowest sense of that word; how often was it Satan casting out Satan—one form of evil expelling another, men finding food for pride and vain-glory in the very advances in wisdom and self-restraint which they had made†—and thus those very victories which they had

---

the later Clement's *Cohort. ad Gentes*, and Eusebius, *De Laud. Constantini*, c. 14, p. 760, ed. Reading.

* See Origen's admirable words in his reply to Celsus (*Con. Cels*, l. 7, c 59, 60,) showing how at the best the philosophers were ἰατροὶ ὀλίγων, but Christ the ἰατρὸς πολλῶν.

† The well-known passage of Cicero (*De Nat Deor* l. 3, c

won over fleshly sins, helping to make them slaves of spiritual wickednesses—of the seven worse spirits which take possession of the house, empty and swept and garnished; from which the one spirit of sensual lust has gone out, but which has not been occupied by any nobler guest.

And if, brethren, even *our* struggles, after an inward conformity to a higher rule, are what they are —if with all the helps at our command, we yet win no step without an effort, if oftentimes our premature hymns of victory over this sin or that are changed into confessions of a shameful defeat, and we, who went forth with victorious garlands too early wreathed about our brows, have to come home and put ashes upon our heads, how must it have been with them? how continually must it have been a seeing of the better only with a greater guilt to choose the worse! Surely the confession of the Jewish Pharisee that was zealous for the law and for righteousness must have been the confession of unnumbered souls in all the world, wrung out from a deep heart-agony, from the sense of defeats repeating themselves with a sad uni-

---

36) has been often quoted. Men justly thank the Gods for the external commodities which they enjoy, but, he proceeds Virtutem nemo unquam acceptam Deo retulit. Nimirum rectè, propter virtutem enim jure laudamur, et in virtute rectè gloriamur. Quod non contingeret, si id donum à Deo, non a nobis haberemus.. *Nam quis, quod vir bonus esset, gratias Diis egit unquam?* At quod dives, quod honoratus, quod incolumis. Jovemque Optimum Maximum ob eas res appellant, non quod nos justos, temperantes, sapientes efficiat, sed quod salvos, incolumes, opulentos, copiosos.

formity, of ever deeper entanglement in the defilements of the flesh and of the world—"That which I do, I allow not; for what I would, that do I not; but what I hate, that do I....I delight in the law of God after the inward man; but I see another law in my members, warring against the law of my mind, and bringing me into captivity to the law of sin which is in my members. O wretched man that I am! who shall deliver me from the body of this death?"

Such voices, no doubt, did make themselves heard. For indeed we shall not err, if contemplating the times which went before the Incarnation, we affirm that there had been two cries which had long been going up into the ears of the Lord of Hosts—*two* cries, although one was far more distinct and articulate than the other. There was the voice of appointed prophets and seers, watchers on the mountains of Israel, waiting for a Sun of Righteousness, who, as they surely knew, should in his time scatter the world's gloom, and shed healing from his wings. There was their voice, who, knowing this, would yet out of a mighty sense of the present evil around them and within them, have fain hastened the time,—psalmist and prophet who exclaimed, "Oh that the salvation were given unto Israel out of Zion!" "Oh that thou wouldest rend the heavens and come down!" But there was another, a more confused cry, of multitudinous tones: it oftentimes knew not what its own accents meant; it was often rather a groan within the bosom of humanity, which asked not, and thought not of a listener, than a voice sent up unto heaven. It was a cry which only infinite wisdom and infinite love would have interpreted into that cry for heavenly help, which indeed at the heart it was; a cry needing infinite love to pardon all in it which made it rather a cry against God, than to Him. But that love it found. He who said long before, "I have seen, I have seen the affliction of my people," saw also the affliction of a world hopelessly out of the way, translated its confused voices into an appeal unto Himself, and sent forth his Son to be the Saviour of the lost.

And then, what not alone the Law could not do, in that it was weak through the flesh, but what all wisdom had been equally impotent to effect, for it underlay the same weakness, He did; what they could not give, he gave. For here we come back again to a point which I have pressed already, but which yet is so important, that I shall make no apology for pressing it once more, which is this,—that the prerogative of our Christian faith, the secret of its strength, is, that all which it has, and all which it offers, is laid up in a person. This is what has made *it* strong, while so much else has proved weak, that it has a Christ as its middle point—that it is not a circumference without a centre,—that it has not merely a deliverance, but a Deliverer,—not a redemption only, but a Redeemer as well. This is what makes it fit for wayfaring men; this is what makes *it* sun-light, and all else compared with it but as moon-light,—fair it may be, but cold and ineffectual; while here the light and the life are one; the Light is also the Life of men. Oh how great the difference between submitting ourselves to a complex of rules, and casting ourselves upon a beating heart; between accepting a system, and cleaving to a person. And how tenfold blessed the advantages of the last, if that person is such a One that there shall be nothing servile in the entire resignation of ourselves to be taught of Him, for He is the absolute Truth—nothing unmanly in the yielding of our whole being to be wholly moulded by Him, for that he is not merely the highest which humanity has reached, but the highest which it can reach —its intended and ideal perfection, at once its perfect image and superior Lord.

They felt this, that help must lie in a person, that only round a person souls would cluster,—those who, when they would fain make a final stand for the old beliefs of the world, and prove if these could not even now be quickened to dispute the world with the youthful Christian Church;—they felt, I say, this, who set about marshalling, not merely rival doctrines to the Christian, but rival benefactors to Christ. If *He* went about Judæa doing good, they also would point to sages of their own, who travelled on like errands to the furthest East. This is, no doubt, the meaning of that half-fabulous life of Apollonius, which just as Christianity was rising into notice and evident significance, made its appearance;—this the explanation of that revived interest in Pythagoras, which then found place. The votaries of the old religions felt that in this respect they must not come short of that which they would oppose; and rightly—however weak and flitting and unreal the phantoms which they conjured up to their help.

For, brethren, had we a system only, it would leave us just as weak as other systems have left their votaries. We should have to confess that we found in ours, as they in theirs, no adequate strength—that not merely now and then, and at ever rarer intervals, we were worsted in our conflict with the sin of our own hearts, but evermore. Our blessedness, and let us not miss that blessedness, is, that our treasures are treasured in a person, and are therefore inexhaustible—in one who *requires* nothing but what first He *gives*—who is not for one generation a present teacher and a living Lord, and then for all succeeding a past and a dead one, but who is present and living for all—as truly for us in this latter day, as for them who went up and down with him in the days of his flesh. Our strength and our blessedness is, that what we have to know is "the truth as it is in Jesus;" that what we have to learn is to "learn Christ;" that what we have to put on, is to "put on the Lord Jesus Christ" and the righteousness which is by Him.

LECTURE VII.

THE FOUNDER OF A KINGDOM.

HEBREWS XI. 10.

A city which hath foundations, whose builder and maker is God.

WE have seen the manner in which He who was "the Desire of all nations," met and satisfied the yearnings of men for an inward peacemaker, for one who, by the mighty magic of his word and Spirit, should change the tumult of man's soul into a great calm; who should heal the hurts which each man was conscious that he had inflicted upon himself; who should set each man free from the bondage to those lords many, his own lusts and inordinate affections, under whose cruel tyranny he had come. But besides these longings for harmony and health and freedom in the region of his own inner life, there are other longings and other desires which crave satisfaction. For each, besides being simply a man, is also a man among men: besides the sinful element which so perplexes his own inner life, in the relation of one part of it to the other, of the higher to the lower, which so threatens his true life with destruction, not from foreign, but from intestine, enemies—the same sinful element acting outwardly in himself, and in every other man, disturbs and perplexes his relation to them, and theirs to him. That which remains in himself, unsubdued, of evil, that which exists of the same in every other man, brings about a collision between two selfishnesses. "From whence"—in the wonderfully simple, yet profound language of Scripture, language applicable to the pettiest village brawl, and to the mightiest conflict that has ranged one half of the world against the other —"from whence come wars and fightings among you? come they not hence, even of the lusts that war in your members?" (Jam. iv. 1.)

At once the question has presented itself to every thoughtful man,—it eminently did so to the great spirits of antiquity,—Is the warfare of these encountering selfishnesses the necessary, the only condition of society? Is it our wisdom to acquiesce in it, satisfied if this evil will allow itself to be kept within certain bounds—to be so far restrained, that a society, a living together of men for social conveniences unattainable in their isolated state, becomes possible? And is society such a fellowship of men that have holden back, by mutual consent, so much of their selfishness and evil, as would render habitation within the same walls or in the same neighbourhood impossible, and would thus defeat them of the gains which they desired by this combination to attain?

There have never been wanting,—there were not wanting of old,—those who dared to avow this wolfish theory of society for their own—that is, as a theory: for no community of men has ever subsisted upon it; no sooner have they attempted to put it in practice, than, biting and devouring, they have presently been utterly consumed one of another. And they who even avowed it as a theory were few—a profligate sophist of the old or the new world, a Thrasymachus* or a Mandeville;† the exceptions and not the rule. For rather it was truly seen that the fellowship of man with man, so far from being an artificial product of his wants, something added on to his true humanity, that lay circular and complete in himself already,—something therefore which he might have foregone without any necessary imperfection,—is that rather which constitutes the very humanity itself—animals *herding*, men only *living*, together. It was seen that this fellowship is the sphere in which alone his true life, that which belongs to him as man, can unfold itself—‡in which alone he can reach, it is little to say, the perfection of his being, but without which he cannot be conceived otherwise than as a monster, such a monster as the world never saw. It was truly perceived of that other condition of absolute isolation, that, so far from being the state of nature, it is rather a state so unnatural that no man has ever perfectly reached it—the most absolute savage not having become an isolated unit, not having been able to strip himself bare of all moral relations—being at most able to act as though he had not, but never able to cease

---

* Plato's *Republic*. † *Fable of the Bees*.

‡ As is remarkably witnessed in the words, *civilized*, *civilization*. The civilized man, as contra-distinguished from the savage or utterly degenerate man, is essentially the *civis*, belongs to a *civitas*.

from having, these. And they understood therefore that not this tamed selfishness was the idea in which the state consisted, and on which it reposed, but that there was another to which every state and fellowship of men, as it deserved the name, as it would be any thing better than a pirate's deck or a robber's den, must be a nearer or more remote approximation: a condition in which men were holden together by invisible ties,—by sanctions which not the flesh, but the spirit owned to be binding,—by common rites,—by sanctities which men dared not neglect,—*by a god Terminus keeping the boundaries of fields,—by a dread of vengeance, not as the mere human recoil of outrage on the wrong doer, but as being itself divine,—a condition in which men have felt that they were one people, not so much in their common interests and common aims, or even in their common history and descent and language, as in the one tutelar Deity that overlooked their city, and to whom they had confided its keeping.

If it was so—if there was this sense existing in the hearts, showing itself in the acts, of men, that the relations between man and man rest on something out of sight, are spiritual relations, not those of force, or fraud, or convenience—that men do not huddle together as cattle, to keep themselves warm, nor band together as wild beasts, that they may hunt in company; that law is not a result of so much self-will which each man might have kept, yet for certain ad-

---

* Sophocles, *Antigone*, 450—160.

vantageous considerations throws into a common stock, but that rather there is a law of laws, anterior to, and constituting the ground of, each positive enactment— if men had any sense of this divine order, which they did not themselves constitute, but into which they entered; which to accept was good, which to deny and fight against was evil,—if they did thus believe in a kingdom of righteousness and truth, and that we were ordained for that, (in the words of the father of Roman philosophy, Nos ad justitiam esse natos,)—if there was any true feeling that those lusts and desires, so far from being the ground of the state, the cement which held it together, were rather the element of decay which was ever threatening its dissolution, and were to be denied as the violations of the humanity, not recognised as its essentials; then we have implicitly here the acknowledgment of, and the yearning after, the kingdom of God.* They who believed this,

---

* Thus Cicero (*De Legg.*, l 1, c. 7.) Universus hic mundus una civitas communis Deorum atque hominum existimanda. Cf. *De Fin.*, l 5, c. 23, and the glorious passage in Juvenal (*Sat.* 15, 131—158,) one of the noblest in antiquity on the fellowship of men with one another, as resting on their divine original. I may be excused for quoting a few lines·

                Separat hoc nos
A grege mutorum, atque ideò venerabile soli
Sortiti ingenium, divinorumque capaces,
Atque exercendis capiendisque artibus apti·
Sensum à cœlesti demissum traximus arce,
Cujus egent prona et terram spectantia. Mundi
Principio indulsit communis conditor illis
Tantùm animas, nobis animum quoque· mutuus ut nos

believed in "the city which hath foundations," in that only one which can have everlasting foundations, for it is the only one whose foundations are laid in perfect righteousness and perfect truth—the city "whose builder and maker is God," which Abraham looked for, and because he looked for, would take no portion in the cities of confusion round him, but dwelling in tents witnessed against them, and declared plainly that he sought a country—the city of which *we* already are made free, and which it was given to the latest seer of the New Covenant, ere the book was sealed, to behold in the spirit coming down from heaven in its final glory. (Rev. xxi. 2.)

And can we say that there were not such thoughts and expectations stirring in the hearts of men—that the idea of a perfect state, as well as of a perfect man, had not risen up before the eyes of them, the men of desire, the souls to which any spirit of higher divination was imparted? Were not the latest speculations of the wisest sage, those to which he fitly came after he had accomplished each other task, concerning this very thing? Nor needs it to press that derivation

> Affectus petere auxilium, et præstare juberet,
> Dispersos trahere in populum, migrare vetusto
> De nemore, et proavis habitatas linquere silvas,
> Ædificare domos, laribus conjungere nostris
> Tectum aliud, tutos vicino limine somnos
> Ut collata daret fiducia, protegere armis
> Lapsum, aut ingenti nutantem vulnere civem;
> Communi dare signa tubâ, defendier iisdem
> Turribus, atque unâ portarum clave teneri.

of *religion* which would make it the band and bond, which binding men to God, binds them also to one another; for it is a derivation at the least questionable;* and the fact, to which such an etymology would give only an additional proof, is unquestionable without it—I mean, that the invisible ties were those in which every state was acknowledged to consist, so

---

* Nitzsch (*Theol. Stud. u. Krit.* v. 1, p. 532) seeks elaborately to prove that, according to the genius of the Latin language, the only possible derivation of *religio* is Cicero's (*De Nat Deor.*, l. 2, c. 28.) Qui omnia, quæ ad cultum Deorum pertinerent, diligenter retractarent *et tanquam relegerent*, sunt dicti religiosi, ex relegendo. It will thus have for its first meaning, the conscientious anxiety and accuracy in the performances of the divine offices. The passage which best explains how the word obtains a wider meaning is this from Arnobius (*Adv. Gen.* l. 4, c. 30·) Non enim qui solicitè *relegit* et immaculatas hostias cædit ... numina consentiendus est colere, aut officia solus *religionis* implere. This etymology was called in question by Lactantius, who derives the word not from relegere, but religare, to which derivation allusion is made in the text. He says (*Inst. Div.*, l. 4, c. 24.) Hoc vinculo pietatis obstricti Deo et *religati* sumus, unde ipsa religio nomen accepit; et non ut Cicero interpretatus est, a relegendo. He has Lucretius on his side, to whose words he alludes:

arctis
Relligionum animos *nodis exsolvere* pergo.

Augustine, too, who at first had consented to Cicero's etymology, inclines at a later period (*Retract.*, l. 1, c. 13) in favour of the other. Freund (*Lat. Worterbuch*, s. v.) without expressing himself at all so strongly as Nitzsch has done in regard of the absolute inadmissibility of the other derivation, yet accepts as certainly preferable the Ciceronian.

that with their weakening it must grow weak, with their perishing it must perish; while to strengthen and to multiply these, was justly regarded as the noblest mission of its noblest sons. What if here too heathendom had but the negative preparation, and Judaism the positive? what if the Jew could point to a state which did realize, though through his own sin most inadequately, this kingdom in its unripe and early beginnings, and if he was upheld by the sure word of prophecy, that one day the King of this kingdom should be revealed, and should reign in righteousness; while for the heathen they were for the most part dreams to which he could impart no reality, realities which tarried infinitely farther behind the idea which they professed to embody—this was only according to the distribution, in God's manifold wisdom, of their several parts to Jew and Gentile, in the preparation for Christ's coming; to the one being already given the stamina and rudiments of that which afterwards should unfold itself more fully, to the other being given little more than the expectation and the want—yet both so conspiring to prepare the way for his appearing.

This want and this expectation Christ came to satisfy; for He came not merely to awaken a religious sentiment in the minds and hearts of his disciples, or to declare to them certain doctrines of which before they were ignorant; but to found a kingdom, as He Himself declared from the first; as St. John, the herald of His coming, had declared before Him; "The kingdom of God is at hand;" "The kingdom of God is among you." For this term, "kingdom of God," we must not impoverish as though it were merely a convenient abstraction to express the sum total of the religious sentiments, opinions, feelings, actions of his disciples. But this kingdom, as it is *a kingdom*, points to a visible fellowship, and the embodiment therein of a number of persons, constituting an organic whole, owning a single head. And as it is a kingdom *of God*, it declares God to be its author and its founder; it declares itself to be lifted above the caprice of men, neither having been made, nor yet being to be marred, by them; which they indeed may deny, but which cannot deny itself, nor by their denial be annulled.

The practical Roman saw as much as the natural man could see of this in a moment—that the question at issue between Christ and the world was not a question of one notion and another, but of one kingdom and another; and seeing, he came at once to the point, "Art Thou a king then?" And that empire which tolerated all other religions, would have tolerated the Christian, instead of engaging in a death-struggle with it, to strangle or be strangled by it, but that it instinctively felt that this, however its first seat and home might seem to be in the hearts of men, yet could not remain there, but would demand an outward expression for itself—must go forth into the world, and conquer a dominion of its own—a dominion which would leave no room in the world for another fabric of force and fraud; for it was *his* dominion who, sitting on his throne, should scatter away all evil with his eyes; who had said in a thousand ways, "All the horns of the ungodly will I break, but the horns of the righteous shall be exalted."

It is quite true that this kingdom, in the men who at any time compose it, may misunderstand and mistake itself, even as it has often done. There are times when it caricatures itself into a popedom, when knowing rightly that it ought to have a real and outward existence, yet it will not believe that it has this, or is a kingdom at all, unless it can outdo the kingdoms of the world on their own ground, and in their own fashion; unless it can be a kingdom like unto them, and greater than they in their kind of power and magnificence and glory. It is quite true that times arrive when it cannot believe in its own oneness, unless it can see that oneness represented to it in a visible Head. Yet this only proves that times may arrive, when, through the sin of its members, its consciousness of itself as God's Church grows weak, when it has only too much lost hold of the great truths on which it was founded, and which it was intended to proclaim; and having done so, does, by an inevitable necessity, act over again the unfaithful request of the children of Israel, when they desired a king to go forth with *their* armies, as one went forth with the armies of the nations, and would not believe, unless they could thus see him there, that "the shout of a King was among them." (1 Sam. viii.) And the reaction from this error must not make us to count that this kingdom can only be spiritual when it ceases to be real, when retiring into the hearts of men, and dwelling there apart, it claims no more the world for its possession, and each region and province of man's actual life for its own.

But to return. This kingdom, as it was a consummation of all that men had ever hoped in the way of a kingdom of righteousness, as it was a protest and witness against the evil into which each kingdom of the world, each fairest polity of man's founding, was ever presently degenerating, was not all. Christ came to give more than this; to give not merely a kingdom of truth for some men, but for every man; to found a fellowship which should be for men as men, which should leave out none, which should call no man common or unclean. This indeed was new, not merely in fact, but even in theory; for it had hardly risen over the horizon of their minds who stood in wisdom and in goodness upon the mountain-summits of the world. The Greek ever left out the barbarian, the freeman, the slave, the philosopher, the simple. The highest culture of some was ever built upon the sacrifice of others; they were pitilessly used up in the process. So far from men themselves producing the thought of a universal spiritual fellowship, even after it was given, they were long in making it their own. Thus Celsus mocks at the madness of the Gospel, (for so to him it showed,)—adduces as enough to convince its author of a shallow impracticable enthusiasm, that he should have proposed such a dream as this, that Greeks, and Barbarians, and Lybians, and all men to the ends of the earth, should be united in the reception of one and the same doctrine.

Nor can we greatly wonder: the sense of diversity

was so strong, that which was differencing men was so mighty, the intellectual superiority of the Greek over the Barbarian was so immense, that we cannot be so much surprised to find one thus mocking at the scheme for bringing all men into one, as the shallow dream of an enthusiast's brain. Such it must have seemed to him, who had not insight enough to perceive that the real ground of separation between men lay, not in natural distinctions of race, of customs, of language, but in different objects of worship, in the gods many of polytheism. These were what kept men apart, and rendered their union and communion impossible. They were not at one in the highest matter of their lives: how should they be in the lower? And if this *was* the ground of division, then the walls of partition might yet be thrown down, would indeed fall away of their own selves, when once there was revealed to faith one God and Father *of* all,—one Christ, a common object of love and adoration *for* all, in whom the affections of all might centre,—one Spirit, effectually working *in* all. Then indeed the Babel mischief, the confusion of spirits, whereof the confusion of tongues was only the outward sign, would cease; even as for one prophetic moment on the day of Pentecost, in the gift of tongues, it *had* ceased,* in sign that the Church

---

* Grotius Pœna linguarum dispersit homines (Gen. xi.,) donum linguarum dispersos in unum populum recollegit. In the Persian religion there was the expectation of a day coming when with the abolition of all evil, ἕνα βίον καὶ μίαν πολιτείαν ἀνθρώπων μακαρίων καὶ ὁμογλώσσων ἁπάντων γενέσθαι. (Plutarch, De Is. et Osir., c. 47.)

which that day was founded was for all nations and tongues and tribes. The distinctions between men were indeed infinite, reaching far down into the deeps of their being, yet not to that being's centre; and in the regeneration, in that mighty act of God's, which does not obliterate distinctions, but reconciles them in a higher unity, they might all, so far as they were elements of separation, be annulled. When to all alike it was permitted to say, "We are Christ's, and Christ is God's," then the secret of a fellowship was imparted, which should include all nations, in which there should be neither wise nor simple, Greek nor barbarian, bond nor free, but Christ should be all in all.

Of all this the world had, beforehand, scarcely the faintest intimations—the poorest parodies. Yet such parodies perchance there were; and we may be allowed to trace dim indistinct yearnings even for this, for the breaking down of the middle wall of partition, for the making of twain one new man. Thus there were already in the centuries anterior to our Lord meeting-places for the Greek and Jew. Remarkable in this respect was the existence of such a city as Alexandria, where the Jew and Greek met, and sought to exchange to mutual profit the most precious commodities each of his own intellectual and spiritual land, the Jew making himself acquainted with Greek culture, the Old Testament Scriptures becoming accessible to Greek readers. Yet still these meetings were intellectual only: no true blending did or could have followed from them. It is the fire of charity which must melt, ere there can be any real moulding into one. In vain had the whole East and West jostled violently together; they had hardly mingled any more for this. A certain surface civilization had ensued, which was common to both; but hearts waited for more prevailing bands than those which even an Alexander could weave, ere they would knit themselves together in one. And as far as any practical realization of the hopes which at any time the world cherished from this it now was further off than ever. The iron kingdom, the fourth beast, dreadful and terrible and strong exceedingly, had broken all other, and was stamping the residue under its feet; until it seemed now as if brutal force was all that remained, or that had a meaning any more, and as if the world only could be prevented from falling into pieces by those links and bands of iron, which were forged around it.

But how hateful such a world was to live in, how intense a loathing it inspired in each nobler spirit, the works of Tacitus seemed preserved to us especially to tell. For surely this is the key-note of them, the predominant thought,—this indignation and scorn, which all words, even his own, seem weak to him to utter, at the sight of the high places of the earth, the seats of blessing, the thrones of beneficent power, occupied by the meanest and basest of their kind,—till we feel, as we read, this conviction to have been branded as with burning iron on his soul, that it were better ten thousand times not to be, than to witness the things which he has witnessed, and to bear the things which he has borne.* Nor on his soul only was the conviction branded, but on those, we cannot doubt, of multitudes besides, whose more dumb agony found only its adequate expression in his words.

But these failures, these shipwrecks of the world's hopes, these issues of things so different from the promise with which they started, this agony, this despair, they were not for nothing. They were part of that severe discipline of love to which the world was being submitted: they helped to constitute that fulness of time in which the Son of God should come, and coming, find acceptance. Not till the world's pride and self-confidence were thoroughly broken, would it have been prepared to humble itself under his cross, would it have accepted that cross for the standard round which it rallied. For the breaking of this pride two great experiments had been going forward at the same time, had run through, as they gave a moral meaning to, all the anterior history of the world— experiments which needed both to be thoroughly and fairly tried. Of the Jewish it concerns us not here to speak at large: it was this, if righteousness could come by the law; if there was a law which could give life— an external rule of conduct, even though of divine appointment, which could sanctify and save—if there was not a weakness and falseness in man, which would defeat and frustrate it all. This was most needful, and only through the process of this could a Saul ever have been transformed into a Paul.

* Agricola, c. 2, 3, 45.

But the other, which may not seem to us so directly of God's ordaining, yet was so indeed: for it was of its very essence that He should not mingle in it so far, should seem to have less to do with it;—that those to whom it was given to try it out should walk in their own ways, and be left to their own resources. The experiment was this, whether man could unfold his own well-being out of himself—whether art or philosophy or institutions could give it to him; whether in any of these he could truly find himself and the good for which he was made. And of this experiment we cannot say that it was unfairly tried, or imperfectly worked out. All which was required for its success was there, and had been given in largest measure. God had raised up men of the most glorious gifts, of the mightiest strength of will; and surely had deliverance lain in aught which man could unfold, by his own strength, out of his own being, the world had been indeed redeemed, and had found the fountain of salvation in itself.

But fair and flattering, full of the promise of success, as the results showed oftentimes for a while, there was ever a worm at the root of this glory of the world. The moment of highest perfection was evermore the moment of commencing decay. How deeply tragic, though in different ways, the histories of the Greek and Roman world! how had the paths of glory led one and the other, though by diverse ways, to the grave of all their moral and spiritual independence; the intellectual conquests of the one and the worldly triumphs of the other, however diverse, yet having agreed in this, that they alike left the victors enslaved, degraded, and debased—the Greek a scorn to the Roman,* and the Roman to himself. And now the fresh creative energy of an earlier time had all departed and disappeared: and that springing hope, which contemplated its objects, if not as attained, yet at least as attainable, was no more. The world had outlived itself and its attractions — †saddest of all, had outlived even its hopes; the very springs of those hopes seemed to be dried up for ever. Yet was not this all without its purpose and its blessing. It was something to be shut in to the one remedy, all other devices having failed,—to have come thus to the husks; for this alone would have sent back the prodigal of heathenism to claim anew his share in the rich provision of his father's house. This was the emptiness, of which Christ's coming should be the answering fulness. In all this agony, this mighty yearning of souls, the gates of the world were being made high and lifted up, that the King of Glory might come in. Only in such an utter despair, in such a sense of decrepitude, of death already begun, would the world have welcomed aright the Prince of Life, who came to make all things young, and out of the wreck and fragments of an old and decaying world, to build up a fairer and a new.

* See such passages as Cicero *Pro Flacco*, c. 4; Juvenal, *Sat.* 3, 58—113, 10, 174.

† Augustine: Mundus tantâ rerum labe contritus, ut etiam speciem seductionis amiserit.

And such he built up indeed. "They went astray in the wilderness out of the way, and found no city to dwell in: hungry and thirsty, their soul fainted in them. So they cried unto the Lord in their trouble, and he delivered them from their distress. He led them forth by the right way, that they might go to a city of habitation." And this city of habitation, this kingdom, was all which they *had* asked for, or could ask. It was a *free* fellowship, the constraining bands of it being bands of love and not of force; and He that founded it fulfilling the idea of the true spiritual conqueror of men, who should subdue all hearts not by force or by flattery, but by the mighty magic of love—as some of old had been reaching out after this, when they dreamed of Osiris, that he went forth to conquer the world not with chariots and with horses, but with music; for so had they felt that the power which truly wins must be a spiritual one, an appeal to the latent harmonies in every man—that in a kingdom of heaven law must be swallowed up in love,— not repealed, but glorified and transfigured, its hard outline scarcely visible any more in the blaze of light with which it is surrounded.

It was a *large* fellowship—larger than the largest which the heart of man had conceived; for it should leave out none, it should trample upon none: He that was its Head should "be favourable to the simple and needy, and preserve the souls of the poor." Nay, it should be larger than this, for it should embrace heaven and earth. That whereof the great Italian sage had caught a glimpse, that φιλια,* that amity or reconciliation of all things, whether they be things in heaven or things on earth, had found its fulfilment. Henceforward heaven and earth, angels and men, constituted one kingdom, "his body, the fulness of Him that filleth all in all."

It was a *righteous* fellowship. If aught of unrighteousness was *within* it, it was there only as a contradiction to the law of that kingdom, and presently to be separated off; even as all of unrighteous that was *against* it was in due time to be taken out of the way; for it in its weakness was yet stronger than the strongest. It was only weak as the staff of Moses was weak; which being one, and an instrument of peace, did yet break in shivers all weapons of war, the ten thousand spears of Pharaoh and his armies.

And being this righteous kingdom it was also an *eternal* kingdom, having in it no seeds of decay, a kingdom not to be moved, which should endure as long as the sun and moon endureth, of the increase of which there should be no end.

To this city, brethren, ye are come—the city of which such glorious things are spoken, the city of our God. Not only prophet and king of Israel, but sage and seer of every land, have desired to see the things which we see, and have not seen them—so truly are

---

* Porphyrius (*De Vitâ Pythag*.) Φιλιαν (κατέδειξε) πάντων πρὸς ἅπαντας, ειτε Θεῶν πρὸς ἀνθρωπους—ειτε δογμάτων πρὸς ἀλληλα—ειτε ἀνθρωπων πρὸς αλληλους. See Baur's *Apollonius von Tyana und Christus*, p. 194.

they the best things which man can conceive, or God can give. And what do they require of us but a walk corresponding? Citizens of no mean city, whose citizenship is in heaven, we must not show ourselves unworthy of so high an honour. It is the very aggravation of the sinner's sin that he deals frowardly in the land of uprightness; and because he does so it is declared that he shall not see the majesty of the Lord. (Isai. xxvi. 10.) We baptized men are in this "land of uprightness," in this kingdom of the truth. For it is not that we *shall* come, but in the sure word of Scripture, we *are* come to Mount Zion, the city of the living God, the heavenly Jerusalem, and to all the glorious company which is there.

And surely the apostle's argument which he drew from this ought to stand strong for us, his exhortation to find place in our hearts; "Wherefore we receiving a kingdom which cannot be moved, let us have grace, whereby we may serve God acceptably with reverence and godly fear." (Heb. xii. 28.)

LECTURE VIII.

CONCLUDING LECTURE.

1 THESSALONIANS V. 21.

Prove all things; hold fast that which is good.

It needs not, I trust, to remind you, brethren, that in these lectures which are now concluding, we have been engaged in the seeking to discern the prophecy of Christianity, which has run through all history. I have traced in them, so far as under the conditions and limitations of such discourses I might, the manner in which the old world was in many ways blindly struggling to be that better thing which yet it never could truly be, except by the free grace and gift of God,—to come to that new birth, which yet it could not reach, until power for this mighty change was given it from on high. We have asked ourselves whether we could not discern an evident tending of men's thoughts and feelings and desires in one direction, and that direction the cross of Christ, a great spiritual under-current, which has been strongly and constantly setting that way; so that his bringing forth of his kingdom into open manifestation, if in one sense a beginning, was in another, and in as true a sense, a crowning end.

And it has cohered intimately with the purpose of these lectures, which, according to the purpose of their founder, should assume more or less of a *defensive* character, to urge the apology for our Christian faith which is here. It has been to me an argument for the truth and dignity of his mission who was its author, to find that in *Him* all fulness dwelt, all lines concentred, all hopes of the world were accomplished. For surely the King of Glory shows to us more glorious yet, when we are able to contemplate Him not merely as the Prophet and Priest and King of the Covenant, but as the satisfier of vaguer, though not less real, aspirations, of more undefined longings, of more wide-spread hopes—when looking at *Him*, we take note, with the inspired seer, that on his head are *many* crowns,—and, looking at his *doctrine*, that not Israel only, but the isles also had *waited* for his law.

This my subject I have now brought to a close; or at least I dare not, at this latest moment, open it upon another side. I may perhaps more profitably dedicate the present opportunity to the considering of some ways in which our recognition of the intimate relation between all that has gone before and all that now is, between the hopes of the past and the fulfilments of the present, may practically and usefully influence our study of antiquity. For indeed a Christian view of the ancient world, which shall neither despise it, because it is not what it could not be, itself Christian, because its grains of finer gold, of purer ore, are mixed with so much impure and debasing; nor yet on the other hand to glorify it, as though its imperfect anticipations of the truth were as good as, or rendered superfluous, the manifestation of the perfect image of God in his Son, or its faint streaks of light were as truly an illumination as the day-spring from on high; this true it is most profitable for us that we should win. It may preserve us from extremes and exaggerations on either hand, into which we are in danger of running. It may preserve us, too, from a listless, careless, unfruitful study of that which, unless we neglect the plain duties that lie before us, must form one of the chief occupations of several, the most precious and least recoverable years of our lives,—years in which our minds are to be built up, if built up at all; in which, more than in any other, our characters are being moulded, and are receiving that impress which they shall bear to the end.

The exaggerations to which I allude are twofold. There is that, first, against which one is almost unwilling to say a word, springing as it so often does, out of a state of mind in which there is so much that is admirable,—giving witness for a moral earnestness, without which men would have been scarcely tempted to it; I mean the exaggeration of those, who in a deep devotion to the truth, as it is a truth in Christ Jesus, count themselves bound by their allegiance to Him, by his Name which they bear, his doctrine which they have learned, his Spirit which they have received, to take up a hostile attitude to every thing, not distinctly and avowedly Christian, as though any other bearing were a treason to his cause—a betrayal of his exclusive right to the authorship of all the good which is in the world. In this temper we may dwell only on the guilt and misery and defilements, the wounds and bruises and hurts, of the heathen world; or if aught better is brought under our eye, we may look askant and suspiciously upon it, as though all recognition of it were disparagement of something better. And so we may come to regard the fairest deeds of unbaptized men as only more showy sins. We may have a short but decisive formula with which to dismiss them: we may say, These deeds were not of faith, and therefore they could not please God. The men that wrought them knew not Christ, and therefore their work was worthless—hay, straw, and stubble, to be utterly burned up in the day of the trial of every man's work.

Yet is it in truth a violation of the law of conscience, to use so sweeping a language as this. Our allegiance to Christ as the one fountain of light and l fe, demands that we affirm none to be good but Him —no goodness but that which has proceeded from Him: but it does not demand that we deny goodness, because of the place where we find it—because we find it, a garden-tree in the wilderness; but rather that we claim it for Him, who was its true source and author, and whom it would its·f have gladly owned as such, if, belonging to a happier time, it could have known Him. We do not make much of a light of nature, when we allow a righteousness in those, to whom in the days of their flesh the Gospel had not come; we only affirm that the Word, though He had not yet dwelt among us, yet being the light which

CONCLUDING LECTURE. 301

lighteth every man that cometh into the world, had lighted them. Some glimpses of his beams gilded their countenances, and gave to them whatever brightness they wore; and in recognising this brightness, whatsoever it was, we are giving honour to Him, and not to them; glorifying the grace of God, and not the powers of man.

I can well understand how in the earnestness and exclusiveness of a first love to Christ, and to that word of Holy Scripture which directly testifies of Him, all teaching of all other books, in which is no explicit mention of his name, should appear valueless to us; and all else taste flat and dull, because we taste not there the sweetness of that One Name which is sweeter than all. Yet were it good for us to see that, without going back one jot from this entire devotedness to the Lord of our life, which every where looks for Him, and finds every thing savourless without him—a devotedness too precious to be foregone, and for which no other gains would compensate—that without, I say, going back from this, we might yet enlarge the sphere of our Christian sympathies, and take a wider range of objects within it. To this end let us learn to cultivate a finer spiritual ear, and one which shall be more quick to catch the fainter echoes and whispers of his name, which are borne to us from other fields than those of Scripture; let us learn to look for Him even where *they* thought not and could not have thought directly of Him, whose pages we may hold in our hand. Let us aim to take keener note of the manner in which all things pointed to Him, all things were asking for Him—the world passing judgment on itself,* and out of its own lips at once condemning itself and demanding its Redeemer,† demanding him in frequent acknowledgments of the vanity of all things, in confessions of its own incurable evils,‡ in voices of deepest sadness and despair,—as theirs who by word or solemn rite declared plainly that it was better for man never to have been born than to live; or, if he lived, that then the gods had no better boon for him than an early death—§ and

---

* Cicero (*Tusc. Quæst.*, l. 2, c. 22) In quo viro erit perfecta sapientia, (*quem adhuc nos quidem videmus neminem sed philosophorum sententiis*, qualis futurus sit, *si modo aliquando fuerit*, exponitur,) is igitur, &c. Compare Theognis, 615, Οὐδένα παμπήδην ἀγαθὸν καὶ μέτριον ἄνδρα τὸν νῦν ἀνθρώπων ἠέλιος καθορᾷ.—Even supposing a man were to reach the highest goodness, this could only be, as was confessed, through a long process of anterior mistake and error. he must be as a diamond which is polished in its own dust. Seneca (*De Clement*, l. 1, c 6.) Etiam si quis tam bene purgavit animum, ut nihil obturbare eum amplius possit aut fallere, ad innocentiam tamen peccando pervenit.

† Seneca (*Ep.* 52.) Nemo per se satis valet ut emergat. *oportet manum aliquis porrigat*, aliquis educat

‡ Thucydides, l. 3. c 45, Seneca, *De Irâ*, l. 2, c. 8.

§ Compare the remarkable fragment of Euripides, quoted in the original by Clemens of Alexandria (*Strom.*, l 3, c. 3,) and in a Latin translation by Cicero, (*Tusc Disp*, l 1, c. 48.)

Ἔδει γὰρ ἡμᾶς, σύλλογον ποιουμένους,
Τὸν φύντα θρηνεῖν, εἰς ὅσ' ἔρχεται κακά·
Τὸν δ' αὖ θανόντα καὶ πόνων πεπαυμένον
Χαίροντας, εὐφημοῦντας ἐκπέμπειν δόμων.

Compare Herodotus, l 5 c 4 Pliny, *H N*, l. 7, c. 1 and

this not in the Christian sense of death as a passage into life, but only as the harbour from the world's wo, the anodyne of the world's pains.

Let us take note, too, of the manner in which the language of philosopher and of poet seems often marvellously overruled to have a deeper significance, to bear the burden of a larger and completer thought, than it is possible that they who uttered it could have had in their mind, or could have attached to their words. As for instance, when it is said* that the highest righteousness must be approved in extremest trial, that if we would know certainly whether one be indeed a lover of the good, he must be set in those conditions, in which to abide by the good shall bring upon him every outward calamity, shame and loss and scorn and torture and death, all which he might have avoided would he ever so little have gone back from that good; the righteousness which he chooses must be stripped utterly bare of every ornament, yea, must seem to the world as the extremest unrighteousness, and then only it will be seen whether he loves it for its own sake—to us Christians shall not this possible case at once present itself as an actual one?

---

c. 41. Si verum facere judicium volumus, ac repudiatâ omni fortunæ ambitione decernere, *mortalium nemo est felix*, Pindar, *Pyth*, 8, 131.

* By Plato (*De Repub.* l 2, c. 4, 5) I have not seen it noted how the reverse of the picture, the perfectly unrighteous man, whom Plato draws, is almost as remarkable a prophecy in its kind, of Antichrist, and of the deceitful glory which will surround him.

Shall we not catch here, as many indeed *have* caught,* a prophetic word about the cross, and about Him who even in this way was proved, by ignominy and scorn and suffering and death, whether He would love the good and hate the evil; and who did by a distinct act of his will choose for his portion that righteousness to which all these were linked, and which could only lead Him by roughest paths to the shamefullest and bitterest end? Or when another expresses his conviction that a sacred Spirit dwells with man, yea, not *with* him only but *in* him, a Spirit which is not his own, however freely it converses with him, a Spirit which treats him as he treats it,† shall we refuse to acknowledge here a word which was reaching out after that Spirit, the Spirit of the Father and the Son, which, dwelling in God, does also dwell in sanctified souls; which, if we grieve, will grieve us, which, if we continue to provoke, will utterly forsake us? And in many such ways as these we may disentangle

---

* Grotius (*De Verit. Rel. Christ.*, l. 4, c. 12:) Et verò lætius esse honestum, quoties magno sibi constat sapientissimi ipsorum dixere. Plato, *De Republica* 11 *quasi præscius*, ait, ut verè justus exhibeatur, opus esse ut virtus ejus omnibus ornamentis spolietur, ita ut ille habeatur ab aliis pro scelesto, illudatur, suspendatur denique. Et certè summæ patientiæ exemplum ut exstaret, aliter obtineri non poterat.

† Seneca (*Epist.* 41:) Sacer intra nos spiritus sedet, malorum bonorumque nostrorum observator et custos, hic prout à nobis tractatus est, ita nos ipse tractat...Quemadmodum radii solis contingunt quidem terram, sed ibi sunt unde mittuntur, sic animus magnus et sacer, et in hoc demissus ut propius divina nossemus, conversatur quidem nobiscum, sed hæret origini suæ.

the golden threads of a finer woof than its own, which were running through the whole tissue which the ancient world was weaving for itself; we may delightedly observe how the cross of Christ was as an invisible magnet, drawing hearts to itself by a mighty, though secret, attraction, in ages long before it was openly lifted up, an ensign for the nations.

Let us remember too how little the world could have done without these preparations which sometimes we are tempted to despise. Difficult as was the world's reception of the word, and its transition to the faith, of Christ, how much more difficult would it have been if the way had not been thus prepared. What another thing would it have been, if the word about the Son of God, where it first was delivered, besides strengthening and purifying and enlarging, had needed also to create, the very foundations of religious belief and ethical science on which it rested; if it had been needful for it to be not merely the seed, but the soil, —having first to form the very ground in which it should itself afterwards find room and depth to germinate. If instead of finding a language ready at hand which it could appropriate, and needed only thus to rescue for itself,* if, instead of this, all nobler words and

---

* Thus not merely the more obvious, but the more recondite rites of heathenism, have been made to set forth far better things than themselves. For example, the mysteries yield the substratum of language and imagery and allusion to each word of the following noble passage, in which Clement (*Cohort. ad Gent.*, c 12,) is exhorting the Gentiles to become μύσται of Christ ’Ω τωι ἁγιων ὡς αληθως μυστηριωι ω φωτος ανη-

signs, all which spoke of worship, of religion, of sanctity, of initiation, of atonement, of piety, had been absent from it, how different the case would have been. And with the absence of the *things*, there would also have been inevitably the absence of the *words* which are their correlatives; since language is no more than thought and feeling permanently fixing and embodying themselves; it is but as the pillars of Hercules, to mark how far the conquests of spirit have advanced.

No one can have thoughtfully perused the modern records of missionary labour among savage tribes, and the almost insurmountable hinderances opposed to the reception of the Gospel by languages, if they deserve the name, stripped of each nobler and deeper element,—languages in which is no speculation, no distinction, no hoarded thought, no embodied morality, no unconscious wisdom,—no terms, in short, but for the barest needs or the vilest doings* of the animal man, without

ρατου. δᾳδουχουμαι, τινς ουρανους και τον Θεον εποπτευσας· ἁγιος γινομαι, μυουμενος· ἱεροφαντει δε ὁ Κυριος, και τον μυττη σφραγιζεται, φωταγωγων και παρατιθεται τω Πατρι τον πεπιστευκοτα, αιωσι τηρουμενον. Ταυτα των εμων μυστηριων τα βακχευματα· ει βουλει, και συ μυου, και χορευσεις μετ' αγγελων αμφι τον αγεννητον και ανωλεθρον και μονον οντως Θεον, συνυμνουντος ἡμιν του Θεου Λογου.

* Languages like one of the North-American Indian, which possesses a word for a tomahawk, but none for God; or that of a tribe in Australia, which with the same deficiency, has yet a word to describe the process by which an unborn child may be destroyed in its mother's womb. On all this subject of language rising and falling with the rise and fall of people's moral and spiritual life, and on the speech of savages as not being the primal rudiments, but the ultimate wreck, of a language, there is much of deep interest in De Maistre's *Soirées de St. Petersbourg, Deux. Entret.*

feeling that a miserable necessity is imposed on the Truth when it must weave for itself the very garments in which it shall array itself, and is in danger of losing its treasures in the very attempt to communicate them,—so wretched are the only channels through which it can convey them. And considering this, he will esteem it to have been an infinite mercy, yea a very primal necessity, that the Truth, where it uttered itself in that which should be its normal utterance for all future ages of the Church, where it first took body and shape, should have found, as regarded language, vessels ready prepared for its new wine, and only waiting for a higher consecration,—an inheritance which it had but to make its own, entering upon it, as the children of Israel entered upon vineyards which they had not planted, and wells which they had not digged, and houses which they had not built, of which yet they became the rightful possessors from henceforth.

Nor can we doubt that by *that*, which we with our fuller knowledge, our larger grace, are inclined to slight, many were preserved from defilements, in which otherwise they had been inevitably entangled. This salt may have been powerless to give the savour of life to that with which it came in contact; but that progress of corruption, that dissolution of social and personal life, which it was unable ultimately to arrest, it yet retarded for a time.* It preserved many a man

---

* The consideration of the Greek philosophy as a προπαιδεια for the reception of the absolute Christian truth, is a more recurring one, and takes a more prominent place, in the writings of the later Clement, than perhaps in those of any other

for something better than itself, and in not a few cases of which we have distinct record, handed over in due time its votaries to the school of Christ. To mention teacher of the early Church. Thus he speaks of it in one place as a step to something higher (ὑποβάθραν οὖσαν τῆς κατα Χριστὸν φιλοσοφιας, *Strom.*, l. 6, c. 8) Again, as a preparatory discipline, and ordained to be such by the providence of God: (ἐκ τῆς θειας προνοιας δεδόσθαι, προπαιδευουσαν εἰς τῆν διὰ Χριστου τελειωσιν, *Strom* , l. 6, c. 17,) and so again as an anterior culture of the soil of man's heart for receiving the seed of life: προαθαιρει ναι προεθιζει την ψυχην εἰς παραδοχην πιστεως, (*Strom.* l. 7, c. 3.) It would seem from more passages than one in his writings, that he felt it needful to defend himself for the so high appreciation in which he held the philosophy of Greece, ἥν τινες διαβεβληκασιν, ἀληθειας οὖσαν εικονα ἐναργη θειαν δωρεα ν Ἕλλησι δεδομενην. There were those who warned against its attractions, as being those of the "strange woman" of Prov. v. 3—8, "whose lips drop as a honeycomb, and her mouth is smoother than oil." (*Strom.*, l. 1, c. 5) The heathen philosophers were according to them the "thieves and robbers" which " came before" Him who was the true Shepherd of men (*Strom.*, l. 1, c 17.) Tertullian may be taken as a representative of the more intolerant view (*Apol.*, c. 46) Quid simile Philosophus et Christianus ? Græciæ discipulus et cœli ? famæ negotiator et salutis ? verborum, et factorum operator ..interpolator erroris, et integrator veritatis ? furator ejus et custos ? Whatever exaggeration there *is* in the language of Clement, yet this I think is certain, that his strong expressions have their rise in a deep and solemn feeling, that nothing anywhere which is good, by which men have been kept back from any evil, or prepared to any good, but must be traced up to God He dared not trace it to any other, thus speaking of this very thing his words are, παντων μεν γαρ αἰτιος των καλων ὁ Θεός. (*Strom.*, l 1, c. 5) And that he did not make the difference between the two a mere question of degree is plain from such expres-

but a single example. Few who have once read, will forget the manner in which the falling in with the *Hortensius** of Cicero kindled the young Augustine, and inflamed him with a passionate love of wisdom. What a moment it was in his life when he lighted on that treatise, how greatly did it serve to arrest him in that downward career which he was then too rapidly treading, to hinder him from utterly laying waste his moral life! How did it set him to the seeking for goodly pearls, though the goodliest of all, the pearl of great price, he was not yet to find! He himself in after years describes all this, with thankful ascriptions of praise to the guiding hand of his God, and telling how that book, though it did not and could not bring him into the inmost sanctuary of the faith, yet was to him in the truest sense a porch to that auguster temple not made with hands, into which at a later

---

sions as these. Χωρίζεται ἡ ‘Ελληνικὴ ἀλήθεια τῆς καθ᾿ ἡμᾶς εἰ καὶ τοῦ αὐτοῦ μετείληφεν ὀνόματος, καὶ μεγέθει γνώσεως, καὶ ἀποδείξει κυριωτέρᾳ, καὶ θείᾳ δυνάμει · θεοδίδακτοι γὰρ ἡμεῖς (*Strom.*, l. 1, c. 20.) That other was the wild olive which had need, ere it bore any nobler fruit, of insertion upon the good (*Strom.*, l. 6, c. 15,) words which may suggest a comparison with that most eloquent passage at the end of the first book of Theodoret, *De Græc. Affect. Curat.* And those remarkable words have been often quoted in which Clement likens heretics and founders of human systems to the rabble rout that tore the body of Pentheus limb from limb: *so they* tore the truth, and then each boasted of the fragment in his hands as though it were the whole (ἑκάστη ὅπερ ἔλαχεν, ὡς πᾶσαν αὐχεῖ τὴν ἀλήθειαν.)

* Otherwise called *De Philosophiâ.* It has been lost, all but a few unimportant fragments. The subject was the superiority of philosophy to eloquence.

day he should be privileged to enter; and did at once hand him over to the searching of the Scriptures, though as yet his eyes were holden, and he found not in them till a later day their hid treasures of wisdom and of knowledge.*

But I spoke of exaggerations *on either side* into which we were liable to fall. To take the very oppo-

---

* *Conf.*, l. 3, c. 4: Usitato jam discendi ordine perveneram in librum quemdam cujusdam Ciceronis, cujus linguam ferè omnes mirantur, pectus non ita. Sed liber ille ipsius exhortationem continet ad philosophiam, et vocatur *Hortensius*. Ille verò liber mutavit affectum meum,...et vota ac desideria mea fecit alia. Viluit mihi repentè omnis vana spes, et immortalitatem sapientiæ concupiscebam æstu cordis incredibili.

He has very interesting acknowledgments (*Conf.*, l. 7, c. 9, 20, 21) of the effect which the Platonist books exerted upon him at the great crisis of his life that went before his conversion,—what he found in them, and what he did not find,—where they helped, and where rather they hindered him, concluding with this declaration of the things which he had looked for there in vain. Hoc illæ litteræ non habent, Lacrymas Confessionis, Sacrificium tuum, Spiritum contribulatum, Cor contritum et humiliatum, Populi salutem, Sponsam, Civitatem, Arrham Spiritûs Sancti, Poculum pretii nostri. Nemo ibi cantat: Nonne Deo subdita erit anima mea? ab ipso enim salutare meum· etenim ipse Deus meus, et salutaris meus, susceptor meus, non movebor ampliùs. Nemo ibi audit vocantem. Venite ad me qui laboratis ...Et aliud est de silvestri cacumine videre patriam pacis, et iter ad eam non invenire, et frustra conari per invia, circùm obsidentibus et insidiantibus fugitivis desertoribus cum principe suo leone et dracone: et aliud tenere viam illuc ducentem, curâ cœlestis imperatoris munitam, ubi non latrocinantur qui cœlestem militiam deseruerunt, vitant enim eam sicut supplicium.

site extreme to this of painting the old world to ourselves in lines and colours of unredeemed blackness, we may dwell exclusively on the fairer side which it presents, shutting wilfully our eyes to each darker and more revolting spectacle which it displays. We may find in its art and its literature that which gratifies our taste, and out of a lack of any deeper moral wants, we may come to say with the poet, " Beauty is Truth, Truth Beauty," and where we find beauty and proportion and harmony, may be ready to pardon the absence of every thing beside; just as those Italian literati at the revival of learning, who preferred calling themselves brethren in Plato to brethren in Christ, to whom the groves of Academus were far more than the waters of Siloam, and the cultivation of taste than the promotion of holiness—men who so mourned over the vacant thrones of Olympus, that to them a heaven opened, with angels ascending and descending upon the Son of man, seemed but an insufficient compensation.

But such a nearer acquaintance with the world which was before and out of Christ, as these studies faithfully pursued must give us, will teach us that if there are sides on which heathen mythology stands related to, and has the recollection and intimation of, something higher than itself, there are also other sides upon which it lies under the influence of man's corruption, is itself the outgrowth of his foolish sin-darkened heart, with the impurities of its origin cleaving to it,—does itself help distinctly to mark his downward progress toward idolatry, and toward the losing of the Creator in the creature,—is often only the strangely distorted resemblance, never more than the faint prophecy, of the coming truth. And if so, we shall feel that to linger with *that* is ridiculous, whose only worth is that it hands on to something better than itself, and is capable of being translated into a nobler language than its own. So too we shall feel that if the ancient philosophy had glorious ethical precepts, yet were they but adumbrations of the truth, since they wanted, for the most part, that body and substance which action alone could give them; as is plain from unnumbered confessions and complaints on all sides heard, that the world's physicians had not healed themselves, much less their patients; as is plainer still in the colossal character which sin had assumed* at the time of Christ's appearing, till it sat as it were incarnate in the person of a Tiberius on the throne of the world.† In all this we shall behold

---

* In its two great aspects of lust and cruelty: the passages in proof of the first may remain unquoted, but what a picture of the last, this account of the gladiatorial games and of the manner in which they had grown ever bloodier, presents! (Seneca, *Ep.* 7:) Quidquid ante pugnatum est, misericordia fuit: nunc omissis nugis, mera homicidia sunt...Plagis aguntur in vulnera, et mutuos ictus nudis et obviis pectoribus excipiunt. Intermissum est spectaculum? interim jugulantur homines, ne nihil agatur.

† With only slight exaggeration Seneca compares the aspect of the world in which he was living to that of a city taken by storm (*De Benef.*, l. 7, c. 27·) Si tibi vitæ nostræ vera imago succurret, videberis tibi videre captæ cummaximè civitatis faciem, in quâ omisso pudoris rectique respectu vires in con-

how feeble all the barriers which the world's wisdom could raise up, to stay the overflowings of the world's ungodliness and evil.*

But to imagine yet a third position; we may read these books, not indeed setting them up in our affections against the truths which ought to be dearest to us, nor on the other hand slighting them, because not themselves Christian; but failing altogether to trace in them any relation at all to the great facts of

---

silio sunt, velut signo ad permiscenda omnia dato. Non igni non ferro abstinetur: soluta legibus scelera sunt, nec religio quidem, quæ inter arma hostilia supplices texit, ullum impedimentum est ruentium in prædam. Hic ex privato, hic ex publico, hic ex profano, hic sacro rapit: hic effringit, hic transilit: hic non contentus angusto itinere, ipsa quibus arcetur evertit, et in lucrum ruina venit. Hic sine cæde populatur: hic spolia cruenta manu gestat: nemo non fert aliquid ex altero. Compare his 95th Epistle.

* Thus the atrocity of the gladiatorial shows was by heathen moralists abundantly felt and understood. Cicero indeed makes but a feeble protest against them (*Tusc Quæst.*, l. 2, c. 17:) Crudele gladiatorum spectaculum et inhumanum nonnullis videri solet; et haud scio an ita sit, ut nunc fit. But Seneca more distinctly (*Ep* 95:) Homo, *sacra res*, homo jam per lusum et jocum occiditur, et quem erudiri ad inferenda accipiendaque vulnera nefas erat, is jam nudus inermisque producitur, satisque spectaculi in homine, mors est. Cf. *Ep.* 7. And Lucian, in a collection of the notable sayings of Demonax, a cynic philosopher of the second century, tells of him, that once when the Athenians were planning a spectacle of the kind, he told them that they must overthrow the altar of Pity, before they proceeded further in this matter. Yet with all this it remained for an unlettered Christian monk to put a stop to these bloody shows.

the spiritual life of man. We may read them, forgetting that the meaning of books is to make us understand something else besides books, that we miss their significance to us, when they have their end in themselves, when they do not hand us on to life and to action; when they explain to us no mysteries of our being, help us in no struggles of our souls, make clear to us no dealings of our God.

There was a time in our lives,—yet a time which we who are here present should now have left behind us,—when this might have been natural enough, when it would have been premature to begin to meditate on the moral problems which these works present, or to do more than first to master their difficulties, and those overcome, to walk up and down admiring and enjoying the strange and wondrous world into which they had helped to introduce us. But the time is gone by, when that alone was our task. Further duties are ours—to study that classical antiquity in the light which our Christian faith and experience throw back upon it, with an open eye for its moral good and for its moral evil, with an entire confidence that in Christ and in his Gospel is given to us the touchstone which shall enable us to recognise—the sharp and dividing sword which shall enable us unerringly to separate between—the evil and the good, the false and the true.

Let us feel that not by some strange inconsistency, some traditional usage which we will not abandon, but cannot defend, it has come to pass that a literature and philosophy, not Christian but heathen, hold the place which they do among *us*, members of the Church of Christ—are at this day contemplated, as they *have* been contemplated in time past, by each wiser and more thoughtful man, as an indispensable organ for all higher education, necessary instruments for the cultivating of the complete humanity.* Let us feel that this only could have been, inasmuch as they stand in some real and intimate relation to the innermost fact of our lives, to our Christian hope—a relation of defect it will often be, yet a relation not

* The intimate connexion between the Reformation and the revival of classical learning, with the zeal and success of the Reformers in promoting this last, all will remember—Melancthon's especially, to whom beside other titles of honour, this of Præceptor Germanniæ was added. There is a very interesting letter of Luther's, in which thanking a friend, who had sent him a Latin Poem which he had composed, and had at the same time expressed his fears that the cause of Classical literature would suffer from men's zeal about Theology, Luther replies that it should not so with his consent: Ego persuasus sum, sine literarum peritiâ prorsus stare non posse sinceram theologiam, sicut hactenus ruentibus et jacentibus literis miserrimè et cecidit et jacuit. Quin video nunquam fuisse insignem factam verbi Dei revelationem, nisi primò, velut præcursoribus baptistis, viam pararit surgentibus et florentibus linguis et literis. Planè nihil minus vellem fieri aut committi in juventute, quàm ut poesin et rhetoricen omittant. In ea certe vota sum ut quàm plurimi sint et poetæ et rhetores, quod his studiis videam, sicut nec aliis modis fieri potest, mirè aptos fieri homines ad sacra tam capessenda, quàm dextrè et feliciter tractanda...Quare et te oro ut et meo (si quid valet) precatu agas apud vestram juventutem, ut strenuè et poetentur et rhetoricentur. (Luther's *Briefe*, v. 2, p. 313. De Wette's edit.)

the less, which should not be overlooked or denied. And these things being so, let us understand that we fall below our position, we fall short of the purpose with which these books were placed in our hands, when we fail to regard them in such a light as this. And in this light to look at them will not mar nor hinder that free spontaneous joy in them which in earlier times may have been ours. We may keep that earlier delight, and yet, keeping it, may pass on to a deeper and more meditative emotion. For indeed with what livelier interest shall we occupy ourselves with this classical antiquity, when we feel that it is not disconnected with the highest things of our life, the most solemn questions which can employ us as baptized men.

How many will be the thoughts and emotions, and all of them purifying and ennobling, which these studies in this spirit pursued, will awaken and cherish within us! Thus surely a divine compassion will oftentimes stir in our hearts, as with an ear made open by love, we drink in the voices of the world's deep disquietude, its confessions of an intolerable burden,* its

---

* In none perhaps so frequent and distinct as in Lucretius. There is a very interesting lecture in Keble's *Prælectiones*, on the witness for and craving after that which Christianity only can give, that is to be found by those who know how to look for it, in the reputedly atheistic work of the great Roman Poet. He dwells on the many passages in which he expresses his deep dissatisfaction with life, and with all which life could offer—a dissatisfaction which yet was not, like that of so many on the score of the fleeting nature of life's pleasures and the

acknowledgments that if there be nothing prouder, so also there is nothing more miserable, than man.* And these we shall not go far without meeting: for however the prevailing tone of that heathen world may be lightsome and gay, a summons to enjoy the present, to pluck the roses of life ere they wither, yet if only we listen aright, we may detect that in its laughter there is heaviness; and oftentimes that laughter is followed by a sigh drawn from deeps of the heart far deeper than those where its smiles were

little of them which a man in his brief space could enjoy—but had its rise rather in a sense that these very pleasures, even in fullest measure, did never truly satisfy or fill the soul (*Prælect* 35) Campus hic ferme nobilium est poetarum, ut nænias canat ac querimonias de vitæ flore fragili ac caduco. Habet autem Lucretius noster illud, ni fallor, proprium ac modò non singulare, quod non tam breves et augustos incuset ævi in terris agendi limites, quàm ipsum vitæ hujus statum, vel optimæ actæ. significet, rem eam unicuique hominum et fuisse, et fore semper, molestissimo omnium oneri. This is but one of the many memorable passages of the kind, 3. 1016:

<blockquote>
Deinde animi ingratam naturam pascere semper,
Atque explere bonis rebus, *satiareque nunquam*,
Quad faciunt nobis annorum tempora, circum
Cùm redeunt, fœtusque ferunt, variosque labores,
Nec tamen explemur vitaï fructibus unquam ;
Hoc, ut opinor, id est ævo florente puellas
Quod memorant, laticem pertusum congerere in vas,
Quod tamen expleri nullâ ratione potestur.
</blockquote>

Compare 3. 1066—1097

* Pliny (*H. N.*, l. 2, c. 5) Nec miserius quidquam homine, nec superbius.

born.* Surely we shall find in these cries of a constant unrest, a thousand confirmations of his word, who, heathen as he was, yet likened man in his separation from God, to a child torn from its mother's arms, and which nowhere could be well, till it was given back to those arms once more.†

Again, as we acquaint ourselves with the lamentations of mourners for their dead, lamentations so deep and so despairing, as to explain to us all the meaning of that sorrowing without hope, which by the apostle is attributed to the heathen;‡ as we hear too the

---

* Compare Herodotus, l. 7, c. 46, *Iliad*, 17 446, *Odyss*, 18. 129, Lucretius, 5. 222, Moschus, *Idyll.*, 3. 106, Sophocles, *Œdipus Col.*, 1225, Virgil, *Georg.*, 3. 66. There is a striking collection of passages in which the vanity, the sorrow, the burden of life, are acknowledged, in Plutarch's *Consol. ad Apollon.*

† Dio Chrysostom, *Orat.* 12, p. 405, ed Reiske.

‡ How affecting a picture does Augustine give of what his feelings were, when, in the time during which he was still moving in the element of heathen life, the friend of his soul was taken from him (*Conf.*, l. 4, c. 4) Quo dolore contenebratum est cor meum, et quidquid aspiciebam, mors erat. Et erat mihi patria supplicium, et paterna domus mira infelicitas et quidquid cum illo communicaveram, sine illo in cruciatum immanem verterat. Expetebant eum undique oculi mei, et non dabatur mihi; et oderam omnia, quia non haberent eum, nec mihi jam dicere poterant: Ecce veniet, sicut cùm viverit quando absens erat. Factus eram ipse mihi magna quæstio, et interrogabam animam meam, quare tristis esset, et quare conturbaret me valde, et nihil noverat respondere mihi. Et si dicebam: Spera in Deum, justè non obtemperabat, quia verior erat et melior homo quem carissimum amiserat, quàm

wretched consolations of miserable comforters, the slight palliations of sharpest sorrows, which were all that, with all their kindness, they could suggest, we shall know how to prize the oil and wine, the strong consolations which are stored in the Gospel for each bruised and smitten heart.

Or a compassion profounder yet will stir within us, as the voices reach us, which proclaim that the very citadel of hope was lost, voices of an utter uncertainty about all things, and these coming from some of the earth's noblest spirits, who asked of themselves, and could give no satisfying answer to their own question, whether there was indeed a God governing in righteousness,* or whether all was not given over to the blindest chance—whether they who did his will were a care to Him; whether they survived the grave, and if there were indeed any future and happy seats reserved for the names of the just.

And even that of impure which we shall encounter, as we must encounter it, there, proving, as it often has done, fuel of dark fires in unholy hearts, setting

---

phantasma in quod separare jubebatur. Solus fletus erat dulcis mihi, et successerat amico meo in deliciis animi mei.

* The reader will remember the way in which the *De Naturâ Deorum* concludes, and the entire indecision in which all is left. Pliny (*H. N.*, l. 2, c. 5) is more explicit yet in his open confession of an utter skepticism in any moral government of the world: Irridendum verò agere curam rerum humanarum illud quidquid est summum. Anne tam tristi multiplicique ministerio non pollui credamus dubitemusve? Cf. Lucian's *Jupiter Tragœdus*, c. 17.

them as with sparks of hell in a blaze, it shall not be to us, who go not to seek it, who unwillingly encounter it, this incentive and provocative to evil. Rather shall this impure itself conspire to the same ends with all else which there we meet. It shall make us feel, in its light we shall more plainly see, what hideous sores there were to be healed, how deep a corruption to be subdued, when men could thus glory in their shame, and some comparatively pure in their lives, felt that in their works it was not merely so permitted, but so expected, that they should write.* And intruding, as often that unholy does, among the fairest creatures of genius, rising up like a plague-spot upon their foreheads, who were among the most gifted of their age and nation, it shall teach us a solemn lesson, even this—how much of moral insensibility may co-exist with highest capacities of intellect—how little the sense of beauty by itself avails to preserve purity of heart,—how needful it is that hearts should be in better guardianship than this—how the highest of this earth's yields us no security against the lowest; it shall teach us that if there are pinnacles of heaven above every man, and *that* in him which prompts him to ascend them, so also are there abysses of sensuality yawning beneath his feet, and that in him which tempts him to engulf himself in these.†

* See the elder Pliny, *Epist.*, l 4, ep 14, l 5, ep. 3.

† I borrow these remarkable words from the answer of one, whose position gave him full right to speak, to the proposal for publishing an expurgated edition of the Classics for the use of schools. Rather, he says, he would have the works as

CONCLUDING LECTURE. 321

Nor will this be all; there will mingle in these studies thoughts and feelings of a liveliest thankfulness to God, as amid the great shipwreck of the Gentile world, we recognise the planks by which one and

the authors wrote them, and encountering with his pupils any of those passages which, in such an edition, would have been omitted, he would make them the occasion of some such comment as the following: "This lesson they teach you, that refinement of intellect will not purify the heart; that great mental endowments may co-exist with great moral insensibility, that vigour of understanding and delicacy of taste will not reform the world. You see that these have been tried and found wanting. Something more is needed. You may conclude also that the depravity of an age and country was great, in which those who were the most distinguished by their intellectual endowments and literary culture, thought themselves not only *licensed*, but *expected* thus to write. It follows that you have in these passages an evidence of the divine power and purity of that influence which *did* what all the wisdom of the world could *never do*. It is Christianity, and it alone, which has really *expurgated* the literature, not only of Greece and Rome, but of the civilized world. These passages are the trophies of the triumphs of Christianity. They show us, as in triumphal procession, what fearful enemies it has conquered. *Without* them you might have asked what social good has the Gospel done? What moral blessings have we derived from it? These passages forbid, they *answer*, those questions. They remind you from what, and into what you have been delivered, and by Whom. Therefore, had we expunged them, we should have diminished the strength and glory of that very cause which we desire to serve. Being what they are, I fear not that you should pervert them to an improper use. God forbid that you should dwell on them with any other feelings than those of sorrow mingled with

another attained as we trust safely, and through the mercy of a Saviour whom as yet he did not know, to the shore of everlasting life—thankfulness mingled, it may oftentimes be, with something of a wholesome shame to ourselves, as we contemplate the faithfulness and fealty to the good and true, which even in the world's darkest hour have been shown by them, whose knowledge was so little, and whose advantages so few, as compared with our own. And perhaps it shall seem to us then, as if that Star in the natural heavens which guided those Eastern Sages from their distant home, was but the symbol of many a star which twinkled in the world's mystical night,—but which yet, being faithfully followed, availed to lead humble and devout hearts from far off regions of superstition and error, till they knelt beside the cradle of the Babe of Bethlehem, and saw all their weary wanderings repaid in a moment, and all their desires finding a perfect fulfilment in Him.

thankfulness. Horace, had he lived when you do, would have been a Christian, and had he been a Christian, he would not have written thus; but if you who are Christians, *love to read*, what he, had he been one, would have *loathed to write*, you, who ought to Christianize him, heathenize yourselves."

THE END.

www.ingramcontent.com/pod-product-compliance
Lightning Source LLC
Chambersburg PA
CBHW051629230426
43669CB00013B/2232